Free, Melania

Free, Melania

The Unauthorized Biography

Kate Bennett

FLATIRON
BOOKS
NEW YORK

FREE, MELANIA. Copyright © 2019 by Kate Bennett. All rights reserved. Printed in the United States of America. For information, address Flatiron Books, 120 Broadway, New York, NY 10271.

www.flatironbooks.com

The Library of Congress Cataloging-in-Publication Data is available upon request.

ISBN 978-1-250-30737-8 (hardcover)
ISBN 978-1-250-30738-5 (ebook)

Our books may be purchased in bulk for promotional, educational, or business use. Please contact your local bookseller or the Macmillan Corporate and Premium Sales Department at 1-800-221-7945, extension 5442, or by email at MacmillanSpecialMarkets@macmillan.com.

First Edition: December 2019

10 9 8 7 6 5 4 3 2 1

For Tess Bennett.
The best person I know, my whole heart.

Nothing is so firmly believed as that which we least know.

—MICHEL DE MONTAIGNE

Contents

x   Contents

Author's Note

The reader will note that to a large degree, Barron Trump does not appear in this book. I don't believe being born to public figures should render a child fair game for public scrutiny; instead, I agree with Chelsea Clinton, who rose to the youngest Trump's defense in 2017, that first children should "have the private childhood [they] deserve." I have included him where his presence helps frame Melania Trump as a mother, and as a factor in her decision-making processes, but I have refrained from writing about him separately. I hope the reader will respect this decision and my attempt to be sensitive.

Free, Melania

Introduction

Being first lady of the United States is, when you think about it, a terrible job. The role is undefined, often unfulfilling, and unpaid. With it come impossible-to-meet expectations from an impatient and critical public that acts like the worst kind of stage mother, demanding precision and perfection and the adoption of a look that is neither too fashionable nor too bland.

A first lady is expected to be smart, but not too outspoken about her views; kind and empathetic, but not syrupy or weak; aligned with a cause, but not one that is too polarizing or off-putting; supportive of the president, but not a Stepford wife; traditional, but not old-fashioned. It's a bit of an oxymoron, the first lady, because the Constitution assigns her no formal role in the executive branch, yet she is supposed to be a role model and a leader, simply because of the man she married. If she does nothing, she's criticized. If she does too much, she's assuming responsibilities of the president. Frank Bruni, an opinion columnist for *The New York Times*, recently described the role of first lady to me like this: "If the administration is a sedan, the first lady would be the hood ornament. If it was a mansion, the first lady would be the topiary bushes bracketing the front stoop."

Most first ladies with a bold personality have hidden it, adopting a persona instead. Barbara Bush was a dominating matriarch with fiery opinions, but America preferred to see her as a white-haired grandmother who liked pearl necklaces and straw hats. She went with it. Nancy Reagan was Ronald Reagan's frosty second wife, slim and chic and upper-crust. She embraced it. Hillary Clinton, a culturally inclined woman, spearheaded the redecoration of the Blue Room; added a sculpture garden to the White House, which was viewed by thousands of visitors; and championed the display of American arts and crafts, but she was publicly known as a tough, careerist woman who intruded in her husband's administration.

Melania Trump is vastly different from her predecessors. Nearly three years into her tenure, she has proved to be one of the most private and guarded first ladies in modern history. Her secretive nature has given rise to myriad theories about her public persona, her role in the White House, and the state of her marriage. She is unwilling to concede even a morsel of unscripted emotion or vulnerability that would crack the fortress. The secrecy makes the American public anxious for her: Is she happy? Does she hate her life? Does she have feelings?

When she spurned her husband on the tarmac in Tel Aviv via the hand swat seen around the world, remained suspiciously silent after headlines touting her husband's alleged infidelities, or publicly called for the firing of a key West Wing staffer, most people conjectured that she was motivated by her romantic feelings for her husband. These people miss the point. Melania is the only one in Trump's orbit who can flick his hand and get away with it. She is the only one who can say what she thinks to his face. She is the only one who can and does give advice and opinions contrary to his, and she can do so without suffering a barrage of name-calling tweets in the days that follow. She is, essentially, untouchable.

It was Melania who told Trump that the zero-tolerance policy of removing children from their parents at the border was cruel and untenable. It was she who emphasized the opioid crisis was an emergency, one that required more federal funding. And it was, again, Melania who told Donald Trump who was conniving behind his back, whom he shouldn't trust, who didn't deserve to be in the White House orbit. Opinions—she has a few.

She can and does lead by her intuition and not by a preconceived or publicly held notion of what a first lady should be. The secret to Melania Trump's confidence and to her survival as first lady? She doesn't care what anyone thinks about her. Whether people assume she is complicit in Trump's beliefs and actions by being married to him and staying married to him or whether they think she is standing by his side because she is a noble adherent to traditional marriage—it doesn't matter to her.

She just does what she wants to do. As goes Trump and his rule-breaking presidency, so goes Melania and her rule-breaking first lady–ship.

In many ways, her defiance, and at times her patent disregard for the norms of the role, define her as an unlikely feminist. Why should she have to do what is expected of her simply because she is a woman and the spouse of a president?

In recent history there hasn't been a more secretive or compelling first lady than Melania Trump. Melania, the second immigrant first lady (the first was British-born Louisa Adams), has broken the mold: not moving into the White House was unheard of, staying out of the spotlight right after becoming one of the most popular women on the planet was mystifying. Nearly three years into the Donald Trump presidency, Melania is an enigma. Is she smart? Wickedly. Has she learned how to manipulate the media? Completely. Does anyone know what goes on behind those sunglasses? Read on.

Donald Trump may possibly be the most bullheaded and bloviating president this country has ever seen, but Melania has a remarkable place of importance in his world and thereby in the rest of the world. Whether she's mad at her husband or softened by his private kindness, she is not a hood ornament.

1

The Speech

"Don't feel sorry for me. I can handle everything."

—MELANIA TRUMP

When a presidential candidate's wife gives a speech—a speech as significant as, say, the one she gives at the party's national convention—there is a right way to do it and a wrong way. The right way is to work with at least one, if not several, speechwriters, seasoned ones, to come up with the best and most effective means by which to communicate a message, sending drafts back and forth until a version is agreed on by the principal—with luck, weeks in advance of the big night. That leaves time for the speech to make its way up the chain of command, through campaign aides who comment and edit, cut or elongate, add insight and experience, and polish the tone. The communications team of the candidate will go over every line, every anecdote, aiming to get ahead of potential gaffes or land mines. Eventually, the speech will land with the candidate's chief of staff, who typically has the final say, or sign-off, and then it goes to the candidate for the okay. A smart candidate knows not to tangle with his or her spouse, so any edits the candidate makes will go back to the chief of staff, whose name is associated with the suggestions, covering for the candidate.

By the time the candidate's spouse takes the podium, the speech has likely been read by at least twenty people, all of whom will have made notes, and most of whom know better than the candidate's spouse does what will resonate in a convention hall during the most amped-up political rally of a candidate's career. Most candidates' spouses do not have their own speechwriter for the campaign, instead using the services of one or two members of the candidate's own team.

But not Michelle Obama. She would have her own.

Sarah Hurwitz, the Harvard Law–educated speechwriter used by Michelle Obama for close to a decade—and who before that worked for Hillary Clinton and John Kerry—used to say that she would sit with Obama's words and ideas and voice to "marinate" in them before she ever sat at her keyboard to spin them into prose. Hurwitz and Obama would conduct lengthy conversations about the speech topic, the location of the speech, the audience for the speech, and the tone, the first lady often setting the initial idea for Hurwitz, who would then take the ball and run with it. It was Hurwitz's job to be inside Michelle Obama's head, to know her personal stories so that she could weave them into her speech, crafting it from the seed of an idea to an occasion for mass adulation. Hurwitz's voice had to be hidden so that Obama's could shine through. By many accounts, Hurwitz devoted her life to speechwriting for Obama; she was doing more than just a job, she was writing words that would build the legacy of one of the most popular first ladies in modern history. Michelle Obama was a political wife who could move the needle on her husband's popularity. Hurwitz knew the pressures, but she also knew Michelle Obama. One of the first speeches Hurwitz wrote for Michelle Obama, the 2008 Democratic National Convention speech in Denver, Colorado, would be her most important—and her most difficult. Hurwitz understood that the weeks she spent on its creation, the hours she passed listening to Obama tell her story of growing up on Chicago's

South Side, the myriad drafts that went back and forth after she took Obama's own first pass into her watchful care, the minutes leading up to its delivery—all of it would make Michelle Obama's the most successful and discussed speech of the convention. That was obvious. What Hurwitz didn't know was that the speech resulting from her hard work would be used by another candidate's spouse, who would deliver the most heartfelt portions of it at her own husband's national convention almost eight years later.

Less than an hour after Melania Trump stepped away from the podium in Cleveland, Ohio, wrapping up a speech to the 2016 Republican National Convention, Jarrett Hill, a freelance journalist in Los Angeles, busted her: "Melania stole a whole graph from Michelle's speech. #GOPConvention," Hill tweeted, with a link to a recording of Melania's speech and a photographed excerpt from Michelle Obama's 2008 Democratic National Convention speech, with the section that Melania's speech cribbed highlighted.

"That you work hard for what you want in life; that your word is your bond, and you do what you say and keep your promise. That you treat people with respect," said Melania, talking about what her parents had taught her.

And Michelle?

"That you work hard for what you want in life; that your word is your bond and you do what you say you're going to do; that you treat people with dignity and respect, even if you don't know them, and even if you don't agree with them."

Melania went on:

"We need to pass those lessons on to many generations to follow, because we want our children in this nation to know that the only limit to your achievements is the strength of your dreams and your willingness to work for them."

Michelle's speech was basically the same:

"Barack and I set out to build lives guided by these values, and pass them on to the next generation. Because we want our children— and all children in this nation—to know that the only limit to the height of your achievements is the reach of your dreams and your willingness to work for them."

It was a needle-off-the-record moment.

For three to four hours after Hill's tweet, disbelief set in for the Trump campaign staff. According to one member of the team I spoke with, none of them had seen a copy of Melania's speech before she delivered it. Not a one. This was unheard of. There wasn't enough time or hands on deck to do so, they said. And if someone did read it, which this person conceded might possibly have happened without his knowledge, that person certainly didn't vet it or have the political chops to know to vet it. If it was looked at—and no one believes that it was—the idea to compare it to, say, the most recent speeches of similar importance by candidates' spouses just didn't pop into anyone's head. It was the proverbial wrong way to do a spouse speech on a stage this large.

"Wait, did she just . . . ?" they whispered to one another. "Nah. No way . . . right?" But, yes, she did.

It was doubly stunning because Melania had otherwise done a good job with the speech, delivering it with clarity, the words (whosever they were) heartfelt and impassioned. It had set the right tone, and it introduced Melania to the country and to hard-core Republicans, who before this evening knew little about their candidate's third wife other than that she was pretty and dressed well.

And Melania did share, for once throwing off the armor of privacy. She discussed the country of her birth, Slovenia, her parents—her mom who taught her about fashion, her dad about business and travel—and her even more elusive sister, Ines. I'm willing to bet 99 percent of the public didn't even know she had a sister. Melania showed some glam, just a touch to inspire aspirational envy, the type fashion magazines aim to hit: not enough for you to be actually jealous of the actress in the cover story, but enough for you to want to read about her face cream, her workout routine, and where she buys her clothes. "I traveled the world while working hard in the incredible arena of fashion," said Melania with her thick, exotic accent. This was, after all, Ohio. She said she had lived in Paris and Milan, pronouncing the latter "Mee-lan," the "right" way.

Her white sheath dress was by a Serbian designer named Roksanda Ilinčić. It also had just the right touch of celebrity sparkle—a feminine flounce at the hems of the sleeves, a discreet exposed zipper up the back for some sex appeal. Like Melania, Ilinčić was born in a country that was part of the now former Yugoslavia, and she left. It's unlikely, however, that Melania intentionally picked a Roksanda dress because of her shared heritage with the designer; more likely, she simply saw it for sale online, liked it, and scooped it up at its retail price of $2,190. (By the next day, it was sold out.)

Beyond her white dress—with its cheeky subliminal message of wanting to be America's bride—Melania delivered the conservative gut punches she had planned for the speech to land. She talked about becoming a United States citizen in 2006, and she said how much she loved this country. The crowd went wild. By the time she got to her sentence thanking veterans, pointing out former senator Bob Dole, a GOP icon, the audience was beside themselves with patriotic whooping and applause, made more intense when a frail and wheelchair-bound Dole was helped to his feet to wave back to her in gratitude.

She brought it home going on about her husband, the leader she knew him to be, the committed fighter, the successful TV star who just wants you to be like him, to get a little slice of the economic pie. He is a tough guy, she admitted, but he also has a heart. This part, really, only Melania could attempt with success. She gave him the emotional cred in the way a wife could. Tough guy? Sure. But Melania says he's a private softie.

She said he wanted prosperity for everyone, of every race and economic background, that he had compassion for all mankind. Out there, in the rest of America, particularly Hillary country on either coast, there was a collective "huh?" But in the arena, to his fans, true or not, she drilled it home: "I have seen the talent, the energy, the tenacity, the resourceful mind and the simple goodness of the heart that

God gave to Donald Trump." She closed with some foreshadowing: "There will be good times and hard times and unexpected turns. It would not be a Trump contest without excitement and drama."

She wasn't kidding.

Trump had made the unconventional move of showing up at the RNC arena to introduce his wife, when typically the nominated candidate stays away from the convention hall until the final night and his own big speech. Not Trump. "Ladies and gentlemen, it is my great honor to present the next first lady of the United States. My wife, an amazing mother, an incredible woman, Melania Trump." She walked out to Queen's "We Are the Champions." Trump watched the speech live in real time from a private room backstage. "She's nailing it," he said to his aides, one recalled, endlessly proud, and even himself a bit surprised with the accuracy of her delivery. Maybe a little too surprised. Who knew this speech would be so good? Certainly no one in the room where Trump was watching—none of whom had read it. Melania, as she is wont to do, had told her husband and his closest aides that she wanted to do this speech on her own, write it by herself, do as much as she could without help. They found it admirable. But if there had been even one more seasoned national campaign veteran on Trump's team, he or she would have thrown their body in front of the train of that idea, done anything to prevent the I've-got-this attitude from being acted on. At such a significant stage in the campaign, it's a massive no-no to allow a candidate or candidate's family members to so much as be overheard making an offhand remark on their own, much less write a speech for the party convention on their own.

Yet Melania said she wanted to go it alone if she could, and so Trump said to his team, "Let her."

When Trump walked onto the stage to kiss Melania and escort her off, both were glowing, beaming, literally basking in the spotlight. He had let his wife flex her independence in front of a massive audience. She had done the near impossible: made Trump likable and human.

The Twitter revelation of copied passages had picked up steam.

A few dozen of Hill's mere 1,800 followers retweeted it, then a few hundred, then a few thousand. Melania's speech was Monday, July 18; by Friday, July 22, the news was everywhere, and Hill was a star. His follower count ballooned, and every media outlet from CNN to *The New York Times* was crediting him for the biggest scoop of convention week: holy shit, the woman who wants to be first lady just plagiarized a speech from the current first lady. It was headline gold.

Melania, meanwhile, was devastated. "Beside herself," as one aide put it to me. Yet there was no slamming of doors, throwing of vases, blind rage, or berating of staff. Instead, she became despondent, racked with guilt. "She felt like she had let the team down," says someone who worked on the campaign and was involved with Trump messaging. "All she wanted to do was get up there and give a great performance and deliver a big win." Melania wasn't calling for a head on a platter—that's what Trump was doing, wanting to know who had let that happen, why his wife wasn't given more help, why had she been left out to hang? That's what they, the handful of overworked, underexperienced aides were there for, Trump said, to make sure these sorts of things never, ever happened.

The truth was that even if Melania had asked for it, there was no help to give. Trump's "team" was literally fewer than ten mostly politically unseasoned staffers. Unlike Hillary Clinton, who had a team with years and numerous campaigns under their belt, Trump had basically no one. "We were all running around doing eight million things just to handle him," said one of Trump's top campaign advisers, who admits the team was woefully spread thin. "There wasn't the capacity of staff. We could barely prep our own candidate for the party convention. That's not an exaggeration." Melania and her speech had fallen through the cracks. Melania was an afterthought—on the biggest night of her public life.

Meanwhile, Trump apologized to his wife profusely. "He felt really bad and responsible for what happened," said the former aide. He was mad, sure, but not at her. He has always wanted Melania to be her best and to feel strong and capable in her capacity as his wife.

Whether or not he is successful at achieving this, ask anyone who knows him well and they will tell you he makes time to ensure Melania is as professionally comfortable in her role as she possibly can be.

As he was groveling to his wife for having put her in a vulnerable position, simply because his team lacked the people or experience needed to bolster her speech, she was wallowing in guilt because she didn't deliver for him. "He felt genuinely sorry; she felt responsible," says a former aide. To use a Trumpian metaphor, he had cut the red ribbon on a new skyscraper that looked perfect and shiny on the outside, but the workers had forgotten to build the scaffolding to hold it up, and it crumbled. Imploded, really.

Perhaps the worst of it was that Melania herself had no idea she was regurgitating Michelle Obama's speech while she was delivering it. The speech's primary writer was a woman named Meredith McIver, a small-time in-house writer at the Trump Organization who was a ghostwriter for Trump's books, including *Trump 101, Trump: How to Get Rich*, and *Trump: Think Like a Billionaire*. Trump said he trusted McIver with handling his book writing because she used to sit outside his office, and "my door is always open, so Meredith has heard everything."

McIver knew Melania by the simple fact she was the boss's wife, and McIver was essentially one of Trump's assistants; she was in the family, so to speak. In the acknowledgments section of *Think Like a Billionaire*, McIver had even thanked "Melania Knauss" (it was 2005, before the wedding) for her "kind assistance." Clearly, there was a rapport between the two women.

Melania also wasn't interested in sharing her big moment with the campaign team, most of whom she didn't personally know well and, with the exception of Sean Spicer, didn't like all that much. The campaign had initially suggested using a speechwriter from RNC circles, and there were early drafts sent to Melania, written by two professional speechwriters. But she didn't find them to her taste. And, like her husband, she was loath to trust anyone she didn't personally know. But she knew McIver.

Melania's insistence on writing the speech herself as much as possible made McIver, or so it was thought, something of an asset. If Melania wasn't going to be comfortable with words from stranger speechwriters, at least she had a "writer" was the general consensus within the Trump campaign team. And that was about as much thought as they gave it.

McIver knew how to string sentences together, at least in a voice that Trump approved of (i.e., his own), and she was considered by Trump to be capable in the English language. What no one knew at the time, especially Melania, was that McIver would snag pivotal passages from Michelle Obama's DNC speech.

There are some who believe, however, that Melania was aware that she was reading plagiarized parts and just assumed she wouldn't be caught. But those who were present for the incident claim that simply was not the case; Melania was a lamb to the slaughter. "I know she gave specific instructions on what she wanted the speech to be," a friend of Melania's who was aware of her thinking at the time tells me. "Unfortunately, someone within the organization put her in a very compromised and uncomfortable position." Her friend, who has known her for almost two decades, says there's nothing in Melania's character that would point to her being a straight-up plagiarizer. There are those who disagree with Melania, many who think her motives are shadier than others might imagine, but in truth she has little of the truth-fudging habits of her husband. The "big" lies she's been busted for—the campaign's claim she earned a college degree, for example—are almost commonplace, at least for Washington, where there are senators who have embellished everything from their ethnic makeup to their military service. Not to excuse Melania's occasional falsehoods, but she's not ever going to say that noise from windmills causes cancer, or that the president of Russia didn't know anything about U.S. election meddling.

The morning after Melania's RNC speech, Jason Miller, at the time the Trump campaign's senior communications adviser, released a statement: "In writing her beautiful speech, Melania's team of writers took notes on her life's inspirations, and in some instances included fragments that reflected her own thinking. Melania's immigrant experience and love for America shone through in her speech, which made it such a success." First of all, there was not a "team of writers." Phrasing it that way might have made it easier to buy time while the campaign tried to come up with a fall guy, but it only helped fuel the rumors that there wasn't a team at all. To say there was a team was an invitation for the media to hunt for a team, realize there wasn't one, and catch the campaign in even more lies.

That spin, to put it mildly, did not work. Ironically, the Republican National Committee's attempt to fight back on the speech was a massive crash and burn, too. Sean Spicer, then the RNC's communications director, put up the truly laughable—and now infamous—*My Little Pony* defense. Speaking to Wolf Blitzer on CNN, Spicer claimed that only a small portion of Melania's speech was like Michelle's. He said that Melania's words were universal, common phrases. And to prove it, he read off some similar quotes from "others," including John Legend, Kid Rock and, yes, Twilight Sparkle from *My Little Pony*. "Twilight Sparkle said, 'This is your dream. Anything you can do in your dream, you can do now.' If we want to take a bunch of phrases and run them through Google and say, Who else said them? I can come up with a list in five minutes. And that's what this is," an amped-up Spicer said to Blitzer. What it really was? A total head-scratcher. Spicer was trying to push the narrative that maybe Hillary Clinton had done it, that her camp had run Melania's sentences through plagiarism-detection software, which identified the words as Michelle Obama's. It was a weird and stupid defense. No one bought it. And it had the added consequence of birthing a tangential headline associating the RNC's lead comms guy with fictitious pastel-colored ponies.

Trump's campaign manager at the time, Paul Manafort (who would go on to be sentenced to 7.5 years for a variety of federal crimes, from tax evasion to obstruction of justice), took the bizarre line of defense a step further and wouldn't even accept the speech was anything like Michelle's, even though it so clearly was. "The speech was very effective," said Manafort, after a full two days of everyone not talking about the speech's effectiveness. "The controversy you're talking about is not meaningful at all." But it was, and someone on the team should have shot the growing story down as quickly as possible with a mea culpa and a statement from Melania saying something along the lines of how sorry she was.

But the campaign, and Trump, kept giving it legs.

Trump attempted to laugh it off, also a bizarre tactic. He tweeted, "Good news is Melania's speech got more publicity than any in the history of politics especially if you believe all press is good press!"

The story held the news cycle until it became clear someone had to do more to mitigate the damage. Trump, finally having realized his team was incapable of doing anything other than pointing fingers and talking about magical ponies, called for someone to step up and take the blame, because he couldn't stand watching Melania get hammered. She was getting eviscerated.

At best, she was accused of being too detached to have read her own speech and unaware where the content was from; at worst, she was a thieving trophy wife, assuming that the general public would not remember Michelle Obama's speech from eight years ago. "Make Plagiarism Great Again!" was one headline; "Thanks, (Mrs.) Obama!" was another.

After almost two full days of trying to bat it away, Trump finally realized that it wasn't going to happen. Michelle Obama was too beloved, plagiarism was too strong a charge, and Melania didn't have a deep bench of skilled supporters (see Spicer passage above) to successfully spike it. The pivot came in the form of a letter on Trump Organization letterhead, not Trump Campaign letterhead, from McIver. By not linking it to the presidential campaign, the letter distanced Trump's team from the stench of the whole thing and made it easier, they hoped, for the public to believe it was some corporate pencil pusher who goofed and not, say, the "seasoned" folks behind team Trump.

McIver said it was she who helped Melania Trump put her speech sentiments on paper and craft the final draft. "A person she has always liked is Michelle Obama," said McIver in her letter. "Over the phone [Melania] read me some passages from Mrs. Obama's speech as examples. I wrote them down and later included some of the phrasing in the draft that ultimately became the final speech. I did not check Mrs. Obama's speeches. This was my mistake, and I feel terrible for the chaos I have caused Melania and the Trumps, as well as to Mrs. Obama. No harm was meant."

The letter was . . . strange. And, if it is to be believed, exposes the unprecedented and haphazard method by which the campaign had set up crafting Melania's most important speech.

McIver went on to write that the public statement was her idea. But no one believed that. She got to keep her job with the organization, though she said she offered her resignation. "Mr. Trump," wrote McIver, "told me that people make innocent mistakes and that we learn and grow from these experiences." The letter also revealed that McIver, in her sixties at the time of the RNC speech incident, was not a particularly gifted wordsmith and was somewhat rudimentary in her communication efforts. McIver liked to write, sure, but was she capable of crafting prose that expresses the deep thoughts and intense feelings of someone else, of "marinating" in them to ensure a powerful and important public speaking achievement? Nope.

It was widely assumed the dealmaker had struck one with McIver, who turned down several interview requests about the incident. Trump probably told her that if she came forward, explained, and took the blame, yeah, she'd be a professional pariah, but he wouldn't fire her or publicly trash her.

Sadly, it wasn't the first time Trump threw McIver under the bus. In 2006, Trump sued Timothy O'Brien, author of the Trump biography *TrumpNation*, for libel. As part of the suit, Trump was deposed in

2007 by O'Brien's legal team, who asked whether in his books Trump had knowingly inflated his net worth by billions of dollars, something *TrumpNation* discussed. Trump called the financial exaggeration a mistake, but not his. "[It was] probably Meredith McIver," said Trump in the deposition. (Trump would go on to lose his case against O'Brien.)

Though she remains a mysterious—and mysteriously silent—character in Melania's most embarrassing public reveal, McIver is, at the time of writing, still employed by the Trump Organization.

The RNC speech, which Melania, like so many candidate spouses before her, had practiced delivering over and over and over again—more than she'd rehearsed anything in her life—turned out to be her worst nightmare come true. "She fell victim to an inexperienced political team," says an insider. "Needless to say, it's a situation none of us would want to find ourselves in." Suffering humiliation and degradation, giving people a reason to stereotype her, and being the focus of a country's ire and laughter—all of the things Melania had sought to avoid through lean participation in her husband's campaign came flooding her way.

The speech debacle drove Melania deeper into hiding. She essentially became the Greta Garbo of the campaign, just wanting to be left alone. But that was not an option.

2

———

The Reluctant Campaigner

"The politics, well, it's a tough business and you need to have a very thick skin."

—MELANIA TRUMP

It was more than a year before the RNC speech debacle, June 16, 2015, to be exact, that Donald Trump stood at the top of an escalator on the mezzanine level of Trump Tower in midtown Manhattan, put his two thumbs up in the air, and directed his wife to get on, going so far as to give her a slight push at the small of her back before she stepped on for the ride down. As Neil Young's voice blared over a sound system, reminding people to keep on rocking in a free world, Melania Trump, dressed in a two-piece white strapless outfit, got on the escalator that took her to the area where her husband would deliver the speech announcing his official candidacy for president of the United States.

The escalator ride should have told us everything we needed to know about Melania. That she was calm, stoic, and reserved—and that she never, ever faked a smile. She could have been taking the escalator down a level from the shoe department at Saks Fifth Avenue for all that her expression revealed.

Just before the entrance, Trump's undisputed favorite child, daughter Ivanka, had warmed up the relatively small crowd assembled in the lobby of Trump Tower. "Welllllcome, everybody," said Ivanka from the podium in her deep, breathy voice. "Today I have the honor of introducing a man who needs no introduction." She talked about him being a legend, about his power, about his success—"I can tell you, there's no better person to have in your corner."

Trump's other kids were there, too: Donny, Eric, Tiffany, even Barron, who was nine at the time. Melania stood off to the side of the elevated stage, carpeted a royal blue. Trump spoke for forty-six minutes, mostly about how badly America was doing compared with the rest of the world. "When was the last time you saw a Chevrolet in Tokyo?" he asked the group of assembled supporters, many of whom, it would later be revealed, were the product of a talent company the campaign had hired to cast most of the attendees, offering them fifty bucks to wear Trump T-shirts and carry Trump signs. "Wow, that is some group of people. Thousands," Trump had said when he first took the podium. There were maybe 150.

It goes without saying that it's likely none of those in attendance had ever seen a Chevy on the streets of Japan—not that it mattered to Trump. He also talked about ISIS having "the oil" that "we should have taken." And about the wall, saying he would make Mexico pay for it, soon to be a familiar refrain. He went on and on about business and trade and how Obama had basically ruined everything, getting madder and madder with each example, a buildup of white saliva forming in the right-hand corner of his mouth, a bright distraction on his deeply red-orange face. "It's so nice to say I'm running as opposed to 'if I run, if I run'—I'm running," Trump said in between screeds on Yemen, building tariffs, Saudi Arabia, fracking, and what a nice person he is, goddammit. When he was done, closing with how he would make America great again (just seconds after literally saying, "Sadly, the American dream is dead!"), the Trump family hit the stage from the side, one by one, lining up to hug him. Tiffany went first, then Ivanka, then a handshake to Don Jr., a kiss for Don's then wife, Vanessa, pats on the head for a couple of their kids; then it was Barron's turn, and Melania, who gave him a stiff and awkward hug, took her turn as he kissed her cheek. Jared followed, and Lara and Eric Trump brought up the rear. Melania stood there, hovering near Barron, as cameras flashed. She smiled at first and then stopped.

Maintaining a smile merely for effect was not a Melania thing to do. She was not a faker—not then, not during the campaign, and not as first lady. The number of times people to this day ask me, "What's wrong with her? Why does she look so angry?" when they see her unsmiling, standing next to Trump as he stops to talk to the press on his way to the helicopter is a lot. What most people don't understand is Melania's heritage and the country in which she was born. In Slovenia, smiling a nongenuine smile isn't really a thing. Admittedly, it's a tad disconcerting when shopping in an outdoor market, making eye contact with a vendor, asking a hotel bellhop if they mind carrying a heavy bag, or soliciting a waiter about what he suggests from the menu. "We just don't always feel like we have to pretend to be when we aren't," one of Melania's old high school classmates from Slovenia told me.

Though her smiles were less frequent than the pinned-on grins radiating from her stepchildren and their offspring that June day at Trump Tower, Melania was not necessarily *un*happy, she was just, as she often is, doing what felt natural. Mostly, Melania was just glad Trump had finally thrown his hat in the ring. "Good job," she told her husband in his ear before they walked off the stage. "Thanks, baby," he responded.

There's a common misperception that Melania was against Trump's running for president. That she didn't want him to do it. Not true. She very much pushed him to run, in part because she did actually believe he would win and do a good job, but she was also tired, really tired, of listening to him talk about it.

The national election cycle is every four years, when newspapers and cable news channels fill with speculation and think pieces and takes on potential candidates, polls of Americans about what needs to be fixed, what they like, what they fear, what they want to have more of or less of. And so it went in the Trump household during their eighteen years together: each time an election was approaching, Melania would have to listen to her husband go on and on about what was wrong with the country; how he would do it better; how he had predicted this, this, and this would happen, and it did. When they met, Bill Clinton was just starting his second term. Melania had to hear about Clinton, then George W. Bush, and then Obama—all the while listening, nodding. Finally, she essentially said, "Okay, so if you can do it better than all three of these guys, do it already."

Think about it this way: by the time Trump took the oath of office, it had been seventeen years since Melania had posed in a bathing suit on a rug in a fake Oval Office for a glossy magazine, dropping innuendos about what a primo first lady this babe would be. In some ways, the leap from men's mag hottie to White House occurred in the blink of an eye—but for Melania, it was an epic journey. How many times could she be asked what she thought about her husband running for president? In 2000, he toyed with the Reform Party and running on a ticket with former wrestling performer turned governor Jesse Ventura or with Oprah Winfrey. In 2004 he was considering a run "very seriously," he told the press; in 2008 he dropped hints that he would run as an Independent. In 2010 it was *The Apprentice* that prevented him from going forward with pursuing the Republican nomination. "Ultimately, it's hard to give up a top-rated television show," he said. Each time, Melania also had to answer what she might like about living in the White House. "In 1999, when they asked what kind of first lady I would be, it was out there that I'd be traditional, a Jackie Kennedy or Betty Ford. But that was 1999. A lot has changed."

By the time talk of 2016 was in full swing, Melania was more inclined to say "put up or shut up" than to talk him out of it or, as some have suggested, to beg him not to. "He was always thinking about it," she said.

It was now—finally—time. He was getting older, she told friends; when he started thinking earnestly about a presidential career, he'd just hit his fifties; now he was seventy.

She had lost patience with his waffling. It was fish-or-cut-bait time, and she was pushing him to finally drop his line. One close adviser says Melania's goading had a big impact on his ultimate decision to enter the race.

Melania genuinely believed he would win, too. "If you run, you will win," she told him, over and over. She was way ahead in foreseeing the movement that Trump could create and how the focus on the flashy part of the Donald was hiding a charisma and machismo that would draw voters. "They would prefer to joke about his hair than about what he achieved," she said. Yet she did hold his feet to the fire and forced him to consider the seriousness of a presidential run before he embarked on it.

She needed him to know from her perspective what running for president would mean. "You really need to think about it," she told Trump, according to two friends who know how deeply she wanted her husband to understand the consequences for their family and the life they knew of campaigning for months; of reporters picking through every aspect of his life and his family's life, revealing his personality; of losing friends; of experiencing isolation. He had to grasp there were legitimate emotional things to ponder.

Most of those issues directly impacted her. Even if Donald Trump had wanted to be president, by many accounts being first lady was not something Melania Trump aspired to. This wasn't her dream. Her dream was actually quite akin to what she had: a rich husband; cushy life; happy child; multiple homes; glamour when she wanted it, privacy when she didn't; independence. Having a husband run for and ultimately win the presidency sort of felt like a gross inconvenience for Melania. Was she happy for her spouse for achieving his dream? Yes. But she greeted the rest of it with a heavy sigh.

But when he did finally announce his campaign, Melania was supportive, as she had promised she would be if he did the work of deep consideration. Still, she laid some ground rules. Most of them Trump knew were coming, simply because he was well aware of the kind of person he married. Melania wouldn't be cajoled into campaigning or threatened into it. She wasn't going to be prodded to attend events by overzealous staff members or Washington political consultants claiming to know best. She and she alone would choose which events she would attend and what she would say or not say. She didn't care that first ladies were historically important players for corralling voters and that Trump was already woefully behind when it came to support from women. Her approach was, quite frankly, unsuited to a political wife; more than that, it was unheard of.

From the start of the twentieth century, first ladies, or potential first ladies, were essential to their husbands' platforms. Immensely popular for the most part, a candidate's spouse was the perfect opener at a hard speech about policy or the ideal closer for a speech about cultural issues; she was as good alone preaching to a local Rotary Club as she was with a gaggle of local politicians' spouses, standing behind their men. Jackie Kennedy had a virtual cult of campaign trail wannabes who followed her to the White House, pillbox hats and minidresses growing exponentially with the rise of Jackie's signature bouffant, chin-length hairdo. Hillary Clinton worked the campaign as part hard-charging modern woman, wife, mom, and lawyer and part fierce defender of her "man," when he was faced with allegations of infidelity. Laura Bush, while not immensely comfortable with making speeches in front of big crowds, worked the hell out of small donor groups, showing off an approachability and likability that ultimately made her a favorite of Republican voters. Michelle Obama was so good on the trail that in 2008 she earned the nickname "The Closer." Michelle was used to commanding an audience. As a former hospital executive with degrees from Princeton and Harvard, she was gifted with words and solid at delivering a resonating message. However, like Melania, she put limits on her campaign participation, insisting that her two daughters came first on her schedule. She also knew quite well that when she did show up for a speech, she would handily knock it out of the park. Michelle's conversion rate was legendary; the number of voters who registered or signed up to volunteer on the Obama campaign after a Michelle speech was always high.

In terms of campaign participation, small, medium, or large, Melania didn't really want any of it.

"You don't manage Melania Trump in the way it's discussed when you're normally managing or handling a high-profile political spouse," a political veteran who worked on the Trump campaign told me. He had initially dabbled in attempting to get Melania to play along with some political events—but quickly saw it was like talking a brick wall into being something besides a brick wall. "She rejects *any* efforts to be managed or told what to do."

Melania had decided long ago, around the time Barron was born in 2006, that if her husband actually ever did run, she would still remain home and take care of their son. It wasn't a convenient excuse. Melania didn't like nannies living in the penthouse with them. With the exception of a night nurse when Barron was a newborn and an extra nanny for daytime when he was an older baby and toddler, she did most everything herself, says a friend.

Melania was there to shepherd Barron to soccer and baseball practice, liked dropping him off at school, enjoyed when his friends came over to play—she had no desire to take a maternal sabbatical for the sake of her husband's political objectives. She wasn't about to leave her son to eat corn dogs at the Iowa State Fair. (She did eventually go to Iowa with Trump, first for a campaign event in Council Bluffs and then for the caucus in February 2016 in Des Moines. Wearing a red dress and matching red coat draped over her shoulders and her giant diamond ring, Melania sat uncomfortably in a plastic chair at the Ramada hotel next to Trump, a blank, not-overly-excited-political-spouse face, awaiting returns.)

Seasoned political watchers and campaign veterans said it was weird that Melania wasn't on the trail, and a lot of them chalked it up to the campaign's concern that "traditional values" Republicans in America wouldn't take kindly to a third wife who was a former model. That wasn't it. Inside Trump world they longed to get Melania out there, because they knew behind the diamonds and the heels and the lip gloss was a warm woman with a story to tell. A story about the American dream, about immigration, about the human side of their candidate from the woman who had a child with him.

And even if—if—they hated her, they would probably still come out just to listen to this curiosity of a woman who could somehow manage being married to a man many undecided voters considered a jackass loudmouth. Either way, the campaign would have preferred her on the trail. "We weren't purposefully trying to hide her, no," says the aide. She just kept a distance from the role of campaigner.

Melania for years has told people that being married to a man like Trump meant not morphing into him, absorbing his life, but doing the opposite. "She's very independent," says the campaign staffer, clearly catching the drift early on in the election cycle that Melania wasn't playing when she said she wasn't going to be active. The "independent" line was a familiar refrain with Melania, who used it both as a calling card and a prophylactic to get people to stop poking around about why she was staying out of the campaign.

She did make a few appearances on the trail, however, mostly at Trump's debates, even once in a while taking a solo turn at a rally. Her first speaking appearance with him came in November 2015 in Myrtle Beach, South Carolina, a full five months after his Trump Tower announcement of his candidacy. Her parents, Viktor and Amalija Knavs, were there, too, and he called them up on stage with Melania, Barron, Ivanka, Jared, and Tiffany.

"Would you like to say hello?" Trump asks his wife in front of the screaming crowd of thousands. Her body language clearly indicates no, she does not. But she does. "Good evening. Isn't he the best?" she says, pointing to Trump. "He will be the best president ever. We love you." And that was that.

He did the surprise call-over move again in February 2016, also in South Carolina. She was better this time, but no less shocked by the unplanned invitation. "I said say a few words, Melania. There's only about forty million people watching. Say a few words," as Trump recalled the morning after he had fear-teased his wife into talking about him on the campaign trail. "She got up and she spoke beautifully."

What she actually said was, "Congratulations to my husband; he was working very hard. And he loves you, we love you, and we are going ahead to Nevada and we'll see what happens." Then she handed the mic back to Trump.

"Melania, what she puts up with, oy," was the way she was introduced by her husband a couple of weeks later in New Hampshire. He was thanking her, I think, but it came out in a way that made it sound like even her own husband felt sorry for her. "So Melania, thank you, honey, thank you," Trump said, clasping her shoulder and shaking her a little like she was an old war buddy.

She'd been through a lot, though, sort of like a war buddy. During the second Republican primary debate in September 2015, Trump straight up didn't mention her in his introduction, which wouldn't have been a big deal if each of the other ten candidates on the stage hadn't gushed over their own spouses.

"I'm Donald Trump," he said. "I wrote *The Art of the Deal*. I say not in a braggadocious way, I've made billions and billions of dollars."

As the campaign unfolded and Trump picked off those ten other challengers, there were attempts by Trump's team to get Melania more involved, but they were weak and almost never succeeded. "There might have been the odd ask here or there or a 'Hey, it would be great if,' but there was never a hard sell," says a Trump campaign source on how gently they handled Melania. They would sometimes ask Trump to ask his wife himself, but that was hardly ever successful, mostly because Trump doesn't like wasting his time on something he knows isn't going to go his way. "I think there was a recognition on his end that he knew his wife better than anyone and that he knew what she would be interested in or not interested in."

It also mattered what worked with Barron's schedule. If he was out of school on a break and her parents could stay with him in New York, then Melania was more likely to attend an event. Slovenian mothers are notorious for not being able to let go of their children; Melania is no exception.

She didn't miss the Trump family interviews, though—making sure to be present for a *Today* show town hall in April. Ivanka, of course, talked the most of all the kids (see chapter 13), but Melania got the last question: "What's the one habit you wish he'd give up?" "Let's see," she thought, looking at Trump, sitting next to her. "Retweeting," she said, laughing in his face, demonstrating early on that she is probably the only one in his life who can do so and get away with it. He laughed too, a little.

Although Melania was not present for events on the trail, she followed the campaign with intense scrutiny from home: whether it was the polls, how Trump spoke to another candidate, or threats only she could see coming. "I'm very political in private life," Melania said in an interview with *Harper's Bazaar,* "and between me and my husband I know everything that is going on. I follow from A to Z."

"She never allowed herself to fall into the political trap that most spouses do in the first place," says a campaign source. "That trying to program all of her movements that plenty of wives tend to do. She never did that." Because unlike most other spouses (most humans, really), Melania cares not at all what other people think about her. It's a skill that she has honed—one that ultimately drew Trump to her and that allows her to remain married to him—and that forms a protective shell for her as first lady.

When she did fall into the "trap" or did something she wasn't comfortable doing, it felt like it. In April, in Wisconsin, ahead of that state's primary, Melania, looking gaunt, gave a stilted speech about Trump that was basically all declarative sentences strung together. "He's a hard worker. He's kind. He has a great heart. He's tough. He's smart. He's a great communicator. He's a great negotiator. He's telling the truth. He's a great leader. He's fair. As you may know by now, when you attack him, he punches back ten times harder. No matter who you are, a man or a woman, he treats everyone equal. He's a fighter."

When she was done, Trump mouthed to her, "Wow, so good!" like she was a toddler who had just said her ABC's for the first time. "So beautiful," said Trump, taking the mic from her. "She said, 'Do you mind? I wrote something.' I said, 'Do you want me to read it?' and she said, 'I don't want you to read it.'" So she read it.

Those rare appearances were mostly orchestrated by Hope Hicks, Trump's trusted aide. Hicks was the interface with Melania, making sure that the events Melania did want to attend went smoothly and that travel and logistics were handled for her so she wouldn't be bothered. Kellyanne Conway also helped in that space, but it fell predominantly to Hicks to handle Melania.

Melania liked Hicks—the two women shared similar qualities. They were both jaw-droppingly pretty, stylish, quiet in public, good at keeping secrets, close to their immediate families, and favorites of the candidate. Melania, like Trump, also trusted Hicks's instincts. She felt that if Hicks was asking her to participate in an event, she had already calculated Melania's time, hours away from Barron, the need for her presence, and how her being wherever she was asked to be would affect her husband's mood, on a scale of aloof to he needs her or he'll lose his shit.

Of course, the campaign trail inevitably got thorny for Melania as the election neared. In July, she delivered the partially plagiarized RNC speech, and the very next day a story ran that the official GOP Web page biography about her was inaccurate. It was. It said she had obtained a degree in design and architecture from the University of Ljubljana, which she had not. She dropped out after one year to pursue modeling. The Web site came down. Actually, the spiel that she had graduated college was a thing for Melania since she'd been in New York and started dating Donald Trump, who is obsessed with education status, prone to spouting off the names of Ivy League schools his appointees attended and suggesting people with better college pedigrees were naturally smarter. The embellishment of Melania's college career was likely influenced by Trump, in the same way it was probably he who advised her to shave a few years off her age when she landed print stories in magazines after they got together.

Less than two weeks later came the real humdinger of humiliation. The *New York Post* ran old nude modeling shots of Melania, a particularly shocking one on its cover, with the brutal headline: "*The Ogle Office.*" "You've never seen a potential first lady like this!" raved the cover line, next to a picture of Melania, photoshopped blue stars covering her nipples, her own hands barely hiding her private parts, naked below the waistline. Inside, there were more photos. One from the front, one from behind, Melania looking over her shoulder, in high heels, hands pressed against the wall. They were . . . not good.

Melania had done the shoot in 1996, and the images had run in a French magazine in 1997. "Melania was super-great and a fantastic personality and she was very kind with me," the photographer, a bon vivant with a lean photography résumé named Jarl Alexandre Alé de Basseville, said. He added he was "celebrating the female form" when he took the shots, as male photographers who take naked pictures of up-and-coming models and starlets often do. Alé de Basseville would do time in federal prison for money laundering in 2007.

The shoot happened shortly after Melania arrived in New York, when work was scarce. More models do nude shoots than don't, especially ones trying to break into the industry, and while the shame and secrecy attached to those I-did-what-I-had-to-do photos isn't as intense as it used to be (remember former Miss America Vanessa Williams?), Melania Trump isn't necessarily a woman the current feminist brigade gets jazzed to rally behind.

That these images existed wasn't necessarily a surprise, but the rumors of who leaked them was. There remains to this day a strong indication that it was Trump himself who tipped off the *New York Post* to the photos, using his longtime friend Roger Stone to deliver the goods. (As of this writing, Stone is currently awaiting trial, scheduled for November 2019, on charges of lying to Congress, obstruction, and witness tampering by the Department of Justice.) The theory goes that

Trump was trying to head off a bad week on the campaign. He was embroiled in a nasty public battle with the Gold Star parents of fallen army captain Humayun Khan. So he did what he often does when he wants the conversation to switch to something else: he throws out something new to the media and sits back and watches as it does the trick.

But this time, the idea that he would throw his naked wife under the bus was almost so gross and salacious, and the photos so B-movie bad, the press ultimately spent very little time discussing them. Melania has not commented on how she thinks they got into the hands of the tabloid and onto the cover, but friends say she still refuses to believe Trump would do that to her. As for Stone, she's not so sure.

Trump, who has a long history of wanting everyone else to appreciate the beauty of the women he is with, responded to the photos saying, "Melania was one of the most successful models and she did many photo shoots, including covers and major magazines. This was a picture taken for a European magazine prior to my knowing Melania. In Europe, pictures like this are very fashionable and common." That last part, at least, is true.

The very next day, Monday, August 1, the *Post* dropped more pictures from the same shoot; this time the photos of Melania, again naked, showed her locked in an embrace with another naked model, a woman named Emma Eriksson. "*Menage a Trump*," screamed the headline.

Oddly, though, the photos sort of tanked. In the whirl of an already nasty campaign getting nastier by the day, somehow the public didn't feel like piling on by making fun of Melania Trump. Instead, many felt sorry for her. Liberals and feminists had a difficult time bashing a woman whose nakedness was being shamed on the cover of newspapers. Doing so felt dirty. It fell once again to Jason Miller to spin away the bad news about Melania, just as he had during the uproar over her plagiarized convention speech. But he didn't have to say all that much because photos from twenty years ago were much more forgivable than copying and pasting words Michelle Obama spoke about her husband.

"They're a celebration of the human body as art. There's nothing to be embarrassed about with the pictures," Miller said on CNN, sounding a lot like the photographer who took them. "She's a beautiful woman."

A year before the photos came out, Barbara Walters asked Melania in an interview if her modeling photos—the ones of her naked on a rug in British *GQ*, for example—were too hot for the American public to handle for their first lady. "I don't think so," Melania answered. "I think people will always judge. Maybe they will say, oh, the past that you have, the way you were modeling . . ." She trailed off before adding that she was just doing a job.

The naked photos, however, were too much for her to explain away. Instead, humiliated, defeated, embarrassed, and scared for her young son, she all but disappeared for much of the fall, emerging only at the end of September to sit in the audience as Trump debated Hillary Clinton in upstate New York.

Then came *Access Hollywood,* and the dam broke.

3

The Tape

"I'm not a 'yes' person. I'm 'yes,' or I'm 'no.' But I'm not easily a 'yes' person."

—MELANIA TRUMP

Not even seventy-two hours after the biggest scandal of Trump's campaign broke—his leaked private conversation with *Access Hollywood* host Billy Bush about being able to "grab [women] by the pussy"— Melania showed up to his debate with Hillary Clinton in St. Louis, Missouri, in a hot pink blouse, the necktie of which was styled in the fashion commonly referred to as a "pussy bow." The term dates to the 1930s, when fashionable women would sometimes tie an elaborate, showy bow around their neck, snuggled up tight to their chins, in the fashion of a fancy cat wearing a bow.

The Internet went wild.

What Melania had done was wear something in her first public appearance since the infamous *Access Hollywood* tape that made people question exactly what she was thinking—a tactic she would later use to great effect when she became first lady. That *Was she or wasn't she?* kept people guessing. Was she wearing a pussy bow because Trump had said "pussy"?

Just as Melania started to step back out on the trail after the RNC speech debacle, David Fahrenthold, a *Washington Post* reporter, broke the story, getting his hands on a clip from a hot mic during the interview Trump did in September 2005 with Bush, then host of the entertainment program.

The content was beyond lewd: it was grotesque and horribly offensive. With no cameras on him, only a microphone turned on, Trump starts talking to Bush about a married woman he thought was good-looking, which didn't prevent Trump from taking a stab at trying to sleep with her.

"I moved on her like a bitch, but I couldn't get there. And she was married," Trump says. "Then all of a sudden, I see her. She's now got the big phony tits and everything. She's totally changed her look."

He and Bush chuckled back and forth, Trump saying how hot the woman in the soap opera scene he was about to tape was.

"I've got to use some Tic Tacs, just in case I start kissing her," Trump, who had married Melania eight months earlier, says. "You know I'm automatically attracted to beautiful—I just start kissing them. It's like a magnet. Just kiss. I don't even wait." And then, the coda: "And when you're a star, they let you do it," Trump says. "You can do anything." "Whatever you want," says Bush. "Grab 'em by the pussy," Trump says.

It was that last part that sounded the alarm, that went beyond bawdy talk and into sexual assault territory. It would become a rallying cry for women, both those for and against Trump, and a weapon used by his critics and political opponents.

The tape came out so close to the election that Trump's allies were calling the campaign, telling aides Trump would have to drop out, that it was all over. He was dead on arrival.

Melania was livid. By this point in her marriage, she was less concerned that her husband had an imperfect track record of fidelity and more worried the stories of his behavior, like this one, would get out. She was also furious that all she had sacrificed—her privacy, her schedule, time with Barron, her dignity following the leak of old nude photos, and the RNC speech scandal—would now possibly be for nothing. Some dumb, disgusting conversation could take it all down.

The timing of when Trump recorded the interview was also part of her anger and humiliation. In August 2005, just weeks before he said what he said to Bush, she had told Trump that she was pregnant.

Just as she would do when the story about Stormy Daniels broke months later, Melania went cold, telling him, "You're on your own with this one." As she has often said, he is an adult, he makes his own choices, and he knows the consequences. This was no different.

The worst thing Melania can do to her husband is ice him out, ignore him when the chips are down. Melania was Trump's truth touchstone, and she now had zero desire to throw him a lifeline—and he was drowning. She remained unconcerned with rushing to his side or telling him not to worry, which was all he wanted his wife to do.

"Remember," says someone who knows Melania's thinking, "she grew up under communism, a good environment to learn both survival and resistance."

Melania's frosty public demeanor, the unsmiling pout, the icy stare at cameras, was nothing compared with her expression of anger in private. She's not a crier, says a friend, and she doesn't lock herself in a room and sob and scream. Instead, she gets aloof, distant, punishingly stoic. With Ivana, Trump's first wife, there would be fights. With Marla, his second, drama. But with Melania, since conflict was rare, the sting was in the haughtiness of her judgment.

In a knee-jerk response to the disclosure of the *Access Hollywood* tape, Trump, as he tends to do, made it worse, telling the *New York Post*, "This was locker room banter, a private conversation that took place many years ago. Bill Clinton has said far worse to me on the golf course—not even close. I apologize if anyone was offended." I wondered if "anyone" included his wife, who most definitely was.

By midnight, Trump sent out a videotaped apology, which started off better. "I've never said I'm a perfect person, nor pretended to be someone that I'm not. I've said and done things I regret, and the words released today on this more than a decade-old video are one of them. Anyone who knows me knows these words don't reflect who I am." But it ended back on Clinton, an attempt to point the conversation elsewhere. "I've said some foolish things, but there's a big difference between the words and actions of other people. Bill Clinton has actually abused women, and Hillary has bullied, attacked, shamed, and intimidated his victims," Trump said. "We will discuss this more in the coming days. See you at the debate on Sunday."

Melania, silent on the sidelines, avoided the compulsory crisis control. She didn't leap to his side. Instead, she let Trump sweat it for almost another full day before she did the least she could do.

"The words my husband used are unacceptable and offensive to me," she said in a statement released to the media. "This does not represent the man that I know. He has the heart and mind of a leader. I hope people will accept his apology, as I have, and focus on the important issues facing our nation and the world."

Melania had been listening to Trump's aides go back and forth about what to do with the mess, but she didn't say much. Outsiders' opinions weren't important to her; she only trusted her instincts. She agreed to go ahead with the statement only after saying she would not sit with Trump for a taped apology on national television. Says an aide who was around at the time, the public ritual of the wife sitting next to her husband, possibly even holding his hand, wasn't going to go down on Melania's watch. To engage in such a ritual in the heat of her humiliation and ire at the whole episode would require her to be inauthentic. Her critics might want to take a minute and think about how rare it is in this day and age for the wife of a politician not to perform the ritual. Remember Silda Spitzer, after the then–New York governor Eliot Spitzer got busted for using prostitutes? There she was, quietly and uncomfortably standing beside him as he resigned, admitting to being, basically, a philandering john. (They divorced five years later.) Or Dina Matos McGreevey, wife of the former governor of New Jersey Jim McGreevey, who stood next to her husband wearing a light blue St. John suit and pearls while he announced not only that he had been unfaithful but also that he was gay. (They separated a few weeks later.) Or Wendy Vitter, wife of Louisiana senator David Vitter; Wendy stood beside him as he talked about "past failings" in their marriage. Vitter's number had been found in the Rolodex of "D.C. Madam" Deborah Jeane Palfrey. Or Terry Mahoney, wife of Florida congressman Tim Mahoney, who was by her husband's side when he held a press conference admitting to two affairs, one with a former staffer whom he paid more than $100,000 in the hopes of buying her silence. (A week after the public show of solidarity, Terry filed for divorce.) Or even one of the original political spouses to demonstrate a show of force: Hillary Clinton. Who can forget 1992, when Hillary Clinton leaned in to *60 Minutes'* Steve Kroft to tell the world she was never (probably ever) going to not support her husband, Bill Clinton, no matter what women like Gennifer Flowers, who was claiming a twelve-year affair with Clinton, said. "You know, I'm not sittin' here, some little woman standing by my man like Tammy Wynette," said Clinton, who definitely was doing just that. "I'm sittin' here because I love him, and I respect him, and I honor what he's been through and what we've been through together." Less than three years later, President Clinton would be embroiled in a sex scandal with a White House intern, Monica Lewinsky.

There's something to be said for Melania's not doing the doe-eyed stare at Trump's side, especially considering the precedent of beleaguered spouses who opted to do so, or were told they had to.

Melania said okay to the press statement only after Trump had aired his public apology video. Notably, the only emotion the statement revealed is that she found the words he used unacceptable. "I hope people will accept his apology" was also weak sauce. She might as well have been saying she hopes people forgive him for not taking out the trash. There was no beg, no "please," no counterexample of a time he was kind to her, no hint at any personal conversation between the two beyond "he said he was sorry." Bare bones, at best.

But she knew he wouldn't drop out of the presidential race, so she had to do something; otherwise, everywhere she went from that day until Election Day, she would be hounded with questions about how she felt—which she hates. She also knew the women of the Trump base would like her more for not ditching him completely and for not forcing a fake, hand-holding interview (a la that Bill and Hillary Clinton *60 Minutes* interview, where Hillary did the heavy lifting, fixing a problem with superglue to which Bill himself could only apply a Band-Aid—she saved his bacon).

For Melania, the optics weren't as clear. She wore the pink Gucci pussy bow blouse to the next debate, sure, but no one really knows whether she did so to downplay the issue of his using the word, making light of it and thinking the whole thing silly, or whether she did so to signal to women that she, too, was offended by her husband's disgusting choice of words. I initially thought Melania wasn't that cunning (or conniving) to subliminally message either support for or opposition to her husband's reference to grabbing women's pussies. I honestly thought she was just wearing it to wear it. I have since changed my mind. I've observed the many times she has used her outfits as messaging. I don't think she selected the $1,100 Gucci shirt (and matching hot pink pants) by accident. I think she meant to wear the hell out of that outfit.

I also think she wanted it to land in that gray area between Trump supporters thinking she's on the side of her husband and anti-Trumpers thinking she's sending them a silent signal acknowledging their rage. She bought the shirt from the online retailer Net-a-Porter, where she prefers to do her own shopping, and the description of the blouse on the site reads, "Pussy-bow silk crepe de chine shirt." The word was right there. There were think pieces about that shirt and what it might mean. *Vogue* even did an entire slideshow about the pussy bow throughout history; more than two years later, people still wonder whether it was a hot pink middle finger to the people who attacked her husband for making the tape or to her husband for making it.

A campaign spokeswoman said the shirt was not intentional.

Ten days after the *Access* story broke, and with three weeks to go before Election Day, Melania finally talked about how she felt.

Speaking to Anderson Cooper from the living room of her Trump Tower penthouse, Melania said she was "surprised" by the talk on that tape because that isn't the Donald Trump she knows. Looking rigid and forcing a smile, a very un-Melania shimmer of perspiration on her forehead, she went on to describe it as "boy talk" and said it was Bush who had egged Trump on to say "the dirty and bad stuff." She was exonerating Trump.

"I've heard many different stuff, boys talk," she goes on, "the boys, the way they talk when they grow up and they wanna, ah, sometimes show each other, oh, this and that, and talking about the girls. But, yeah, I was surprised, of course." Melania was saying that she wasn't offended in general by the way boys can brag and embellish stories about girls—she wasn't a prude—but she wasn't going to sit there and say she expected the worst parts of her husband's crude attitude to be aired in public.

"People, they don't really know me," Melania told Cooper, acknowledging that she understood well the consequences of her absence from the spotlight. "People think and talk about me like, 'Oh, poor Melania.'" Then she said something that, for me at least, stuck: "Don't feel sorry for me. I can handle everything." I've thought about this statement a great deal since.

Melania showed up to the final debate between her husband and Hillary Clinton, in Las Vegas, wearing a sleek, sleeveless black Ralph Lauren Collection jumpsuit—which had a tie at the neck that some people said was another pussy bow, but it wasn't really. (Sometimes a bow is just a bow.)

Melania would make a few more appearances before the election, but she didn't follow through on the "three or four big speeches" Trump had promised his wife would deliver during a TV interview with George Stephanopoulos. One would think that Trump would understand it's futile to promise a Melania appearance unless Melania has decided to appear.

The most potent, and perhaps poignant, speech Melania delivered during the campaign, post *Access,* happened on November 3, five days before the election, in tiny Berwyn, Pennsylvania, a Main Line suburb outside Philadelphia. It was a last-ditch effort to boost women voters and get them to the polls. Melania was introduced by Karen Pence, a prickly woman who hadn't made many friends within Trump circles. Melania and Karen could not be more different. They were total opposites. Karen was "often," say aides, suspicious, judgmental, and universally critical. Everyone around her and Mike Pence made Karen suspect an ulterior motive. And she was particularly suspicious of the tall Slovenian model who had posed in her birthday suit. To put it mildly, the two women never clicked, says someone who was on the campaign.

Fast-forward to when Melania is first lady and Karen second lady traveling together to Corpus Christi, Texas, several months after Hurricane Harvey to thank first responders and check in on families. I was on that trip as a member of the press pool and remember quite clearly sitting in the back section of the plane, a C-32 military jet that's the size of a Boeing 757, and watching someone who looked a lot like Karen Pence move from the section ahead of ours, typically where aides and advance teams sit, and head toward the back lavatory.

The plane is divided into a handful of sections, Melania's large cabin being first in front, with paneled walls; a private bathroom; a writing table and chairs; a blanket embossed FIRST LADY OF THE UNITED STATES draped over the comfy sofa. The next section is typically for VIP staff (often, Melania's chief of staff and communications director, her operations manager for the trip, and any other cabinet members or senior staff traveling), and then another section or two designated for other staff, depending on the trip. Melania's photographer and videographer, who go with her everywhere, as is the norm, typically sit in the same section. Her photographer, a friendly woman named Andrea Hanks whose background is in fashion photography, not straight news, is a consistent presence in Melania's world and thus in my world and that of fellow reporters. She moves where we do, but she has better access to the first lady, because it is her job to take the official White House photographs of everything Melania does. Always with Hanks is Alexander Anderson, the first lady's official videographer. Like Hanks, it's his job to document Melania's movements, but with an eye to film, because it is he who crafts the short videos of thirty seconds to one minute that are posted to her social media feeds and on the White House Web site.

Also on such flights are the chief military aide, who is responsible for logistics and overseeing the military accompaniments for the trip, which are military aircraft that accompany the first lady's plane; the higher-ranking Secret Service detail; and, in the back section, the press. All of the sections are comfortable, the seats are typically the larger leather ones you see in first class on domestic commercial planes, and the food they serve is very good and nothing like commercial plane food at all—there are lunch bags packed for us on each seat, and longer flights include dinners and snacks, all prepared by the military cabin crew. Sometimes the menu reflects where we're headed: taco salad for a jaunt to Texas, Tennessee hot chicken when we went to Nashville on a hospital visit. The plastic drink cups, which I'm not too proud to admit many of us in the press have taken with us off the plane as souvenirs, are labeled with the presidential seal and say FIRST LADY OF THE UNITED STATES.

But the main cabin where Melania stays during flights is truly spacious and luxe. So it would be weird if Karen Pence, the second lady of the United States, wasn't seated up front either with Melania in her cabin or as close to it as possible. But she wasn't. I watched as she walked back from the washroom to her seat, just a few rows up in the next section, and sat beside her chief of staff. I thought it strange and also telling of their relationship that Melania perhaps wouldn't have offered to share her private cabin. Or, if she had, that Karen wouldn't have accepted. I mean, even if you don't like the person, it would seem the right thing to do for a flight from D.C. to Houston that takes three and a half hours—share the most comfortable space. Michelle Obama and Jill Biden would frequently huddle together on flights, discussing strategy for the public appearance they were about to make or analyzing the success of one they had just made and laughing or chatting with staff.

My suspicions that the two weren't close were confirmed, at least somewhat, I thought, when I noticed upon landing that Melania had not changed out of her tall boots with the four-inch heels, which she had worn getting on the plane.

In an earlier debacle, Melania—gasp—wore her signature So Kate Christian Louboutin heels departing Washington to survey hurricane damage in Texas, and people just about had a heart attack. HOW DARE SHE?! As she usually does, she had changed on the plane from the heels into a more appropriate outfit for that occasion, putting on Adidas Stan Smith sneakers and throwing her hair into a ponytail tucked under a baseball cap emblazoned with the letters FLOTUS. After that, Melania was more mindful of her footwear at all moments of her travel.

Yet this time, on the trip with Karen Pence, Melania didn't change into a lower heel before she departed the plane, and the whole day she almost comically towered over Karen, who wore flats. Slipping into a flatter-heeled shoe wasn't a consideration Melania offered Karen to help offset the height disparity. When the two posed for photos with first responders, the top of Karen's head didn't even reach Melania's shoulder. I would say that Melania didn't mean for the difference to be so great, but I've seen her change shoes to a lower heel or a flat, aware of the company with whom she will be walking or photographed.

The same thing happened again when the two took a trip together in April 2019 to visit military families at Fort Bragg, North Carolina. On the plane, Karen sat with the staff hoi polloi, Melania ensconced in her private cabin. On the ground, Melania wore a tailored military-style jacket with a wide belt, slim slacks, and four-inch heels. Karen wore an untucked, nondescript olive green shirt, loose green pants, and sensible loafers.

However, Karen has had something of a makeover in recent months, whether spurred by having to stand so often next to Melania

Trump, we'll never know for sure. But she has lost weight, thanks to a commitment to the Weight Watchers program, say those who interact with her, and she's apparently also discovered the joys—and fashion options—of Rent the Runway, a rental company for designer clothing.

But back in Pennsylvania, right before the election, Karen opened her brief remarks by rattling off her exhaustive campaign schedule: where she had just flown in from (Iowa) and been stumping the day before (Arizona, New Mexico, *and* Colorado). Melania had just popped over from New York City.

Karen called Melania up to the podium, describing her as "strong" and "amazing" (which she probably actually thinks she is, having to be married to Trump—of whom, it's reported, Karen is not a fan). Melania walked out and draped her arm around Karen's shoulder for about five seconds as they stood together, waving while "Age of Aquarius" played on a loudspeaker—truly the weirdest walkout song, especially since no explanation for why it was chosen or who had selected it was given.

Melania's speech was solid: a rare admission of her feelings about her immigrant status and how, as a young woman, she longed to come to America. Political watchers both in and outside the Trump inner circle smacked their foreheads and commented that Melania should have been doing this all along, been the voice of the American dream, or some überversion of it. Maybe the campaign should have pressured her with intensity to do more appearances, tried harder. While Ivanka had been a potent surrogate, her "story"—Park Avenue princess with an Ivy League education—left something to be desired when trying to reach voters who had faced more of a struggle in life. That's not to say that Melania was perfect—she was nervous, shaky almost, and she stumbled over the words several times. In thanking Karen, she pronounced Indiana, "Indy-AHN-a," and said how happy she was to be in "Penn-sil-vay-knee-ah," pronouncing every syllable. She again used her outfit to message, wearing a soft, flowing baby-pink top with loose sleeves and a simple white pencil skirt. She was talking to women, so playing the sexy vamp wasn't the way she wanted to go.

Melania relied on the teleprompter, but it didn't help calm her nerves. Her sentences were stiff. But the crowd loved her. Kellyanne Conway had helped with the speech, smartly interjecting lines that would soothe Melania as she spoke, parts about Slovenia ("I grew up in a small town in Slovenia, near a beautiful river and forests") and her family ("My parents were wonderful. Of course, we always knew about the incredible place called America."). Conway even had the smarts to inject Ronald Reagan into the speech. "President Ronald Reagan's 'morning in America' was not just something in the United States, it began to feel like morning around the world, even in my small country. It was a true inspiration to me," said Melania. "In 2006, I studied for the test, and become a U.S. citizen. . . . I'm an immigrant. And let me tell you, no one values the freedom and opportunity of America more than me," she shared, calling herself an "independent woman."

She transitioned into what she wanted to focus on if she became first lady: helping kids. "Our culture has gotten too mean and too rough," she said, chiding the bullying of kids and remarking that it's especially troubling when bullies are "hiding" on the Internet. Her statement echoed comments she made to Anderson Cooper during the post–*Access Hollywood* Trump Tower interview: she wanted to help children navigate social media. These comments were the first indication that she was going to shine a light on—and try to stop—the very thing that had given her husband a political bully pulpit: name-calling on Twitter. At the time of her announcement in Pennsylvania, her platform didn't get as much play as it eventually would, once the hypocrisy sank in.

She also said she would help women (something she dropped once on the job). Either way, the speech was long—about sixteen minutes—and impactful. Trump won Pennsylvania by the narrowest margin in that state since 1840. Pundits and experts on elections had anticipated it would swing in Hillary Clinton's favor—in the end Trump edged Clinton 48.18 percent to 47.46 percent. And while Melania's speech might not have been the deciding factor that put him over the edge, it certainly didn't hurt.

One senior campaign aide agrees that Melania would have been a huge asset on the stump, if only she had lifted the tiniest of fingers and done more, given more speeches like the one in Berwyn. She might have had "trophy wife" written all over her, sure, but she also had a compelling and effective story, and for women she might have been a more appealing presidential spouse than Bill Clinton, around whom the affair-with-an-intern odor still lingered. "She has her own set of beliefs and she was her own person," says a former campaign adviser, shrugging when asked why they couldn't get her out there more. "And she's still been more successful in being able to maintain that unique identity than any other wife of an elected official in my lifetime."

It is the norm that a political wife loses herself in the persona of her husband. She's window dressing, there to reinforce his messaging and make it approachable, often to the female demographic. Political wives also tend to be so carefully molded and intellectually influenced by the politician's staff and advisers that they become indistinguishable from the stump-made version of themselves. They have done so many potluck dinners and meet and greets with the local Junior League that they don't know whether the speech they gave on Tuesday is the same one they gave on Saturday. A rinse-repeat behavior develops, which is frankly understandable, because the campaign trail can be brutal, but it's a symptom of losing who you are in order to become who the campaign wants you to be. Melania, by refusing to be anyone's shill, maintained, and still maintains, her authenticity.

By Election Day, Melania was just ready to get it all over with. She, like the rest of Trump's team, and possibly even Trump himself, wasn't 100 percent sure he had put the *Access Hollywood* scandal far enough behind him to win. She arrived at Public School 59, her voting precinct near 57th Street and Third Avenue, wearing a white Michael Kors dress she bought at the designer's Madison Avenue store and a camel Balmain coat with gold buttons she bought off Net-a-Porter. She had the coat "on" in her signature way, draped over her shoulders, arms not through the sleeves. With Trump next to her, she stepped into a voting booth and cast her ballot. Ivanka had gone first, not surprisingly, bringing her oldest child, Arabella, with her and Jared to watch the process. Bringing one or more of her children to public photo opportunities would soon become one of Ivanka's more cloying calling cards—exposing her kids to the scrutiny of paparazzi cameras. Perhaps she did so because it was what she knew herself, growing up the child of Donald and Ivana Trump.

Melania didn't want to bring Barron, feeling like the photographers and cameras at the polling place would be too much. She was savoring every last minute of privacy for the boy, just in case Trump would go on to win the election, since all of that could be lost.

Melania looked down at her ballot the whole time, ignoring everyone, pinning on a smile for half a second. Trump, per usual, couldn't focus. He peered over his ballot station to his wife at hers, like he was cheating off her paper for a test. Memes followed. "See the problem with @realDonaldTrump copying Melania's ballot is that Melania copied hers from Michelle Obama," was one particularly viral tweet.

By the evening, the family had gathered to watch the returns come in at Trump Tower. Melania hadn't spent the day making last-minute calls to supporters and doing radio interviews to push every last voter to the polls, like the rest of the family had. Instead, she hung out with her parents and her son in the triplex, savoring the end of this long and difficult road. Michael Wolff, in his book *Fire and Fury,* said Melania had hoped Trump would lose the election so she could return to "inconspicuously lunching." To the contrary, I've now covered Melania for three years and have never found anyone who could confirm that Melania actually hoped Trump would lose, much less vocalize it. She was really the only one who knew in her gut from the beginning that if Trump ran, he would win. Was she comfortable reconciling her prediction with reality? Perhaps not, but she wasn't actively championing a loss.

A loss wasn't to be. As the night went on, the group gathered in election headquarters—which was also in Trump Tower, just on a different floor—and it became clear that Trump was going to win. When it was final, it was late, cruising past 1:00 A.M., and Melania, exhausted and emotionally spent, had to convince Barron, just at the cusp of the moody tween years, to get dressed and celebrate—at 2:30 A.M. Just before the family piled into SUVs to take them to the Hilton, where Trump would officially claim victory, he called Barron over and retied his shiny white necktie.

Melania had changed from the comfortable clothes she had spent the day in to a white one-shouldered jumpsuit with a ruffle running the length of one side, purchased off the rack at Ralph Lauren's Madison Avenue flagship store for just shy of four thousand dollars. Melania says she decides what to wear by diagnosing how she feels each day. And that day she felt like wearing the one designer that Hillary Clinton had relied on for the majority of the campaign. Clinton was well versed in Ralph Lauren, particularly the iconic American designer's arsenal of tailored pantsuits, many of which he had custom made for Clinton in shades of red, white, and blue. Melania's jumpsuit was RL, but with its sexy shoulder reveal bore no resemblance to the stodgy, androgynous suits Clinton chose. The choice of white was also one of those curious coincidences (which, as I have said many times, I don't believe in when it comes to Melania): it not only represents purity and newness but also was worn by suffragettes. Trump, who has told friends he's always preferred women to wear dresses, not pants, fancied Ivanka Trump's election-night ensemble more than his wife's. Ivanka and Tiffany wore girly blue dresses, very short, hems hitting their legs at the upper thigh.

At another hotel nearby, Hillary Clinton was also wearing Ralph Lauren, a dark gray pantsuit with bright purple lapels to match the purple silk shirt underneath. The vibrancy of the color felt out of place as she conceded victory to Trump.

Melania, meanwhile, was making her own concessions, trying to conflate being independent with having just become the most important spouse in the free world.

4

The Girl from Slovenia

*"There will be good times and hard times and
unexpected turns."*

—MELANIA TRUMP

As intense as the damage was in her marriage to Donald Trump—
the scandals, the adultery charges, the language used in the *Access
Hollywood* tape alone—Melania was loath to consider leaving him,
and even more abhorrent was the idea of divorce. She was, like most
women in Slovenia, not only raised Catholic but also trained to take
the bad with the good, even if the bad was really, really bad. "Neg-
ativism is a national sport, and it does not matter if your cow dies,
as long as your neighbor loses at least two" is an apt description of
the mind-set of your average Slovene, says Slovenian writer Sandi
Gorišek.

One aspect of Melania Trump that people find most troubling is
that she doesn't smile. But if you understand Slovenians, you know
they are not a grinning country. "I don't fake," Melania once said to
me, explaining why she is often photographed unsmiling. "I'm not
someone who smiles or pretends to smile just because there is a camera." In the string of political wives who have stood by and gazed

adoringly at their husbands, frozen smiles pinned on for minutes on end, Melania's stone coldness is, oddly, refreshing. But to really understand the Melania of today, it's important to understand where she comes from.

The road to Sevnica, Slovenia, is neither easy to travel nor direct. Nestled in the mountains of Slovenia, some fifty-three miles west of the country's capital and largest city, Ljubljana, and worlds away from Washington, D.C., it is the hometown of Melania Trump, back when she was Melanija Knavs. The higher the climb up the windy, narrow roads toward Sevnica (pronounced "say-oo-neet-zah"), the more alpine the homes, with fewer and fewer terra-cotta rooftops and more A-line cabins with wooden decks and decorative shutters. Slovenia, population just over two million, is about the size of New Jersey and is bordered by Austria, Croatia, Italy, Hungary, and, to the west, a tiny sliver of the Adriatic Sea.

Melania spent the early part of her life in a modest communist apartment, as did most residents of Slovenia. The apartment was tiny, drab, a signature of communist housing that defined what was then Yugoslavian living. Communism in Slovenia shaped a generation who was willing to settle for, who even expected and was grateful for, the bare minimum. President Josip Broz Tito, the communist leader of Yugoslavia, ingrained in his people that being humble was noble and that standing out was bad. The general thought about Yugoslavia at the time was that if communism was going to be the rule, they had it better than most other communist countries. Tito taught his people to keep their heads down and not lust for anything special. It was a lifestyle that created an intensely private population of mind-your-own-business types. But it also had the effect of producing the odd citizen who longed for a shinier penny . . . or a gilded penthouse.

Back then, Melania's father, Viktor, was working as a chauffeur for the mayor of a neighboring town. He would later become a car-parts salesman for a state-owned company, climbing through the ranks, working the system to ingratiate himself to the local communist party bigwigs. It was simply fact that most leadership at the factories and businesses in town were communist, so if life was better if the boss liked you, you had better like communism. Aligning with the party became a way to get ahead: the money, the power, the resources—all were in the hands of the communists, and Viktor understood that to maneuver his family out of the tiny apartment and into a better life, he had to play along. Young Melania was a diligent observer of how he operated and how committed he was, sacrificing at any cost for his children so that they could live in a good house closer to town, attend good schools, go on beach and ski vacations, and be set, if only slightly, ahead of their peers.

There would later, during Trump's presidency, be rumors that Viktor was still connected to Communism, even on friendly terms with Russian president Vladimir Putin. There was also a conspiracy theory that Melania herself was a planted Russian spy. Neither proves true.

The house Melania spent her later childhood years in is located in one of the posher areas of Sevnica, if there is such a thing. The windy roads in the neighborhood are lined with cozy split-level houses, more San Bernardino than Beverly Hills, but comparatively a nice place to raise a family. There's a balcony, a large attached garage that houses Viktor's beloved Mercedes-Benz, blinds on every window, and a rooftop satellite dish. The place hasn't become the tourist attraction one might have anticipated since their daughter became *prava dama* of the United States, but when her mother, Amalija, and Viktor are in town, security guards have been spotted near the driveway.

Nowadays, a waning part of living in Sevnica is scooping up profits from exploiting its famous former inhabitant, whether that's spurred by actual Melania Trump hometown boastfulness or a healthy desire to capture tourist dollars has yet to be determined, not that anyone cares. Trump himself would be impressed with the shops and businesses that have churned out everything from M-branded hand cream to local Krskopoljc sausages (there is an annual festival in town to celebrate the regional meat). The town's Cafe Julija still makes its Melania dessert, a pastry with white chocolate streaked gold on the outside and warm apple and almond filling on the inside. Competitive spirit launched nearby Kruhek Bakery and Coffee Shop's tarts, served for two dollars a pop with a tiny USA flag stuck on top and the letter M dusted in powdered sugar.

As American as Slovenian apple pie.

Korpitarna Shoes, one of Sevnica's longest and most thriving businesses—there is a statue of a large boot in the center of the traffic circle that leads into town—makes a Melania-inspired bedroom slipper that is sparkly gray flannel with a white faux-fur pom-pom on top. The label on the slipper's inside says WHITE HOUSE.

Ironically, friends say one of the things Melania hates most about her fame is people trying to make money off it. She's learned from her husband: if she can't have a cut of the profits, they shouldn't be earned in the first place. She will legally fight back, and has, when her name or likeness is used without her permission, which is why in Sevnica everything is branded FIRST LADY, WHITE HOUSE, and M, substitutes for the word "Melania." A legal tangle with Slovenian tabloid *Suzy* in the summer of 2016 showed that writing falsehoods about Melania Trump isn't something she lets go of. She's like her husband in this way—only when she threatens to sue for slander, she actually goes through with it. And she wins. After *Suzy* published a story saying Melania had worked as an escort, she hired a pit-bull Slovenian lawyer who went after the magazine, pursuing an apology, a retraction, and monetary damages. Melania won the case for an undisclosed amount of money. "The first lady is very well acquainted with the law in the field of personal rights violations," says her attorney, Nataša Pirc Musar, adding that she admired Melania for her "calm and gentle determination. She is one of the most organized persons I have worked with, and always really well informed about the issues we needed to discuss."

Back when she was a child, Melania and her older sister, Ines, were two bright-eyed little girls who enjoyed after-school activities and their lessons. They went to the local elementary school, Sava Kladinka, where it was impressed on them not to stand out but to be a positive participant in communism. Individuality was not encouraged in children, which for two creative girls was a difficult rule to adhere to. Though remembered not as troublemakers but good little communist daughters, Melania and Ines instead indulged their creativity at home, drawing pictures and helping Amalija sew clothes.

Adult work schedules were also assigned and strictly adhered to, which meant most days would end at 3:00 in the afternoon so families would have time to spend together—another benefit for Melania, who worshiped her older sister and was coddled by her parents. Melania and Ines were thick as thieves, each other's best friend. Though older by a couple of years, Ines was Melania's touchstone; the two shared a bedroom for most of their young lives and would later be roommates as Melania traveled throughout Europe to model and lived in Milan and Paris.

Melania and her sister were enamored with their mother, an exceptionally stylish woman who worked as a patternmaker and cutter at Jutranjka, a state-owned factory that produced mostly children's clothing. She made her own clothes and outfits for her daughters. Under communist rule, trendy clothes were hard to come by at stores, if they existed at all, and they often did not. Amalija, however, insisted that her children be properly and fashionably dressed, even if that meant staying up for hours in the evenings, long after the girls had gone to bed, to sew them cute skirts and tops. Melania and her sister would often participate in the factory's frequent fashion shows, modeling the clothing that the workers at Jutranjka helped put into production. It was here, back in the early 1970s, that Melania got her first taste for fashion and the runway. And it was Amalija who taught her daughters that being even that much better than the rest was worth the extra effort.

Otherwise, childhood in Sevnica was fairly average for Melania. Not knowing any other way of life, communist rule felt normal. "When you grow up, you don't think, 'Oh, I'm growing up under communism,' you understand what I mean?" said Melania. "You're just a kid. You go on the bike, you do gymnastics, you enjoy your friends. My parents provided a great, solid life for our family. I have beautiful memories of traveling." The family was indeed tight-knit: although Viktor was often away in nearby cities for work, he came home to Sevnica to spend weekends with his family. By all accounts, he was a hands-on father and adored his wife, to whom he has been married since 1966.

Her parents' marriage and Melania's conventional childhood had a *tremendous* influence on Melania. She was determined that when she got married, she would stay married (which made Trump a peculiar gamble). After she had Barron in 2006, it was all the more important for her to maintain the normalcy for him that she experienced during her formative years, despite living in extremely atypical circumstances.

Slovenian primary schools run from ages seven to fifteen, during which time Melania developed a real taste for fashion design, poring over the rare glossy magazine that Amalija would at times get her hands on at work and bring home. When she was ten years old, CNN came on the scene, and watching the rest of the world via the cable news network was an epiphany for Melania. The images she saw and the clothes people wore represented something so completely compelling that she set her mind to becoming one of the artists who would create such beautiful designs. Melania's ability to knock out a decent sketch was good. Ines also liked to draw and paint and had inherited a bit of artistic flair, and when Melania later pursued a modeling career, Ines tried her hand at fashion design.

Melania had a knack for understanding proportion and fit, again thanks in large part to watching her mother piece together remnant fabric from the factory into wearable clothes. When she became first lady of the United States, even those who have a strong distaste for her gave her credit for her taste—"she knows what looks good on her" is an oft-repeated phrase. And it is true. Melania has always had the ability to buy off the rack and know inherently what will work with her five-foot-eleven frame. It's a rare sartorial skill that many women think they have, but most don't.

Melania was enthralled by the structure of a garment and how to turn something commonplace into something standout. In a country where there was just one kind of soup, one kind of bread, one kind of button for your shirt, Melania had an active and aspirational imagination. Whether it was adding a pin or a patch, sewing on a tiny cloth flower, or changing a button on a shirt, Melania would quietly but determinedly express her flair for fashion.

She put her nascent design skills to work and, as elementary school and middle school ended, applied as a fifteen-year-old to the Srednja Šola za Oblikovanje in Fotografijo (High School of Design and Photography) in Ljubljana, Slovenia's small but bustling capital city, more than an hour's train ride away from Sevnica. The school was a very competitive technical secondary school, the only one of its kind in the city, and served ages sixteen to nineteen, as most high schools in Slovenia do. The centuries-old school building is impressive even today, and it still operates as a school for kids with a penchant for photography and design.

The school is right in the center of town and features a large cobblestone courtyard, adjacent to a Byzantine church; students pass from classroom to classroom via outdoor hallways connected by balconied archways decorated with columns overflowing with ivy. An amphitheater takes up a large portion of the campus and is still used for concerts and performances, the school taking on the role of cultural hub for the city.

There were only a couple dozen students in each class, thirty tops, and acceptance was difficult, especially for someone who didn't live inside the city limits—but Melania, determined, took the required tests, passed, and got in. The school was exclusive and relatively expensive, says one of her classmates. She recalls Melania as a nice and simple girl who immersed herself in the fashion design courses offered, one of four divisions in the overall program: fashion, industrial design, graphic design, and photography.

Melania didn't socialize after school all that much, but that was mainly because she was rushing to catch the train home in the afternoons, an arduous commute for any teenager, but especially one trying to acclimate to her peers. While it isolated her socially, it also highlighted Melania's early sense of responsibility. Throughout the various stages of her life, people who know her almost always fondly describe her as sort of a wet blanket, not one to hang out or change her schedule to grab a coffee or a drink, never one to stay out too late, always sticking to the rule book. She was a giant nerd, disguised in the body of a five-foot-eleven fashion model.

After a year or so of commuting back and forth to school, Amalija and Viktor relented and rented a small flat for Melania and Ines, who was now also attending school in Ljubljana. Though older, Ines had stayed in Sevnica when Melania went off to school in the big city, but when her sister found success in Ljubljana, Ines soon followed. Hyper-responsible, both teenagers were living on their own, with weekend visits from their mother and stopovers from their dad whenever business took him into the city. They did not throw wild parties. They hardly even had friends over, but the freedom to do nothing but be together was, for the Knavs girls, quite literally heaven. Viktor once gave Amalija a fancy gold bracelet, and when the girls were younger, their parents had replicas of it made, one for Melania and one for Ines, and gave them as gifts under the tree one Christmas morning. Melania would later say the bracelets symbolized their love for one another as a family. Theirs was a strong bond based on loyalty, a foreshadow of the family life Melania would eventually try to uphold, under the most ridiculous of circumstances.

Despite their relative monastic existence as teens, one thing that did help Melania's popularity was modeling. She began working for Slovenia's most well-known photographer, Stane Jerko; he discovered her walking in a school-sponsored fashion show in Ljubljana when she was about sixteen years old. "She was cute," said Jerko in a 2016 interview. "Big girl, long legs, and I said she would be a good model. At the time, I was looking for girls on the street who would be suitable for photography."

It was rare for a young girl like Melania to be modeling, especially for someone like Jerko, who was respected for his work, and not for some creep making a lurid proposition. Her classmates thought it cool. Jerko, who at eighty-one still lives and takes photographs in Ljubljana, was famous for discovering the two Slovenian models who made it to mild notoriety outside of Slovenia, Nina Gazibara and Martina Kajfez, the latter a sultry brunette with piercing blue eyes who bears a bit of a resemblance to Melania.

The whispers that she was modeling for Jerko gave Melania, a bland, soft-spoken student at the school, a bit of an edge, one she desperately lacked in the mid-eighties Eastern European world of permed hair and brightly colored leggings and sweaters. She didn't have boyfriends, and she kept her circle of girlfriends close. A former classmate says Melania didn't abuse the privilege of being exceptionally pretty, nor, as a properly raised Slovenian, did she boast about her modeling activities. Instead, she took a few photographs with Jerko from time to time, enough to cobble together an average portfolio. She brought her own clothes to the studio, and Jerko shot her wearing a handful of different outfits, though barefoot, because he didn't have fancy shoes to fit her size 9 feet.

"She was a very ordinary girl; she had to pretty much make do with herself," said Jerko, which would be a terribly unflattering assessment if it wasn't what would be echoed for two decades to come by those who encountered Melania during her modeling years. Following her career from afar, Jerko said that Melania must have taken the business very seriously and been very dogged in her pursuit of work, because to survive solely on the skills she had would require "nerves and strong will." In other words, it took more than her natural looks.

Several decades later, Melania's beauty can leave people breathless in Washington, D.C. (not a city known for its beautiful people) or

Kansas, but in the world of models, moderate to elite, she was pretty average.

Jerko's photographs show a very different Melania than the one we now know. She's smiling a lot in the pictures, striking poses with her arms at various angles. She is stiff in a cute sort of I'm-a-little-teapot way, more than loose model moves. In some photos she has her hair piled on top of her head in a spiky high ponytail, all bushy eyebrows and strong, pouty mouth. In another series, where she looks the most like she does today, Melania wears a white strapless dress, her hair slicked back in a bun, barefoot and scowling. "These photos somehow triggered her modeling career," says Jerko, sounding a bit surprised himself that things took off for Melania as they did. His chief complaint at the time was that Melania took her schoolwork too seriously. "I wanted to photograph her for the magazine *Nasa žena,* but she did not have time."

Melania was too busy doing the things girls her age did. She and her school pals loved listening to Duran Duran, Spandau Ballet, Men at Work, and popular American or Italian bands. The first concert she attended was Elton John, in Zagreb, Croatia, when she was sixteen. A friend from those years says the feeling in Slovenia after it disentangled itself from Yugoslavia to become its own nation—which officially happened in 1991—was freeing. Suddenly, they were able to have things they didn't have growing up. "Like jeans." She and Melania and other girls their age would often travel about an hour's train trip west to Trieste, Italy, just over the Slovenian border, if they wanted denim or other fashionable items like Adidas sneakers. Now, they didn't have to. Jeans were as tame a status symbol as could be, but they were still practically a prerequisite for a cool urban teenager at the time. Without screaming "I'm hip to the scene," they indicated a smooth transition from communist clothing to "normal" duds. Wearing them, as all the kids at her school did, was one of the ways Melania learned early on to use fashion as a messaging tool. Her voice might not be loud, but her clothing could speak volumes, a skill she would rely on heavily when she began living in the White House.

But the rush of being able to wear Levi's still didn't mean Melania and her peers would abandon their inward Slovenian selves. "We are still very simple, and we don't like to push ourselves into first place," says Melania's old school friend. "In Italy, when we would go, if Italians see a camera it's 'Hi, mama! ciao, ciao!' but we're totally different, totally opposite. We don't show it on our faces—we are closed, and that's how we like to be." Later, one of the chief speculations made about Melania as first lady is that she looks freakin' miserable and hates living in the White House, that her face, for all its beauty, belies a sadness and displeasure with her role. Most people can't believe that her expressions lend themselves to any other interpretation. But ask a Slovenian if "resting bitch face" is a thing in their country, and they will look blankly at you and say, "it's just 'face.'"

A popular expression in Slovenia is "tihi vodi premikajo gore," an idiomatic expression that means "still waters run deep" and literally translates to "silent waters can move mountains." If Melania's quiet stoicism is read by emotionally expressive Americans as some sort of silent protest of sadness and despair, they're wrong. Like most native Slovenians, she's quietly judging you, or plotting her next move.

As her high school years came to an end, Melania had zero desire to move back to Sevnica. She enrolled in classes at the University of Ljubljana, studying architecture and design. But she held tight to modeling as a means to leave her home country and see the rest of the world. Jerko said most of his more successful girls naturally went next to Milan, where they could find more runway work or be paid as a fit model for design houses, meaning you were basically a breathing clothes hanger, meant to stand for hours at a time while a designer or an assistant had you try on outfit after outfit. "If you want to work in Milan, you have to be very good; you cannot be a beginner," Jerko warned her.

So Melania participated in Ljubljana's biggest modeling competition, the *Jana* magazine Model of the Year contest. She was already twenty-two years old at this point, well past the ripe age of modeling contests in America and other parts of the globe, ancient by the standards of the international Ford Models Supermodel of the World contest, probably the most popular and lucrative modeling competition in those days. Still, Melania placed second, behind her lookalike and fellow Jerko ingenue, Martina Kajfez. (Kajfez would go on to have a tepid modeling career for many years, mostly in Italy, before returning to her home country, where, now in her midforties, she resides in one of Slovenia's picturesque coastal towns.) The contest was enough of a boon to her ego and her ambition that Melania dropped out of university after just shy of two years, getting Viktor and Amalija's reluctant blessing to pack up and move to Milan. Ines came along, hoping to break into fashion from the design side.

Melania's headshot from the time makes her look a bit like eighties rock groupie Tawny Kitaen. Her hair is dark and tousled, untamed and messy with bangs put to the side. Her cheekbones are sharp, her eyebrows have been plucked (a little) since her earlier photos, and she's mastered the model mouth—lips slightly pursed and parted, just a hint of teeth showing, not a smile but also not a frown.

"I felt it was kind of too small for me," said Melania of her decision to leave Slovenia for Italy and then Paris and, ultimately, New York. Nothing was holding young Melania back. She was eerily confident and, weirdly, having come from a town with about six stop signs in it, street-smart. "I always felt like, don't lose the momentum with what you want to do," she said of her decision to take her second-place win in a modeling contest and move to one of fashion's most competitive markets. "Go for it. You don't want to turn back and say, Oh, why didn't I do that?" Melania lacked something most small-town girls have: fear. This attribute would serve her well for life with Trump.

5

The Donald

"I had my life. I didn't care about his. I wasn't starstruck."

—MELANIA TRUMP

W hen Melania arrives in New York City in 1996, she's on the wrong side of twenty-two—or sixteen, for that matter. At twenty-six, she's already ten years older than most serious models begin their careers in fashion's competitive market. She also has a new last name: Knauss, the Germanized version of her last name that she felt would be easier for potential employers to pronounce.

Though moving to Manhattan to work as a model was her ultimate goal, her arrival at such a late stage in her career felt like getting to the party just as the other guests were leaving. She could still probably get a drink at the bar and meet a few people, but the band had already stopped playing and the lights were coming up.

Today it's the Stephen Sondheim Theatre, a standard show space on 43rd Street between 6th and Broadway. It's environmentally sound, the first LEED-certified Broadway theater of its kind, renovated in

2009 with sustainable materials. Ironically, its longest-running hit was "Urinetown: The Musical."

But in 1998, it was the Kit Kat Club, inspired by the divey Berlin nightspot from *Cabaret*. The Kit Kat was that raucous kind of dance club where DJs yelled over the music and waitresses passed out horns and noisemakers. It was heavy on strobe lights, and pretty girls in Hervé Léger bandage dresses got in gratis. The ubiquitous nightlife gag of champagne bottles with giant sparklers shooting out of the top was practically invented in clubs like the Kit Kat.

It was a draw for city dwellers as well as the bridge and tunnel crowd, and when night met the daylight at closing, it was often the scene of drunken brawls and police activity. The club's neighbors had for years tried to get the place's liquor license revoked in the hopes of shutting it down. By the time the Kit Kat fizzled out in 2000, not long after a young Shawn Carter, aka Jay-Z, was arrested there for stabbing a record company promoter, the owners of the building were frankly more than comfortable ushering it into its next phase of existence as a theater. But in 1998, it was bumpin'.

Fresh off his second marriage to Marla Maples, from whom he was separated for about a year but not yet divorced, Donald Trump was something of a New York nightclub regular. He was heavy into the dating scene at the time, picking up models, generally enjoying bachelorhood freedom after two back-to-back marriages. He was out, a lot, and almost always with young, pretty girls, many of whom he felt comfortable enough with to hug or kiss or pat on the behind, whether he was given the green light to do so or not. One of the people he was seen with during this period (at his estate, Mar-a-Lago, and in New York City) was Jeffrey Epstein, who would later be charged by federal prosecutors with sex trafficking and sexually abusing minors; Epstein killed himself in his jail cell while awaiting trial.

For a time, almost two years, one of Trump's main squeezes was Kara Young, a model whom Trump met at a party in the Hamptons. Young was well known enough in modeling circles that the romance with the mogul made a few headlines, notably when Trump first started dating her, since she was still involved with a celebrity reporter named A. J. Benza. Trump, not one to be discreet about landing a beautiful woman, crowed about it to Howard Stern during one of their infamous radio interviews: "I stole his girlfriend. I took her away like he was a dog."

On this particular evening at the Kit Kat, Trump was not with Young, but squiring another one of his regulars, a pretty blond Norwegian heiress (somewhat unfortunately) named Celina Midelfart. Midelfart, who looks like Trump's daughter Ivanka, had also become something of a steady. Now in a relationship with a wealthy Norwegian businessman, she has since denied that she and Trump, twenty-eight and fifty-two years old at the time, were ever romantically involved, but they were spotted with regularity for several months in 1998, going to ritzy social events with names like the Million Dollar Beauty Ball at the Waldorf-Astoria, watching polo matches at the Bridgehampton Polo Club, and attending the hot nineties ticket VH1 Divas concert. They even went together to a birthday party for Donald's first wife, Ivana Trump, at another nightclub popular at the time, Chaos, where Midelfart posed with her boyfriend's then seventeen-year-old daughter Ivanka, Donald wedged in between, his arms tightly hugging both blondes. That setup, by the way, is one of Donald Trump's favorite photo ops—whatever woman he is with on one side, his own daughter on the other, gripping both around their waists with equal intensity. It's a pose Melania would soon come to know well.

Trump and Midelfart arrived at the Kit Kat for a party thrown by Paolo Zampolli, an Italian social fixture who at twenty-eight had already founded his own modeling agency, called ID Model Management. Not necessarily the loud-dance-club type, Trump preferred a private party, for which the Kit Kat would sometimes be a venue, for a substantial rental fee. It was September, New York Fashion Week, peak opportunity for red carpets crawling with models and the men who wanted to date them. If there were a club of rich dudes who took it upon themselves to go out every night and scope out beautiful young women, Donald Trump would be its president. He once said of dating, "The hunt is a great thing. We all love the hunt."

Zampolli met Trump several months before that evening and considered him a good friend. The two would later collaborate on several real estate deals when Zampolli transitioned from modeling agent to real estate broker. His big claim to fame was melding the two, using models turned real estate agents as lures for big clients. Zampolli founded a second agency in 2006 called Paramount Realty, where his agents (who looked and dressed like high-fashion models, and oftentimes were) toured properties with clients in a company Rolls-Royce, having lunch with them as part of the agreement. Zampolli crowed about his idea and the basis of its success, "Everyone wants to know a model."

But in the 1990s Zampolli collected for his agency the sort of model that probably wasn't going to reach icon status, or even status status. Still, he cared for his girls and was known more as a social impresario than working agent. Zampolli claims he discovered Melania in Milan in 1996, where she was already doing the model grunt work of bouncing between there, Paris, London, and Berlin for gigs, making a passable living, but with her eyes on the prize of New York City. He takes credit for getting her there.

"She wanted to go to New York—that's what she wanted," says Zampolli, a colorful character who, since the late 1990s, has had several careers and is now the United Nations ambassador to the island of Dominica. Zampolli confides that he still maintains regular contact with Melania and the president, visiting with them at Mar-a-Lago, often posting photos afterward on his Instagram account. "Three months later, she came. She was very determined." Zampolli has an Italian accent on the ridiculous side of thick and in several interviews, including mine, has praised Melania's commitment to finding work and tenaciousness in making it. He's quick to paint her as clean—no parties, no drugs, no booze. "She was someone who had serious dreams to work," he tells me, "just come to New York to actually do her job. She was not going out." Any model over the age of twenty-five still hoping to get work in New York probably also knew that late nights, smoking, and drinking weren't going to do much to help with a nubile glow. Plus, the fashionable look at the time was, quite frankly, the opposite of Melania's. Magazines and designers were hot for superskinny models; grunge was still lingering, and "heroin chic" was the rage. Kate Moss and Amber Valletta graced the cover of *Vogue*'s fabled September issue that year, all collarbones and elbows, ethereal slip dresses, pale blond locks, and gaunt faces. Melania at the time was raven-haired, busty, with full eyebrows, when the rest of the girls were having theirs shaved off and penciled back in. That she was the antithesis of what was "hot" at the moment in fashion likely kept her from getting as many jobs as the waifs from bigger modeling agencies. And, being Melania, she didn't want to turn herself into something she was not by dropping twenty pounds and cutting her dark locks into a pixie. She would rather take her chances getting jobs looking like she looked—a noble game plan, but not exactly one that brought in a large number of gigs.

Still, Zampolli set her up with a roommate, a photographer named Matthew Atanian, in an apartment at Zeckendorf Towers, an eyesore of a massive red brick condo complex in Union Square. Rent was taken out of her contract with the agency, a common practice that helps push models to go on go-sees and find work. There was no sugarcoating it: her first home in the Big Apple was decidedly déclassé. But it had a pool and a gym, and Melania used both on a daily basis. For about two years, Atanian rented Melania that spare room in his apartment. He recalls her as simple, bookish, and a bit shy. After Melania became first lady, Atanian did an interview in which he said her favorite thing to do in the evenings was put on a bathrobe, sit on the couch, and watch *Friends*. Not the worst way to spend an evening, but not exactly getting the most out of the city that doesn't sleep.

Her old roommate from her Paris modeling days, Victoria Silvstedt, who went on to be *Playboy* Playmate of the Year in 2007, has also said Melania was a homebody. "She was always very quiet," said Silvstedt, who said the two wouldn't even allow themselves the guilty pleasure of an infrequent fancy French dinner. "We would run up and down the stairs of our building to work it off."

Atanian described Melania's modeling talent as lacking, saying she was oftentimes stiff, and because of that work was not abundant. Since she was on the older side, Zampolli argues, Melania had success with ad campaigns for things like booze and cigarettes—one of Melania's biggest gets was a billboard downtown for Camels. In the ad she's holding a martini in one hand, a lit cigarette in the other, resting her chin on her hand. She's heavily made up, and looks quite beautiful and glamorous, but the mood of the photo indicates she's bored with you—and would prefer to just sit here and have a cocktail and a smoke. Not that there's anything wrong with these kinds of advertising gigs. In fact, she was probably paid quite well; catalog work can be lucrative, too. Clearly, she wasn't in the high-fashion ateliers and on the sets of overproduced magazine spreads, but she was not, according to those who were familiar with her jobs, a starving model.

Zampolli has repeatedly boasted not about Melania's modeling prowess but about how well she took care of herself "like models should be doing." She ate very little—no junk food—and relied mostly on fruits and vegetables as diet staples. Melania's social life consisted of the rare night out—for example, when Zampolli would invite her to a private event such as the one at the Kit Kat or when she would catch a movie with Zampolli's girlfriend at the time, because, "you know, that's what girls do." She wasn't much of a dater, and there is no evidence she had a serious boyfriend during the time she was in New York. "It was known that I was very tough," Melania said about that time in her life. "Yes, dating, but not *dating*. Maybe a movie or dinner. I was busy. After a long day, the last thing I wanted to do is get ready and go out at ten at night and then be up again at six in the morning. I don't want to feel exhausted." Again, shout-out to *Friends* episodes and terrycloth robes.

For Zampolli, being a modeling agent, especially back then, was more about what sort of access the job could supply, an angle he worked until it was coveted by others seeking the same currency. He became a "fixture," which wasn't necessarily a bad word in the New York club world. A fixture who could also get pretty young models to come to a party made for a pretty sweet occupation, one Zampolli navigated well.

Though ID Models folded in 2008, the Web site still exists, and on it is a tab that links to the "Friends" section, featuring a handful of pictures of Zampolli with semifamous fashion industry people. And Bill Clinton. But Zampolli threw decent parties and knew how to get Page Six regulars like Donald Trump in the door. Years later, at Trump's inauguration, it would naturally be Zampolli who threw the afterparty. Complaining that Washington shut down as a city long before New York and that there would be lots of Manhattanites in D.C. for Trump's festivities, eager to stay up past midnight, Zampolli took over a downtown nightclub called the Living Room and staked claim to the only inaugural party that wasn't a ball and wasn't over by 10 P.M.

But back to that fateful night at the Kit Kat . . . Trump may have arrived with Midelfart, but that didn't mean he felt the need to show her any loyalty. It is a quality he requires others to demonstrate, but not one he practices himself. Case in point: Midelfart, who was already all but dumped that night, whether or not she knew it.

Trump noticed a dark-haired, blue-eyed woman sitting on a couch. He looked at her more than once and looked again. She looked back. "I went crazy," Trump said about seeing Melania for the first time. "I was actually supposed to meet somebody else. There was this great supermodel sitting next to Melania," Trump explained with his usual loose regard for superlatives. "I was supposed to meet this supermodel," saying it enough times in front of Melania that you start to think maybe he's enjoying comparing the woman he actually fell for to a hotter, more successful, and more appropriate-for-him version. But, nah—the great supermodel didn't catch his attention the way the Slovenian did. "I said, 'Forget about her, who's the one on the left'— and that was Melania."

It's become a familiar tale, so frequently do both Trump and Melania recount the icky-meets-cute details of their first meeting. Let us not forget, at the time Donald Trump was fifty-two years old, Melania

Knauss, twenty-eight. She'd had two years in New York to scope out how it operated by the time she met Trump, and she was savvy about the parties that brought older men into the same orbit as pretty young women.

Trump waited for his opportunity. When Midelfart went to the ladies' room, which at a party with five hundred people he knew could take a while, Trump pounced, approaching Melania and talking her up. She claims she knew who he was, but that she was not impressed.

"He asked for my number, but I didn't give it to him. I asked for his number instead," Melania would recall in several interviews throughout the decades that followed. She was proud of herself for the bold move, or at least proud of this story, because she figured if he really wanted her to call him, Trump would give her his real number, not that of a secretary. In the phone number, what he wanted from her would be revealed, she thought. If he isn't serious, she'd know right away. Trump gave her four numbers: his direct line at work, his direct line at home, the number for his private jet, and the number to reach him at Mar-a-Lago. Another telling of this story claims that the reason Melania did not give him her number was that she was repulsed that he would hit on another woman while already on a date. Whether it was independence or moral high ground, the phone number thing was her choice, a reasoning she often uses to this day to justify her decision-making process. As long as she establishes the choice was hers—everything, at least in her mind, is okay.

A week later, after she returned from a photo shoot in the Bahamas, Melania called Donald on his office line. She didn't need to remind him who she was; he was interested and ready to take her out.

She has said many things about what drew her to him, repeating words like "great chemistry," "energy," "vitality" to explain why she was attracted to an older man with a history of being in the tabloids for womanizing and philandering. "Something was there right away." It's helpful at this point to remember this was still the late nineties, and Trump was a magnetic figure. His business prowess was legend, and so was his dating life. He was handsome and skinnier back then, and his ego, while overblown, hadn't reached peak obnoxiousness—this was before *The Apprentice*. It was also before Twitter. Melania was legitimately curious and, say her friends, attracted. She had never been interested in immature men, and she liked that Trump sort of reminded her of her own father. The two were prone to wearing suits and swooping, slicked-back hairdos.

Trump took Melania to Moomba on their first date. A restaurant cum lounge space that epitomized the breezy spending habits of Manhattanites in the late 1990s, it was also notoriously hard to land a table there. "You can't get a Saturday night reservation at Moomba," wrote restaurant critic Ruth Reichl in *The New York Times* in April 1998. "I know. I tried for months." Unless you were famous. If you weren't, you had to settle on crossing your fingers for a rare opening, eating with the super-uncool kids and wannabes in the early-bird hours before the glitterati (i.e., Donald Trump and pretty girl) were seated in the much more chic 9–10 P.M. window. Reichl bemoaned this for about thirty seconds before realizing that eating ahead of the beautiful people at Moomba had its privileges. "It means that by the time the music becomes a throbbing beast dominating the dreary dining room, you are ready to leave." (Reichl gave Moomba two stars out of four.)

Melania would have given it four. She dug it there. "Remember Moomba? It was a great place, wasn't it?" she said recounting her first date with the Donald. "I remember that night like it was two months ago."

Fairly quickly after Moomba, it was evident there was something Donald really liked about Melania. He took her to his Bedford estate in Westchester County, New York, a few days after their first date, driving them himself in his new blue Lamborghini Diablo so she could see the 230-acre property he had purchased three years before for $7.5 million (today it's estimated to be worth approximately $20 million). Built in 1919 and called Seven Springs, the bucolic private estate includes a fifty thousand square foot main house with fifteen bedrooms, three pools, manicured gardens, and room upon room of opulent furnishings—lots of his favorite marble and gold antiques.

If he was trying to impress the steely, independent Slovenian, it was working.

But Trump was sensing something about her, too.

She was sharp but not opinionated. She was available, but not slutty. She was intelligent, but not a know-it-all. She came around when he wanted her to, but she was not clingy. He didn't have to excel at having a sense of humor (which was good, because he didn't have one), nor did he have to ply her with gifts—she wasn't about that. There was an immediate ease that each felt right away in the other's company.

Yet despite the "sparkle," as she later called the feeling she had in those early days, Melania actually broke up with Trump after a few weeks, having apparently spotted his former flame Kara Young coming out of Trump Tower as Melania was about to go in to meet him. The two had planned a weekend away at Mar-a-Lago, but instead, hurt by the presumed betrayal, she gave him the boot.

Melania had already been to Trump's Palm Beach estate at that point and had left items of clothing and other personal effects there for future trips, but now, as Trump's former butler Anthony Senecal recounted to Ronald Kessler in his book, *The Trump White House*, "she called me and asked me to please pack up her things and send them back with Mr. Trump, and I said okay. And then I cleared it with him. He said, 'Do what she wants.' So I packed up her stuff and they went up on the plane [at the end of the weekend]."

Young, the model Melania spied leaving Trump's building, declined to discuss her romantic relationship with Trump for this book, but she did say of her former romantic rival, "She's a good girl. We had our problems, obviously, then. But we are all grown-ups now."

Sometimes the best thing you can do to a guy who hasn't been dumped is dump him. Trump was shaken. By the time the following week was over, Trump had won back his girl, promising her he would be faithful. For Melania, it was enough.

As for Trump, when it comes to just about anything, paramount is his perception of what the other guy thinks, and that went for his relationship with Melania. He went on and on about her beauty to his friends, telling them how he had seen "grown men weep" when she walked into a room, sharing a story about a business rival who turned to look at Melania so longingly he fell off his chair—"on his ass," Trump said. It wasn't good enough that she had to be beautiful in his eyes; she had to be the most beautiful in everyone else's eyes as well. Everyone.

It was behavior Trump had demonstrated before and would repeat again to alarming degrees when he eventually ran for president. But the need to show off his conquests was habitual, it made him tick, it was how he self-soothed. Several years earlier, when he was secretly dating Marla Maples and still married to Ivana, Trump would famously have on hand an actual poster of his hot blond mistress, which he would unfurl at random for friends and business acquaintances, commenting on her beauty and saying the model herself had given it to him. Even if he couldn't admit it at the time, he still got turned on by the reaction of other people to the woman he was bedding.

About Melania, Trump did the same. "She is considered beautiful by the other girls," Trump told Howard Stern. "I mean, they, she's really considered most beautiful, but she's beyond beauty; she's a very nice person." Moments later, he's telling Stern that not only does Melania have no cellulite, she doesn't even know what the word in English means. Notably, while he tells Stern details indicating he can basically pantomime every curve on her body, he gets Melania's country of origin wrong, proclaiming her "Austrian and Romanian" when Stern asks where she's from. This particular Stern interview, by the way, took place in November 1999, more than a year after the two met.

That same month, Trump got some help on the home country of his girlfriend from talk show host Chris Matthews, who hosted Trump for a live town hall–style interview on *Hardball* at the University of Pennsylvania. Trump at this stage was seriously toying with a presidential run, or at least in his own mind he was; he had become more politically vocal about his opinions. Matthews, a celebrity worshiper who understood how to get ratings, saw the town hall as a chance to kill two birds with one stone. Matthews asked Trump whether he was running for president. "I am. I am," said Trump. Then a beat later added, "perhaps." That same year, 1999, Matthews also interviewed actor Warren Beatty, another celebrity interested in getting into politics.

Known in Washington for losing his composure in the company of pretty women, years later Matthews would be raked over the coals after getting caught on a hot mic on MSNBC drooling over Melania after the Indiana primary during Trump's presidential campaign. As live video rolls of Trump walking toward the podium, his wife beside him in a clingy sleeveless white sheath dress, Matthews says, breathlessly, "Did you see her walk?" presumably to his panelists and co-anchors, or to no one in particular. "Runway walk. My God is that good. I could watch that runway show." Brian Williams tries to talk over Matthews so his statement isn't so flagrant, but the moment makes headlines. Later, in a magazine article, Melania said what she thought of the Matthews *in flagrante* incident: "Unbelievable!" She lamented that on the campaign she was only considered for her looks. "That's what I'm saying! I'm not only a beauty. I'm smart. I have brains. I'm intelligent." Then she sighed at the stupidity of the male sex. "I would just say, men will be men."

Matthews liked Melania back when Trump was just a glimmer of a political somebody, too. At the 1999 town hall event, he asked his guest if he had brought someone special, and Trump called for Melania: "Where is my supermodel?" Trump's scanning the front of the audience as Melania, on cue, stands up. "Melania. That's Melania Knauss," says Trump, showing her off to Matthews, who takes the bait. The two men, both more than two decades older than she, spend a few seconds looking Melania up and down. If Matthews had leaned over to literally pat Trump on the back for his conquest, no one would have been surprised, so thorough was the ogle. "One thing that's safe to say about you, Donald, is you know the difference between Slovakia and Slovenia," said Matthews. "I do, I do. Absolutely," said Trump, who probably didn't.

Trump brought Melania into his Howard Stern interview, too, asking the shock jock if he'd like to speak with her, which of course he does. Melania picks up the phone and gets on the air with Stern, who immediately unloads a barrage of embarrassing questions. What's she wearing? "Ah, not much." Do the two of them have sex every night? "Even more," she purrs. And, tellingly, Does she want the mogul to marry her? "I'm not answering that." When Trump gets back on the phone, Stern ribs him about whether he'll actually go through with a third marriage. "I'm a little too concerned, Howard, that she may be too smart. I have to be careful."

Critics of Melania have called her a stupid model (and let's not even get into how misogynistic that is), claiming that she's blind to what her husband is doing. But remember, this is a woman who speaks five languages. She knows that her part—and it is a part—is at times to play the sex-kitten girlfriend of Mr. Big. And it's a part she plays well. She was not going to let her ticket into the world of the über-rich slip away because at times she was called upon to offer up some ridiculous (and often distasteful) show-and-tell. For a woman in her midtwenties who had spent most of her life either growing up in a communist country—where wearing jeans was a sign of rebellion—or struggling as a very average "average" model, being on the arm of Donald Trump, the king of Manhattan, was probably beyond her wildest dreams. Little would she know just how beyond it would turn out to be.

6

The Girlfriend

*"We know what kind of relationship we have. And I
don't think I should be scared of anything."*
—MELANIA TRUMP

Melania Knauss endured being Donald Trump's girlfriend for the
next six years—reveled in it, really. It was a position she very much
enjoyed, say friends. But other acquaintances ribbed her. It was usually something to the effect of, "Why would this gorgeous, independent woman, young and beautiful, want to be with that womanizing
old guy with the weird hair?"

Her response was often that she liked that Trump was a "real man,"
sure of himself, powerful, smart. Viktor Knavs, who was just three
years older than his daughter's boyfriend, was similarly self-assured.
Viktor is known for having a large personality and for his charm. "He
was pretty successful over there," Trump has said of his father-in-
law. "It's a different kind of success than you have here. But he was
successful." Some even see a physical resemblance between the two
men. Both tend toward portly, like a roomy suit jacket, and have a full
head of hair; Knavs, while gray, not blond, also wears his parted to the
side. While the wealth and power of Trump were clearly appealing

to Melania, he also inspired in her a sense of familiarity. Viktor, like Trump, was a decision-maker. Amalija, Melania's mother, was strong, too, but it was Viktor who led the family out of the dregs of lower-middle-class life to a more suburban and comfortable existence. Melania adored her father, lionized him, and little did Trump know that Melania's seeing even a smidge of comparison with Viktor already put Trump ahead of other men Melania had been with.

As Trump learned about her family, Melania got to know his. She met his three eldest children, Don Jr., Ivanka, and Eric, fairly quickly after they started dating and eventually met Tiffany, who was just six years old at the time. Melania liked spending time with little Tiffany, whose mother's divorce from Trump was finalized in 1999. She sat with her at the US Open tennis matches, pulling Tiffany onto her lap, playing with her long blond ponytails while Trump, oblivious, sat beside them engrossed in a match. When the couple went to Mar-a-Lago, they sometimes had Tiffany in tow, again with Melania doting on her, making sure the rest of the children felt comfortable, helping preside over holidays like Easter and Thanksgiving. Melania and Tiffany remain close to this day, in part because of the early years after Trump's divorce from Marla. Melania was around on the rare days Trump had custody of the girl, and that had to have been helpful for Tiffany as she navigated being with her dad without her mom. Melania was, and still is, very conscious of Tiffany's oddball status in the Trump-children dynamic. Tiffany is the only child of Trump's second marriage to Marla Maples, with whom he had an affair while still married to Ivana, the mother of Tiffany's older half siblings. Melania has always tried her best to make Tiffany feel welcomed, loved, and supported—and that all began back in the early days of her dating Trump.

In June 1999, Melania was close enough to both Trump and his family that he invited her to attend the funeral of his beloved father, Fred Trump, who died of complications from pneumonia at the age of ninety-three. To the service at Marble Collegiate Church on Manhattan's Upper East Side, Melania wore a black lace dress with a deep neckline, her long, dark brown hair loose past her shoulders. For modesty, she had on a black cardigan sweater. Although she didn't sit with the family, she wasn't too far behind them at the service, reverent and somber, wearing a large cross necklace. She arrived and left alone.

By this point, Melania had become Trump's constant companion, dedicating a lot of her time to being with him, traveling to Mar-a-Lago and listening to him download at the end of the day about business and real estate. She was still working the occasional modeling job, but she was engrossed in being Trump's girlfriend. Her career, she knew, could only be amplified by her connection with her celebrity boyfriend. That didn't mean she was comfortable with the idea— she prickled at the thought of someone giving her a job solely because she dated Trump—but she was accepting of its being a side effect of being with him.

Melania says the two had great chemistry, and that's why they were together, but the fact is, Melania also liked the power. Dating him had a significant upside for her. She was invited to things; she could walk into a restaurant and be seated at the best tables; she could shop in the best boutiques; she had access to limousines, a helicopter, a beach house, a country house, planes . . . She might have been physically and emotionally attracted to his looks and his style, but she was also drawn by the intensity with which he was able to make people respond to him and grant him what he wanted.

Being Donald Trump's supermodel girlfriend (the "super" became a ubiquitous add-on whenever he spoke of Melania, not necessarily because her work put her anywhere near the league of legitimate "supers" of the era like Cindy Crawford, Kate Moss, Naomi Campbell, and Christy Turlington) afforded her the exposure and fame as a model that she had trouble getting on her own, with the exception of the passable living she made doing jobs in fit work or advertisements and catalogs.

In January 2000, Melania had two major spreads in big glossy magazines. Her raciest, for British *GQ*, was a play on a Bond girl—

but in skimpy lingerie, handcuffed to a briefcase of diamonds, firing a weapon while standing on the wing of Trump's private 757.

Later, the magazine's editor would say he was pitched heavily to feature Melania. "We were bombarded by requests" was how Dylan Jones put it. He said Trump was "very keen" to see his girlfriend in a fashion shoot in *GQ*'s pages. "I guess he was trying to help her modeling career," said the photographer, Antoine Verglas. *GQ* didn't pay Melania for the shoot.

When Verglas shot the feature, ultimately titled a very innuendo-less "Sex at 30,000 Feet: Melania Knauss Earns Her Air Miles," the editors rushed to get prints of the images to Trump for his approval. Verglas wasn't concerned Trump wouldn't like them: "She is easy to photograph," he said of the shoot. "She has no flaws."

The text accompanying the photos wasn't much better in the cliché department, with allusions to the Mile High Club and "in-flight entertainment." Melania, whose last name was still Knauss, was described as a "delectable" "Slovenian supermodel" and Trump's "personal hostess."

She was also described in the story as being twenty-six, yet when the publication hit stands, she was actually four months shy of her thirtieth birthday.

The photos themselves are risqué, for sure, but nothing too sensational for a men's mag like British *GQ*, especially at the time. It frequently featured spreads of scantily clad or even naked models and actresses in its pages. For her *GQ* debut, Melania wears white silk panties, a tank top, and a feather jacket in one shot, walking up the stairs of the jet with an expression like she might kill the bad guy or make love to him, depending on how you look at it. In another image she's on the plane, spilling out of a plunging gold bathing suit, an open briefcase of jewelry in front of her on a white leather couch, and in her hand is a silver revolver. Perhaps the most "fashion" shot is Melania in the cockpit, wearing a fembot-like silver headpiece and a chain-mail dress with dangling silver tags, nothing underneath on top.

Part of the copy written to accompany the photos reads, "Not only does she manage to keep a man fabled for his erections (the latest is the Trump World Tower on New York's First Avenue) on the right flight path, but she's also fluent in four languages. Very handy for those summit meetings." Of course, 2000 was the year Trump was very seriously considering running for president (again) as an Independent. "She's popular, she's brilliant, she's a wonderful woman," he says of Melania, "popular" something of an odd description for her, considering that the most anyone had seen of Melania in that past year was on his arm, at red carpet events, and in the pages of *GQ*.

In Trump's mind, the most romantic thing he could do for his girlfriend was boost her image. It was how he expressed his affection, how he showed he cared. And as with most of the things that inspired him, building a brand also helped his own. When he was with Maples, Trump pushed for her to do a *Playboy* spread, going so far as to personally negotiate what she would be paid. He got them up to a million bucks, but Marla ultimately decided she wouldn't do full nude, and the deal was off. She did, however, with the help of Trump and her personal publicist, get $600,000 for a No Excuses jeans advertisement, an incredibly gauche decision considering she was the most notorious "other woman" of the era. She didn't care, and neither did Trump.

The *GQ* story featured hot shots of Melania, but the words beside them were as much about his political aspirations as about how she looked in underwear: "'I'm going to do everything I can do to see that regular Americans can fly as high as their wings will take them,' says Trump. He's got our vote." This is how the story about a lady spy and sex at thirty thousand feet ends.

Melania also declares how seriously she would take the job of first lady, somewhat hard to swallow coming from a woman dressed in a bikini and pretending to hijack a plane in knee-high black boots. "I will put all my effort into it," she tells readers, "and I will support my man."

Of course, the cover image from this *GQ* story will come back to haunt Trump's campaign. It featured Melania fully nude, lying on a fur rug and draped in diamonds, her backside and part of her nipple exposed. The image, again, wasn't a big deal for a men's magazine: in the early 2000s, models and celebrities were often shot naked.

But the image was saucy enough—and unprecedented for a candidate's spouse—to grab attention more than fifteen years later. The photograph resurfaced during the 2016 presidential campaign during a March social media blitz from a super PAC supporting Ted Cruz, one of Trump's chief competitors, as the Utah caucus neared. "Meet Melania Trump, Your Next First Lady," said the ad, which was basically just a huge copy of the naked Melania photo, with her making bedroom eyes at the camera. It was aimed at conservative voters, primarily in Mormon communities. The stunt launched one of the dirtier tit-for-tats in an already nasty campaign.

Trump went to bat for Melania, but he did so in his signature style: bruising, laced with a threat.

"Lyin' Ted Cruz just used a picture of Melania from a *G.Q.* shoot in his ad. Be careful, Lyin' Ted, or I will spill the beans on your wife!" tweeted Trump. Cruz responded trying to distance himself from the ad, tweeting, "Pic of your wife not from us. Donald, if you attack Heidi (Cruz), you're more of a coward than I thought. #classless," as though that would make Trump stand down, even where wives were concerned. Not so much.

The following morning, Trump used Cruz's tweet against him as proof of his own dishonesty. "Lyin' Ted Cruz denied that he had anything to do with the *G.Q.* model photo post of Melania. That's why we call him Lyin' Ted!" Roger Stone, an adviser to Trump, waded in, too, tweeting, "Melania HOT, Heidi NOT." Trump retweeted a tweet comparing the two women's faces that read, "a picture is worth a thousand words." The photo of Mrs. Cruz is less than flattering beside a polished shot of Melania. The media went bananas. *The Washington Post* wrote that Trump's inability to stop saying mean things about women could cost him (it didn't), and Cruz himself, fired up by the whole thing, told CNN, "Donald Trump will not be the nominee. I'm going to beat him." (He didn't.) Within two months, Cruz had dropped out of the race altogether.

The incident served to spark a campaign scandal—Trump ultimately lost the Republican caucus in Utah to Cruz, not that it mattered in the long run—but it didn't do anything to keep Melania's naked bum out of the headlines. The *GQ* shoot found fresh momentum and earned her a new kind of notoriety, albeit unneeded and sixteen years later.

Fun fact: when Melania's official biography first went up on the White House Web site, after her husband won the election, the *GQ* cover was listed among her professional achievements: "She has graced the covers of *Vogue, Harper's Bazaar, British GQ, Ocean Drive, Avenue, InStyle* and *New York Magazine*." That portion has since been removed, replaced with a less specific graph about her work: "At age 16, she began what would soon become a highly successful modeling career, appearing in many high-profile ad campaigns and working with some of the best photographers in the fashion industry." However, despite the edit, Melania has never implied that she regrets her decision to pose for the shoot or that she is embarrassed by its contents or the contents of any others she had done.

Also in January 2000, another sexy spread of Melania hit newsstands, this time in *Talk* magazine, Tina Brown's now-defunct glossy, a wannabe *Vanity Fair* that for a time was incredibly popular. "A Model First Lady: Melania Knauss Gets Ready for the White House," reads the headline. Printed horizontally across two pages is Melania, lying down on a rug (again), though this time a navy-colored one with a gold presidential seal in the middle, a version of the real deal in the Oval Office. She's wearing strappy gold high heels and a red bikini, her bust almost indecently squeezed out of the top. Her face looks beautiful; her hair perfect—she's the first lady of fantasyland. "I would be very traditional" is the pull quote from Melania at the top of the left-hand page. In the bottom right is a small shot of Trump talking on a red phone in front of an American flag. The text says, in part, "She's 26, a model, and lives in a one-bedroom apartment. For now, at any rate. Donald Trump's girlfriend Melania Knauss is getting ready for the White House." Again, she was almost thirty, not twenty-six.

Ironically, around the time both the magazines came out, Melania and Trump broke up, again. Her friends say that she didn't want to be part of his political ambitions. She wasn't sure that the life Trump wanted in the White House, picked apart at every moment by the press, by his enemies, was what she wanted. She was fiercely and deeply private, even back then. Her business was her business. And while that might sound like a glaring oxymoron, considering she had no trouble showing the world her practically naked body in magazines, there is an important distinction. She was very aware of the line between a public persona and a private one. Her boyfriend was not. For Trump, there was no line. Private, public—it was all one Donald Trump.

His side of the breakup—which of course was available in the tabloids—implied that while he liked Melania an awful lot, he was trying to be serious about this Reform Party presidency thing. *The New York Daily News* did a "Trump Dumps Latest Model" story on the split, writing, "Vetoed by the billionaire developer was leggy lingerie model Melania Knauss, the 27-year-old Slovenian who until this week was thinking she would model herself after Jackie Onassis if she became first lady." (Guys, again, she's not twenty-seven!)

The *New York Post*'s headline was similar, if not cleverer: "Trump Knixes Knauss: Donald-Dumped Supermodel Is Heartbroken." In the *Post*, Melania had shaved two years off her age in the *Daily News*; they listed her as twenty-five.

The tabloids painted her as despondent over the breakup, which sounded more like a plant from Trump's camp than the truth—if Melania was upset, she didn't show it to friends. She kept to her own routine and to her own apartment, which she had since upgraded to a one-bedroom by herself, no longer needing a roommate. She decorated with furniture she bought from Crate and Barrel. "The rent was $2,500 a month," she said. "I picked it out, everything on my own. I still remember, I went to shop for a TV and an air conditioner."

Clearly, the version of the end of the romance that Trump was pushing was that Melania was a "great girl," according to a friend who is quoted (who was probably Trump himself; he liked to call the media on his own or under an alias as a fake spokesperson from the Trump Organization), but "he didn't want to get hooked. He decided to cool it." Eventually, Trump himself confirmed the breakup in a quick interview with *The New York Times,* talking about Melania as if she had disappeared on a fishing trip, never to be seen again. "Melania is an amazing woman, a terrific woman, a great woman, and she will be missed."

The split didn't stick. They kept in regular contact, Trump proclaiming in their private phone conversations how much he missed her, until eventually they were a couple again. Melania would later say, "We were apart for a few months, not long. We got back together." That's Melania speak for it's none of your business. Whether or not she got dumped, she's clear that it didn't bother her or send her into a tailspin. Again, as one of Melania's former Slovenian high school classmates told me, revealing emotional hardship or being dramatic simply isn't something Slovenes do. The joy of being Slovenian is hiding your feelings.

Shortly after Trump and Melania reunited, things got even more serious. If he was testing to see if she would do any of the on-again, off-again shenanigans that he went through with Marla when they would fight, Melania passed.

They now went almost everywhere together, popping up at concerts, movie premieres, dinners at Cipriani, the US Open. In 2001 the couple attended their first White House Correspondents' Dinner in Washington, D.C., Melania in a tight, strapless black-and-white dress. Also that year, Trump took her to the Academy Awards in Los Angeles, where Melania showed off her breasts in a sexy white sequined gown with a neckline that plunged to just above her navel. In 2001, Trump played himself in *Zoolander,* entering the film's faux runway show, the climax of the movie. In the scene, he's on the red carpet being interviewed and next to him, of course, is Melania, looking adoringly at Trump. Photos around this time period show a much more smiley Melania, before she perfected her squinty, icy camera face. She appears happy and engaged, practically the bright-eyed ingenue. Her eyes are wider, her grin ear-to-ear.

Melania was different for Trump; she had something his past wives didn't. Ivana was a conquest, power hungry and focused on success. Marla was flighty, a small-town girl who wielded sexuality to get what she wanted—after a few months of being with Trump, she told friends his Palm Beach estate was now called "Marla Lago." Not in a million years would Melania have spoken like that or demanded that kind of attention. Her aloof independence might have been an act to lure him in, but friends of hers will tell you that Melania has never really needed anyone. Companionship, romance, love—those things were never at the top of her list of aspirations. And if she was a gold digger, as she's often portrayed, or if she indeed worked Manhattan, on the prowl for wealthy men, as many young international models certainly do, she sure as hell didn't leave a trace.

Fine with being a silent witness to the events that swirled around her, Melania eased into her new life, making subtle upgrades to her clothing, shifting from nondescript black cocktail dresses to designer labels, eventually better bags and shoes, furs and (borrowed) diamonds. On one of her trips with Trump to Mar-a-Lago at the private club's annual New Year's Eve gala, Melania was asked about her resolution. "I'm going to eat three square meals a day," she said, sounding very much like the old Melania. "I'm not going to prepare them, of course, but I will eat them," she added, in the tone of the new.

Around 2002, she moved into Trump's palatial apartment in Trump Tower, a very far cry from the bleak communist apartment building she had lived in as a child. Trump's place overlooked Central Park; Melania's old apartment in Sevnica overlooked an asphalt parking lot. Trump has valued the apartment at $200 million; in 2017, *Forbes* put a $64 million price tag on it.

The triplex had been Trump's signature piece of real estate for almost twenty years at that point. He was often photographed there for magazine stories, and he used it as a backdrop during television profiles. He secured the triplex when Trump Tower first opened in 1983 but added onto it, grabbing up two adjacent apartments and expanding to about eleven thousand square feet of living space.

A creature of habit who notoriously dislikes changes to his routine, Trump hardly ever changed a thing about the place, even to this day. The apartment had cycled through two wives already by the time Melania arrived. Trump kept all the decor; redoing it was not an option for the women who lived there with him through the years, whether they liked it or not. It was to remain as gold and ostentatious as it always had been. The mural-painted gold leaf ceilings, the curved white couch in the living room, the low-hanging chandeliers, the cold marble slabs of the fireplace mantels, the Louis XIV imperial French–style furniture all stays the same, even the master bedroom with its bed and twenty-four-karat gold headboard with matching canopy drapes: immovable—only the women change.

Melania didn't mind; she had long been aware that she was in love with a man who stuck to his habits. Trying to change him, as she would often state matter-of-factly, was a fruitless endeavor. "He is who he is" was a common refrain. That's not to say that shoving every bit of gold furniture that could possibly fit into one room was her aesthetic. Quite the opposite, actually. Her preferred style is more minimalist, white, sparse, and slightly modern. But, with most things Trump, she learned to live with what he wanted, even if she didn't.

But Trump kept her in the girlfriend zone for a long time. While she never worried that she would go the way of other Trump girlfriends—or wives, for that matter—Melania was getting antsy for permanence. The life he was affording her as his live-in love felt very much like having the whole package, yet there was something else on her mind. Melania had a ticking biological clock; she wanted a baby.

7
_____

The Business of Becoming
Mrs. Donald Trump

"I'm strong. I'm standing on my two feet very strong."

—MELANIA TRUMP

In April 2004, Melania made her first appearance on *The Apprentice*, Trump's hit NBC reality show, wherein he assigned tasks to a group of willing cast members, each vying to be "hired" by the mogul. The contestants from the female-only team are taking a tour of Trump's gilded penthouse when Melania Knauss enters the living room. There are oohs and aahs and one of the contestants says, "This is, like, rich. Like really, really rich."

"How do you clean a house like this?" asks another, to which Melania responds, smiling, "Well, you have people to clean."

"You're very, very lucky," says one of the women. At that, Melania first laughs and nods in agreement, but then she pauses and quite seriously retorts, "And he's not lucky?" The exchange offers a flash of the smartness of Melania, who is by no means vapid arm candy, even if it's often assumed she is indeed just that. She knows her worth, and highly values it. The art of the deal works both ways—sure, she gets to live in a sweet penthouse with help, but he gets to have a beautiful,

savvy, patient, and committed woman who isn't as demanding as his
first wife or as wacky as his second.

Later, a different group of contestants comes over, and this time
Melania, in a halter-neck silver evening gown, walks in and greets
them, shaking hands. In a side interview, one of the contestants de-
scribes Melania as "a fantastic hostess. She to me is how a royal person
would act. She is the epitome of a gracious woman."

Her television debut a success and her ascension to mistress of the
house complete, Trump decides, after six years, it's time to pop the
question.

Oddly, whenever publicly asked why he got married again after
two very public divorces, Trump has never once mentioned the word
"love," never called Melania his soul mate, and never made it sound as
if their union is anything more than a transaction—or, worse, something she has earned. Trump has admitted that one reason is that Melania didn't pressure him to get married. Her lack of caring whether
he put a ring on it ultimately led him to do just that—because he
thought he owed it to her for not nagging about the whole thing.

"I felt it was the right thing to do, number one, and I think she's
special. If I didn't think she was special, I wouldn't have gotten married." Again, nothing about love. Not, "I fell deeply in love" or "I
loved her so much" or "I love her in a way I knew I couldn't live
without her." Nope. It was the right thing to do, and she is special.
On *Larry King Live,* Trump said of his decision to marry Melania,
"We get along. And I just said, 'You know what? It's time.' It wasn't
a big deal."

Melania, seated right next to him, didn't bat an eye.

Trump used the relationship as a barometer for his business success. "We're together five years, and these five years for whatever
reasons have been my most successful. I have to imagine she had
something to do with that." Again, not the stuff of romance novels,
even bad ones.

While his statement is completely devoid of deep sentiment or,

quite frankly, true love, Trump had a point. Melania made him vir-
ile, powerful, a man worthy of standing by and supporting, but only
when he needed her to, because in his mind he was strong enough to
do so on his own. She, in turn, had to believe he was strong, to put
that vibe out, and be stronger—so strong that his bravado, his past,
his reputation couldn't make a dent in her armor. The exterior had to
match what was beneath the surface for the whole thing to look and
feel convincing. Melania had succeeded at this herculean task, and she
was getting rewarded for it.

She could also take small comfort in knowing that his rationale
for marrying her was slightly better than his explanation for why he
married Marla: because she got pregnant with Tiffany. In 1994 he told
Vanity Fair, "We've been together six years," eerily similar to what
he'll later say about Melania, except for the next part. "If she wanted
to do that—get me by getting pregnant—she could have done it a
lot sooner. We had just gotten back together, and she wasn't using
the pill, and I knew it. I don't feel as though I was trapped. Trapped
would have been not to tell me she wasn't on the pill. I'm not the kind
of guy who has babies out of wedlock and doesn't get married and
give the baby a name. And for me, I'm not a believer in abortion."
Maples gave birth to Tiffany in October 1993; Trump married her
three months later.

Marla was also not as good as Melania at building Trump up, and
she'd often treat him like a dolt whom she got to acquiesce to her
needs. Maples was all, "Look at me; pay attention to me," while Melania's message was quite the opposite: "Look at him; pay attention
to him." Marla and Trump also fought—a lot. They would break up
and date other people in the hopes of making the other jealous enough
to come back, which took its toll, but also worked. Trump would famously crow that during one of their fights, when he left Marla ("not
only that, I left her like a dog," he told *Vanity Fair*), the singer Michael Bolton tries to swoop in, wooing her with promises of love and
romance. Trump finds out, gets jealous, and wins her back. "I do a

Trump number on her. . . . She drops him and comes back to me."
It was common for Marla and Trump to duke it out in the tabloids,
hanging their dirty laundry for everyone to see. He was cruel to her;
she belittled him; rinse and repeat.

Maples, at the peak of their romance, said that Trump was "adorable, with a little-boy quality—I mean, he knows when he's being
too cute and he laughs at himself about it." Melania would not have
described him this way, ever, especially in print. She knew it would
drive him crazy, and not in a good way. It was a difference between
wife number 2 and wife number 3 that Trump was especially tuned in
to, and turned on by.

Melania also had none of the societal aspirations of Trump's first
wife, Ivana. New York socialites would often snicker behind Ivana's
back in the 1980s at the way she swanned about as though she was
European royalty. She wasn't. Trump wasn't crazy about Ivana's need
to be out every night, hitting the party and charity circuit, especially
when he could be home working or watching television. Ivana was
over-the-top in her desire to drip wealth and create a legacy. "I want
nothing social that you aspire to!" Donald had once apparently yelled
at her. "If that is what makes you happy, get another husband!"

Melania, though born in a communist country like Ivana, had none
of Ivana's social fixation. Parties and people tripping over themselves
to be invited to them—not Melania's thing. Grateful for that, Trump
was ready to reward her for not being like his two exes. "That's the
rock," Trump said of Melania.

It was April 26, 2004, the night of the Met Gala, the Costume Institute's glitzy celebration, its guest list orchestrated by Anna Wintour,
editor in chief of *Vogue*. It's basically fashion's annual Super Bowl,
and Melania Knauss, who had never been, really wanted to go. Trump
decided he would take her. Most retellings of the couple's engagement say he proposed to Melania there, at the gala. Or associate the
proposal with him or her wanting to show off new bling on fashion's
biggest night. They are wrong.

In fact, the engagement didn't really have anything to do with the gala, except that it fell on the same date as Melania's birthday. She turned thirty-four on April 26. Before the couple left Trump Tower for the black-tie evening, the theme of which that year happened to be "Dangerous Liaisons," Trump asked Melania to be his wife.

"It was a great surprise," Melania said of the proposal, which was likely true. Friends say that while she was hopeful that one day the two would marry and start a family, she didn't make it a deal breaker. She also knew that the less she nagged him about it, the more likely it was that, someday, he would come around to getting engaged. "She didn't pressure me at all," Trump would say.

In contrast, Marla Maples had pressured Trump so intensely to marry her, she reportedly gave him an ultimatum shortly after their daughter, Tiffany, was born. In a 1990 interview with *Vanity Fair*, when Maples was able to go public as Trump's girlfriend following the scandal and demise of his marriage to Ivana, Marla was asked whether, if she does marry Trump, she would take his name. "That could become a bit of a point of argumentation. But, you know, I always promised my daddy I'd keep my name. Because I'm an only child and he never had a son. I said, 'Daddy, don't you worry,'" said Maples. "So I don't know. Maybe Marla Maples Trump." She talked like this a lot. But Marla needed to be extra public about getting the coveted title of "Mrs." because she hoped it would erase the smear of "mistress."

Through it all, Trump truly disliked the drama of his relationship with Marla; it was never pleasing to him, the roller-coaster romance. It was too much effort. With Melania, none of that existed. "What Melania is so good at, we just have this natural relationship," Trump would explain shortly after he married Melania. "It's like, my mother and father were married sixty-three years. I've always heard you have to work at a good relationship. My father didn't work at a good relationship. He went home. He had dinner. He went to bed. He took it easy. He watched television. My mother, the same thing, she cooked him dinner. And it was just one of those things. It wasn't work, but I always heard you have to work, work, work." He liked that being with Melania was more like what his parents had and less like what he had with Marla, or Ivana for that matter. "I work very hard from early in the morning til late in the evening," Trump said. "I don't want to go home and work at a relationship. A relationship where you have to work at it, in my opinion, doesn't work."

Trump felt Melania truly deserved his largesse, which for him was making an honest woman out of her; bestowing the Trump name was his highest compliment.

To seal the deal, he gave her a massive 12-carat, emerald-cut diamond ring with two tapered baguette diamonds on either side of the solitaire, all set in platinum. It was, as the saying about big diamonds goes, enough ice to skate on. "I picked it," Trump would later say, "but she and I have similar tastes. It's amazing. We just have similar tastes." As though there would be a woman out there who wouldn't like a gigantic diamond ring, but whatever.

The ring was reportedly priced at $1.5 million, but, as Trump later bragged, Graff, the esteemed luxury jewelry house, shaved one million dollars off the price, an exchange that all but guaranteed Trump would publicly speak well of the ring and the jeweler. In a later episode of *The Apprentice,* the contestants pay a visit to the store on camera.

"Only a fool would say, 'No thank you, I want to pay a million dollars more for a diamond,'" said Trump in *The New York Times* story, which was about how celebrities barter publicity for discounts. He told Larry King that he "negotiated hard" for the sparkler. Graff has since denied it offered a discount to Trump.

If Melania cared that the resulting story of the marriage proposal had little to do with romance and love and his utter devotion and more to do with whether her betrothed got a good deal on the rock, she didn't let on. These early signs of whatever it is in her that allows for complete and total keeping of her cool, at least in public, are harbingers of how she will handle life's strangest curveball, still to come.

The couple arrived at the Met Gala red carpet that night arm in arm, Melania in a black satin gown with sheer black lattice corset detail. Her hair at the time was dyed jet-black, and she wore it half up in a voluminous bouffant. From her ears hung massive diamond chandelier sparklers, almost long enough to graze her shoulders. On her wrist were three chunky diamond bangles, one stacked atop the other. And on her left ring finger, her new engagement ring. It was the only piece of jewelry that evening that she could say was hers and not on loan.

Trump and Melania had a few minutes to pose in front of a phalanx of photographers on the steps of the Met. Soon, however, Ivanka Trump, also on the red carpet, hopped in their frame, joining her father and soon-to-be stepmother. Melania doesn't appear to mind, but she's nowhere near as delighted as Trump, who laughs and grabs at his daughter with his right arm, pulling her by the waist into him as tightly as he has Melania enclosed in his left. Trump makes a kissy face in Melania's direction, puckering, but at the last moment, still in kiss mode, turns his head to Ivanka's face, kissing her firmly on the cheek. In the photograph, Melania is smiling, but the three of them together in one frame would not be all smiles in years to come.

Melania fairly quickly embarked on wedding planning, telling people she wanted a simple and intimate affair, not a lot of people, but in a world of Trumpian proportions, that was out of the question. If it was to be simple, it would be simple on steroids.

They decided on Mar-a-Lago for a location, and January 22, 2005, for the date—leaving Melania about eight months to get the entire event together.

But first, like most everyone who did a deal with Donald Trump, Melania had to sign on the dotted line.

Trump had learned the hard way with Ivana that divorce without a good prenuptial agreement was a painful, and painfully expensive, endeavor. By the time he married Marla Maples, he'd learned a thing or two about hanging on to his assets. Marla told the *New York Daily News* in 1997, when the couple was starting the process of divorcing, that she had signed the prenup under duress: "backed against the wall, I really felt at the time that I had no choice." Marla pleaded in the press for Trump to be generous with child support for Tiffany. "I'm praying that he's fair where she's concerned. She's a famous child," she said. "I want to give her a secure home in a good, safe neighborhood, in a good school district. That's all I want." Marla would raise Tiffany predominantly in the posh Los Angeles suburb of Calabasas, California, made more famous in recent years as the hometown of the Kardashian clan.

Ivana, too, had tried desperately to contest her prenuptial agreement with Trump. They had signed one before getting married in 1977, and Trump reportedly tweaked the nuptial agreement through the years, adjusting for the births of children and his mounting millions. At the end of it all, despite Ivana's pleas to get more, the courts ultimately sided with Trump to keep it intact. But the judge who granted their divorce did so by citing cruel and inhuman treatment by Trump to his wife of thirteen years, in large part because of his very public infidelity with Marla Maples.

Trump had technically "won," but his finances, already in jeopardy because of business issues, took a major hit. Even more annoying to him, so had his reputation. Ivana was the publicly jilted spouse, and he was the jerk who left her for a bimbo. "When a man leaves a woman," Trump once opined to *Vanity Fair* writer Marie Brenner, "especially when it was perceived that he has left for a piece of ass—a good one!—there are 50 percent of the population who will love the woman who was left." Trump, for all his bluster, didn't like being seen as a bad guy—unless it helped him make a deal.

Ivana, who truly believed she was entitled to half of Trump's assets, would ultimately walk away with $14 million in cash; the couple's vast 45-room estate in Greenwich, Connecticut; a huge apartment in Trump Plaza; and access to use Mar-a-Lago for one month of the year. Trump would also pay out $650,000 annually in child support for their three kids, it was reported at the time by *The New York Times*. In 1991, when their divorce was finalized, Trump was financially in dire straits—the settlement all but wiped him out. "I'm very happy that this is behind me," said Trump, who was allowed to keep his fifty-room triplex in Trump Tower, even though that had been where Ivana, Don Jr., Ivanka, and Eric had actually been living since Trump left Ivana for Marla. The divorce agreement basically allowed him to kick out his children's mom and move Marla in.

At the end of their union, Marla didn't get as much as Ivana did. As her marriage with Trump deteriorated and rumors swirled that she'd been caught in a flirty clinch with one of her Palm Beach body-guards, she had very little in the way of negotiating power. In the end, it was reported to be about $2 million in settlement cash for her and a generous chunk in child support for Tiffany.

When it was Melania's turn to sign a prenup, Trump made it sound like getting the thing done was better than couples' counseling. He was so happy he didn't have to twist her arm like the last two, he raved that her going along with his demand helped their relationship—a confounding philosophy, but he said after the wedding that the pre-nup made his marriage to Melania stronger. "It's a hard, painful, ugly tool. Believe me, there's nothing fun about it," he said. "But there comes a time when you have to say, 'Darling, I think you're magnif-icent, and I care for you deeply'"—again, no mention of the word, "love"—"'but if things don't work out, this is what you're going to get.'" This is presumably the speech Melania was on the receiving end of before she took pen in hand.

Of course, Melania never imagined she would one day be first lady of the United States, with the burdens and exposure that carries. Bill and Hillary Clinton might not have had a legal prenuptial agreement, but they were inextricably tied together by their ambition to conquer the political world. If you go, I go, was the theme to their marriage, a bond some could argue was much more intense than a prenup. Each supported the other's foundation. Michelle and Barack Obama also did not have a prenup and were similarly entwined, though for years there were rumors that Michelle was so miserable hanging up her powerful corporate career to fulfill Barack's presidential dreams that she was planning to leave him when the White House years were over. Instead, they signed a joint book deal worth $65 million. The ties that bind.

"The beautiful thing is, she agrees with it," Trump told gossip columnist Liz Smith about his fiancée's complacency over the prenup. And really, is there anything more beautiful than a woman who signs a document stating that if her marriage hits the shitter, she won't have any recourse to get funds from the man from whom she is parting? "She knows I have to have that," Trump told Smith.

Melania was also incredibly pragmatic. She was under zero illusion that at least some aspect of her relationship was transactional, no matter how much she loved him or how much he loved her. Part of their "fairy tale" was not a fairy tale but the ages-old story of a rich, older man who bolsters his vitality and ego by marrying a young, beautiful woman/model. He gets the babe; she gets the cash. And although Melania in no way thought about her relationship in this manner, she was smart enough to be aware that in some small way, there was a deal to be upheld. She would maintain her looks, her support, her youth and sex appeal while she was with him, and he would maintain his wealth and power. At her core, Melania is a realist, a girl from a communist country who understands that materialism, for all its allure, isn't wrapped up in romance.

In 2005, before the wedding, Melania was invited to speak to a class at New York University's business school, presumably because by extension she understood the Trumpian way of how to build something profitable. Or they just couldn't get Donald. Either way, during the class she was asked by one particularly ballsy person if she would be with Trump if he weren't rich. Without missing a beat, Melania fixed her cool blue eyes on the student and said, "If I weren't beautiful, do you think he'd be with me?" In other words, don't fuck with Melania. She knows exactly what is up.

It's this sort of complete, 360-degree understanding that elevates Melania beyond the stereotype. Clearly, the student was trying to be snide or even essentially call her a gold digger to her face. Would she be with him if he weren't rich? In her answer, she's basically saying no, she wouldn't be—but if she were some average Jane, he wouldn't be with her either. Again, her recognition of the business side of their arrangement adds a layer of complexity to Melania. And the degree to which she acknowledges that component as a valid and anticipated—and accepted—part of her marriage is not to be overlooked. It signals an insider's savvy that she will demonstrate, even rely on, when she ultimately becomes the most enigmatic first lady in modern history.

In his book *Trump: The Art of the Comeback*, which was released a year before he met Melania, Trump clearly has unresolved issues about women who don't sign prenups or, worse, in his opinion, have the gall to mouth off after they do. "The most difficult aspect of the prenuptial agreement is informing your future wife (or husband): 'I love you very much, but just in case things don't work out, this is what you will get in the divorce.' There are basically three types of women and reactions. One is the good woman who very much loves her future husband, solely for himself, but refuses to sign the agreement on principle. I fully understand this," Trump writes. "But the man should take a pass anyway and find someone else." Translation: screw love if she's not signing. "The other," he goes on, "is the calculating woman who refuses to sign the prenuptial agreement because she is expecting to take advantage of the poor, unsuspecting sucker she's got in her grasp. There is also the woman who will openly and quickly sign a prenuptial agreement in order to make a quick hit and take the money given to her." Those are the three categories in which Trump views women. Oh, and he also thinks they shouldn't gripe and bitch—key to the crux of marital advice he gives pals. Again, from *The Art of the Comeback*: "Often, I will tell friends whose wives are constantly nagging them about this or that that they're better off leaving and cutting their losses. I'm not a great believer in always trying to work things out," writes Trump, just before this gem of a sexist zinger: "For a man to be successful he needs support at home, just like my father had from my mother, not someone who is always griping and bitching. When a man has to endure a woman who is not supportive and complains constantly about not being home enough or not being attentive enough, he will not be very successful unless he is able to cut the cord." Ivana would, years after her marriage was over, write that she became a business-woman in part because she adopted an "if you can't beat him, join him" attitude. She felt that if Trump was always going to work and never be home, she might as well grab a briefcase and do the same. It ultimately led to the end of their union. "My big mistake with Ivana was taking her out of the role of wife and allowing her to run one of my casinos in Atlantic City, then the Plaza hotel. . . . I will never again give a wife responsibility within my business," he said.

Marla also complained about their marriage, a lot, claiming that he wasn't the kind of husband who would come home on time at the end of the day and snuggle with his wife and baby. Trump wasn't that guy. He wasn't even in the same galaxy as that guy. In 1999, after their divorce, Marla told the *New York Post,* "I thought that I could change him. But he won't change."

Melania, however, didn't want to change him, *and* she wanted to sign the prenuptial agreement. By signing it and being happy to do so, she smartly eliminates any concern he might have that she wants to try to do to him what Ivana did (make him feel less powerful) or what Marla did (make him feel like a failure as a husband and father). She immediately elevates herself above her predecessors simply by non-chalantly going along with the one thing most brides to be fight tooth and nail against. And somewhere in the back of her mind, she must know that should the worst happen and she and Trump divorce, she would have a pretty sound legal case for being granted more than the prenup she signed. (Public humiliation by her husband's alleged infi-delities with a porn star and a *Playboy* model? That's got to be worth something.) Melania has almost always, even back then, maneuvered two steps ahead of her betrothed. "I think the mistake some people make is they try to change the man they love after they get married. You cannot change a person," she said. It was music to Trump's ears.

8

The Wedding of the Century

*"To be married to my husband, to someone as successful
as he is, he needs somebody who will tell him the truth."*
—MELANIA TRUMP

It's funny to look back on Melania and Donald Trump's wedding and realize who was on the guest list: Bill and Hillary Clinton, Barbara Walters, Rudy Giuliani, Anna Wintour, P. Diddy, Katie Couric, Gayle King, Matt Lauer, Billy Joel, Les Moonves, Shaquille O'Neal, Jeff Zucker, Chris Christie, Chris Matthews, and Steve Wynn. The list of celebrities is as long as it is weird. Because of course today, while a handful remain Trump allies (Giuliani, Wynn, sort of Christie, maybe Shaq), most are vocal opponents. Anna Wintour won't even put Melania Trump in the pages of her magazine; Hillary Clinton is still seething over her lost election; Chris Matthews spends most weekday evenings skewering Trump; Billy Joel, who wrote a special song to sing at the wedding, wouldn't be caught dead performing at the White House during the Trump administration.

Fast-forward a decade after the "wedding of the century," as the tabloids called it, and a lot of the guests won't be on speaking terms with the bride and groom.

But at the time Melania had no idea how the future would unfold. So she hired a planner and got started on the business of becoming Mrs. Donald Trump (the third). Like most society brides, Melania set her sights on Preston Bailey, then the most well-known, high-end celebrity party designer in the country.

Bailey said that while the time frame to plan the Trumps' wedding was tight at three months out, he was not about to turn down the opportunity. The timing was narrower than most weddings of this size and notoriety because the first planner she had hired didn't work out. Bailey happily stepped in. "I remember we would fly on the private plane many times, planning while we were in the air," says Bailey, who, like Melania, was based in New York. "She usually flew out with her sister, Ines, her parents, or with close friends." Bailey says Melania wasn't an obsessive bridezilla, but she was decisive. "She wasn't fuzzy about what she wanted. She was very clear in her taste level."

Bailey tells me he still recalls how well Melania treated his staff, getting to know everyone's name and displaying warmth that most onlookers now have no way of seeing. "Way before any of *this* happened, she ending up as first lady, what I remember about her is the way she came into my office when my staff was there, how at ease she made everyone feel," says Bailey. "I remember her so clearly being that way, and she treated every one of them the same—she gave them attention. She was so impressive. Even my assistants, she made sure that she spoke to them and she connected to them."

The couple registered at Bergdorf Goodman, Frette for linens, and, naturally, Tiffany. It's somewhat odd, and etiquette experts might say uncouth, for a groom on his third wedding and a thirty-four-year-old bride to be who crows about her independence and is marrying a millionaire to register for gifts. The tradition of a registry really began to help young couples get on their feet with gifts like towels and small appliances, candlesticks, and napkin rings. But Trump insisted, so Melania picked out glassware from Royal Copenhagen, crystal from Lalique, and silver from Tiffany, where a five-piece set of her English

King flatware cost $2,000. Her china service was the Palladium pattern, also from Tiffany and not superornate, considering the decor of the homes she and Trump would live in; a set of twelve pieces cost $1,135.

"I was completely in every, every detail," Melania said of her wedding planning. "I did everything and I wanted to be along to do it because more people have it to tell you, 'Oh, maybe you should do it that way, maybe you should do that.' You know you get confused. And I know what I want."

Later, as first lady, she would say the same thing when it came to how she envisioned events at the White House. Mood boards, fabric samples, test runs with flower arrangements and tastings from the chef—she knows what she wants.

What Melania wanted for her wedding day was elegance, she said—white and gold everything—and tons and tons of flowers.

In fact, that's the only thing Bailey recalls Trump got in a tizzy about: the flowers. One day, Trump had come by the newly reconstructed $45 million ballroom at Mar-a-Lago, where the reception was to be held. Bailey says it wasn't unusual for Trump to stop by and check on things. "He was very much involved. He wanted to see everything," says Bailey of the weeks leading up to the big day. "I remember Mr. Trump as being this very accessible man. You know, one time, I remember him serving us something from the kitchen, just very hospitable. You know, he was very, very, very accessible." But this particular day, he had an issue: the floral candelabras were just too goddamn big. "I do remember clearly that moment of him coming in when we were setting up the design and him being like, "Get those things off the table!"

"I had this idea of creating huge white candelabras at each table, covered in flowers. And Mr. Trump came in and he was like, 'Oh my God. That is too much,'" says Bailey. "But, of course, Melania already knew about the candelabras and how big they would be, and what I remember is she took him to the side and very calmly said,

'This is something that we had already planned,' and 'just wait until you see them when it's all finished.'" Bailey says she talked Trump off the ledge. Friends note that, in general, this is what Melania is especially good at in their relationship: being composed when he goes off the rails. Pamela Gross, a former producer at CNN who is a close friend of Melania's and has been for many years, said, "When he is spinning and thinking and blazing forward, she brings this quality of calm and serenity to him. That calming influence is a really important thing about her character. She is not a frantic person."

"When it all came together, and she explained everything, he loved it," says Bailey.

In the end, the candelabras were quite literally a huge hit, and two graced each of the twenty-one tables. Eight feet tall and gold, they were swathed in white roses, amaryllis, and hydrangeas, dripping with Dendrobium orchids, woven to look like hanging wisteria. At the top of each were long tapered candles. It took two people three hours to arrange just one of them. All of the wedding flowers, more than ten thousand in total, were either flown in to Florida or driven down from New York via specially made refrigerated trucks to keep them from wilting. Bailey insisted the ballroom temperature be sustained at a chilly 50 degrees up until the last minute before guests entered, in order to preserve the freshness of the blooms.

"She wanted something that felt like in a way was a statement, but not too overstated," explains Bailey of Melania's wedding goals. "Two weeks after we first met to discuss her vision, she came back to my office and we set up the tables and everything else and she walked in and she loved it. She really, really loved it. From that moment on, I think somehow we had gained her trust and the communication was very open."

So, apparently, was the budget, which most wedding experts have put at well over one million dollars. Bailey wouldn't confirm that number, but he didn't dispute it either. He did say there were "very few" questions or issues with money being spent on the affair, adding Trump would regularly review the numbers, but he ultimately wanted everything to be what Melania expected, money not an issue. "He wasn't like, 'let's save,'" says Bailey.

Later, of course, Trump would brag to *The New York Times* about the vendors tripping over themselves to offer their services for free or steeply discounted. "Literally, anything you can imagine from photos to flowers to food to jets to airports to diamonds," Trump told the paper in a story that ran ten days before the nuptials. "There's five people who want to do it. In all cases they don't want anything, but they want recognition." Bailey makes it clear he was not one of those people, and Trump paid full price for his services. Trump told the *Times* that famed chef Jean-Georges Vongerichten was doing the food—lobster rolls, crab cakes, and steamed shrimp salad for appetizers, filet mignon with potato-horseradish galettes for entrée—but for free. Vongerichten brought four chefs from his restaurants in New York with him to Mar-a-Lago to prep the meal. He also packed $18,000 worth of beluga caviar, flown in a cooler on Trump's private jet, to use for "beggar's purses," the most luxe of the hors d'oeuvres, with crème fraîche and caviar tucked into tiny blinis tied with a chive bow. The Trump touch came when the chef's assistants brushed each "purse" with a streak of gold leaf to finish them off. The four hundred–plus guests sipped 1983 Louis Roederer Cristal brut champagne, which retails for about five hundred dollars a bottle.

Trump found a jet company willing to supply red carpet treatment and likely less pricey champagne for guests arriving at the private aviation terminal in West Palm Beach—again, at no cost. The kicker was the one thing Trump didn't outsource as a freebie: his wedding coif. "I'll do my own hair." Trump should have been grateful that was all he had to manage, because Slovenian wedding tradition often includes a ritual wherein the groom must perform what's called a *sragna,* demonstrating physical strength by sawing a log. Melania let him off the hook with that one.

Her wedding-day hair would be a huge updo sticking out from the back of her head like a beehive, with detailed loops of perfectly combed and curled sections pinned high enough to form the perfect setting for the hood of her gigantic tulle veil, which Melania herself took a needle and thread to just before the ceremony to secure a section that wasn't cooperating as she wanted it to.

As for the dress, Melania had traveled to Paris for the haute couture shows months before, invited by *Vogue*'s Anna Wintour and André Leon Talley, who served as her guides. While Wintour today wouldn't be caught dead in her Prada dress and sunglasses shopping with Melania Trump, back then the wedding was really a point of pop culture discussion, and Melania even had the mysterious allure of being a relatively unknown, younger, and strikingly beautiful woman marrying Donald Trump. The wedding was strange and epic and intriguing all at the same time.

The trio, Melania, Wintour, and Talley, was looking for a designer who could dream up a gown important enough to feature on the cover of *Vogue* and fit the bride's aesthetic. Melania settled on John Galliano, at the time the designer for the house of Dior. Later that year, after the wedding, Melania would call on Galliano again for a custom gown, this time a white, strapless, beaded couture creation for a charity event she was chairing in New York for the Martha Graham Dance Company. Later in an interview, Melania would praise Galliano for the detail and craftsmanship of his work.

"We went to Paris for one week to the shows," Melania would recall of shopping for her wedding dress. The resulting wedding gown was a strapless creation with a fit-and-flare silhouette (tight on top, flowing outward just below the hips at her upper thigh) and more than one hundred yards of shiny ivory duchesse satin. The dress was massive, tucked up in spots to add design details, ruched in the middle of the bodice and pleated along the sides and the hem, and had a whopping thirteen-foot train—the gown weighed sixty pounds.

"And then they have crystals and crystals," said Melania of the thousands of tiny embroidered stones that caught the light on the neckline and skirt. "They were working 550 hours just to put the crystals on." The gown, all told, was said to cost in the neighborhood of $300,000, but each haute couture creation is one-of-a-kind and almost always considered priceless. She had trouble walking in it and would later say the couple's first dance, to Puccini's "Nessun Dorma," wasn't some ridiculously choreographed thing, mostly because she couldn't move all that much. Trump did dip her, though. And later she changed into a more movement-friendly Vera Wang Grecian-style dress.

A few days before the wedding, Melania reached the pinnacle every model dreams of: the cover of *Vogue* magazine. "Exclusive: Donald Trump's New Bride. The Ring, the Dress, the Wedding, the Jet, the Party," read the cover. Melania was posed, stiffly, as those who criticize her modeling skills often say is her way, leaning against a wall, one hand on her hip, the other by her side, wearing her couture Dior gown and full veil. She is smiling, a real showing-teeth smile—a happy grin that she doesn't normally use for photographs. You can see her diamond engagement ring clearly, as well as the Edwardian-style bib diamond necklace on loan from Fred Leighton jewelers, which she also wore on her wedding day. The *Vogue* cover and the photos that accompanied the story inside were shot by Mario Testino, possibly the most famous fashion photographer of this generation—known for taking portraits of Princess Diana. In October 2012, Melania tweeted a photo of her *Vogue* magazine cover. "My favorite photographer #MarioTestino Happy Birthday! #flashback @ voguemagazine 2005."

Melania Knavs (Knauss) married Donald Trump in a wedding ceremony held at the Episcopal Church of Bethesda-by-the-Sea, even though it would later be revealed that Melania is Catholic. In 2017, as first lady, she visited the Vatican with President Trump and had a brief audience with Pope Francis. During their tête-à-tête, Melania held out her hand, extending her rosary beads, which the pope then blessed, placing his hand atop hers and making the sign of the cross. It was a brief moment, maybe ten seconds, but it was significant; there has not been a Catholic first lady in the White House since Jackie Kennedy. Trump is Presbyterian. It's unclear why the couple chose Bethesda-by-the-Sea for their ceremony, besides that it was pretty and convenient to

Mar-a-Lago. A team of Bailey's floral designers decorated the archway of the giant doors of the church with hundreds and hundreds of white hydrangeas, peonies, and roses.

The ceremony itself held a lot of significance for Melania; it was way more personal for her than the reception. This might have been Trump's third trip up the aisle, but it was her first, and she sincerely hoped it would be her last. She told friends that she had zero doubts about marrying Trump. Whether that was true or not, it was certainly a line she stuck to in interviews. "No, I didn't have any concerns," she would tell Barbara Walters years later when asked if she was worried that Trump's previous marriages were signs this one too wouldn't make it. She replied, "You have to know who you are" to be with him, something she is fond of saying.

As for Trump, he gave at least minimal acknowledgment of his past marital failures and described his plan for his nuptials with Melania: "I'm gonna show up, I'm gonna say, 'I do,' and I'm gonna be a very good husband for a change," said Trump in an interview right before the big day.

During the service, the Metropolitan Opera soprano Camellia Johnson sang "Ave Maria" as Melania walked toward her groom—carefully. The giant dress almost toppled her, but she found her footing before taking a tumble. Her maid of honor and only attendant was her older sister, Ines. For the wedding, Ines was outfitted in a strapless white, custom-made Vera Wang gown with a beige satin belt. She wore an ornate white pearl choker that looked Victorian in era.

Trump's two sons, Don Jr. and Eric, were his best men. Ivanka Trump did a Bible reading during the service, and reality show producer Mark Burnett's eldest son, nine-year-old Cameron, served as a page, dressed in a Dior pageboy ensemble with white silk shorts and white knee-high socks. Tiffany's job was less high-profile: she was asked to hand out wedding programs before the service began. It's still unclear why Tiffany's role was so minimal in the wedding, but as with most things Tiffany Trump, there's a sad footnote of afterthought.

The church's pastor, the Reverend Ralph R. Warren, performed a traditional Episcopalian ceremony at the altar, which was decorated on either side with white flowers. After the couple read their vows, Trump holding the hand of his bride the entire time, the two lit Melania's own baptismal candle. "I was baptized on Donald's birthday, so I think it has a meaning to me and to the family, and I kept it," said Melania of the candle, which her mother brought specially to Palm Beach from Slovenia for the wedding. "Then I will keep it for baby, so I will baptize my baby and the candle will be there." After lighting the candle, Trump and Melania both knelt at the altar and prayed. They maintained eye contact. "We had a little smile, but we were serious, because they are serious words," Melania said of the vows.

When it was time for the groom to kiss the bride, Trump, dressed in a black tuxedo with a large white silk bow tie and matching white silk cummerbund, dutifully did so, planting one on her for a good few seconds, and guests applauded. The couple exited the church as they had entered it, only now showered with white rose petals, Melania still clutching in one hand her diamond cross and rosary, embellished with tiny tea roses. She had eschewed a big bridal bouquet, opting for the holy symbol of Catholic prayer instead. It was more significant, she said to friends.

The ceremony had started at 7 P.M., and afterward guests were shuttled in black limousines to Mar-a-Lago, where most had already spent the day enjoying free spa treatments or golf. Along with the celebrities, politicians, people on the Forbes 400 list, and media titans, were Melania's few personal guests, people she met pre-Trump: essentially just her parents, her sister, and a handful of girlfriends. Her life in New York before meeting Trump (even while dating Trump) was simple and centered on home. She was not a social swan, and she didn't hit the charity circuit like so many wealthy Manhattan wives do. Her circle was small, not because she wasn't a friendly person or because she had few social skills, but because she only wanted to spend time with people who mattered to her and, most important, people she could truly trust.

Spectators lined up behind police barricades in front of the church just to catch a glimpse of the star power—they waited so long many ordered pizzas from their cell phones. "If someone had dropped a bomb on that place, it would have wiped out an entire generation of famous Americans," said the bandleader's wife.

These were, of course, the years that Hollywood loved Trump, or at least tolerated him as a mainstay of popular culture. But Trump thought they loved him. *The Apprentice* was a huge hit, and the idea that this real estate magnate slash reality TV star would one day be in the White House . . . well, it was ridiculous. When that day eventually, and unbelievably, came, nearly all of Trump's celebrity friends would abandon him. It remains a stinging sore spot with the president.

Back then, however, Trump had famous pals, and they adored Melania, liking the way she kept him centered. He wasn't oblivious to having found in Melania a woman capable of putting up with him. "[If] this were just another really wonderful woman, I wouldn't have done it," Trump said when asked ad nauseam why on earth after two hellish divorces would he dare marry again. "This is beyond that." He must have really meant it, because although he and NBC wanted to carry the wedding live, Melania said no way would she have television cameras at her big day. In fact, there was virtually no press at all, and guests were asked not to take photos or video. Only Katie Couric broke the rules, snapping away at the reception. "I didn't have her thrown out," Trump said. "I heard about it a little bit later. But, she was fun. You know, it does happen."

As the Michael Rose Orchestra struck up the forty-six-piece band, the celebration kicked off in the new Mar-a-Lago grand ballroom. At various points in the evening, Tony Bennett and Paul Anka would sing—as would Billy Joel. Joel included in his repertoire a song he wrote called "That's Why the Donald Is a Trump" to the tune of "The Lady Is a Tramp." (*Page Six* wrote about Joel's performance at the wedding, claiming the singer was so "tipsy" he kept losing his place reading the lyrics.)

But the vibe of the wedding was fun and easy and no one minded because they were having a good time bearing witness to yet another over-the-top Trump nuptial. Guests marveled at the detail, the lace overlays on the tablecloths, the flowers, the china. "I wanted to do everything like Louis XIV style because it's my favorite," said Melania about her decor inspiration. Even Bailey, who attended the wedding as a guest, said Melania was able to enjoy the night. "She really let go," says Bailey, who got tons of future clients from that wedding. Bailey admits that for years following the event, his clients would use it as a model for what they wanted him to do for their own weddings.

Bailey said that at one point during the wedding, Ivanka approached him and said, "When I get married, I'm calling you," which she did. "Literally, at six in the morning, the day her engagement was announced, she called me," said Bailey.

But for Melania's big day, the focus was on what she had envisioned, created, and executed, and it was 100 percent to her liking. "That night, I did not get one request from Melania that anything was wrong or upsetting," says Bailey, adding that this was most definitely the exception and not the rule. "She wasn't 'move the light, fix this.' She was completely at ease once the entire ceremony and reception started."

In her later life, the White House staff would say the same of their new boss. Melania's attention to detail and certainty about how she wanted things to look and the mood she wanted to set was discerning—she was a stickler for making sure it was all just as she imagined it would be. She pores over every detail of a table setting or a floral arrangement, asking that everything for a big event be set up the night before so that she can do a walk-through, sleeping well in the knowledge she won't be surprised with mistakes on the day of. The value of this type A behavior means that she tends to be calm and effortless at whatever celebration she oversees, as though the evening had never required hard work or induced stress.

As the reception dinner rolled on, the toasts began. Eric Trump, who ten years later would also get married at Mar-a-Lago and, like his stepmother and sister, also hire Preston Bailey, was warm and welcoming to his new stepmother. He was twenty years old, the youngest child from Trump's first marriage to Ivana. "I know this is the last time I'll ever have to stand up here," he said, raising a glass. It was thoughtful and reassuring to her, even if others in the room might have been willing to bet it wouldn't be the last time. At twenty-seven, Donald Trump Jr., whom everyone still called Donny, was the brattier of the three oldest Trump kids, and he didn't mind being perceived that way. "I look forward to spending many years annoying both of you," he said during his toast, tucking his long hair behind his ear, a prediction that would very much come true. Months later, Don Jr. would himself get married in the ballroom at Mar-a-Lago to Vanessa Haydon, also a model (from whom he is now divorced). The decor at Donny and Vanessa's wedding was as opposite from Melania's white-and-gold vision as could be. Vanessa wanted purple tablecloths and bright fuchsia flowers. When they cut the cake, Donny, ever the frat boy, smeared frosting over his new wife's face. The saving grace of Melania's relationship with Don Jr. would come a few years later, when Barron was a young boy. An only child, he was grateful, and so was his mother, for the rambunctious fun of playing with Don Jr. and Vanessa's five children, some of whom were almost the same age as their uncle.

For Ivanka, letting go of her father to another wife was more complicated. She was twenty-three when he married Melania, and while she liked the Slovenian model a lot more than she did Marla, which was not at all, coming to terms with another alpha female in her family wasn't always easy.

Four years after her own wedding, Melania would attend Ivanka's nuptials to Jared Kushner at the Trump National Golf Club in Bedminster, New Jersey, wearing a sexy, strapless, royal-blue silk gown, a massive starburst-shaped diamond brooch attached to the waistline. Simple and understated Melania was not.

Ivanka was also especially close to her younger brother, Eric, and she felt that if Eric was okay with Melania, which he was, she was fine as well. Years later, when Eric married Lara Yunaska at Mar-a-Lago, Ivanka's husband, Jared Kushner, would perform the wedding ceremony; Ivanka herself designed Lara's engagement ring and the couple's wedding bands from her now-defunct eponymous fine-jewelry line. Forever on brand, that Trump family.

Melania's arrival was all good by Ivanka's standards. Like her dad, she felt that the Slovenian "deserved" to marry into the Trump family after sticking with him for more than six years. Again, the word "love" was rarely used to describe why the couple was together and why they got married. Still, she offered more support for the union with Melania than she had for Marla Maples—who married her father at the Plaza Hotel; Ivanka and her two brothers didn't even show.

"I want to thank my girl" was how Trump opened his wedding toast, addressing not Ivanka, as one might imagine with a start like that, but Melania. "It has been the best six years of my life in every way. My little Melania." It was, at best, worth a cringe. But Trump, with his awkward expressions of emotion, and Melania, with her daddy issues and joyful nuptials, didn't appear to think the toast was anything other than hopelessly romantic.

Just after midnight, it was time to cut the cake. A gargantuan, two-hundred-pound, Grand Marnier–flavored creation many feet and seven tiers tall, the wedding cake was about as Trump as it gets. The facade was covered with three thousand white sugar flowers. "I said 'I want all roses,'" was Melania's instruction to Mar-a-Lago's pastry chef, Cedric Barberet, who met the demand with gusto. It took two months for Barberet and his team to build the cake's platform, as well as the intricate wiring system used to support all the buttercream and yellow chiffon cake with orange zest, which was weighed down with liqueur. Like an actual Trump building, inside the thing was mostly infrastructure. It succeeded in staying upright, of course, and at the wedding it was a centerpiece worthy of oohs and aahs, but sadly it wasn't edible. The tiers weren't deep enough with actual cake for pieces to be cut for the guests, so only the base had "cake" enough for show for the couple to do the ceremonial cutting. Trump winked at the gathered crowd as they cut into the cake, her hands on top of his. "We made a wish," he said.

The top tier was the only other part that was also actual food, and it was preserved for Melania so she could presumably eat it with Trump on their first wedding anniversary, as is tradition. As for the guests, Barberet baked dozens of five-inch-tall spare cakes with the same flavors as the main cake, and slices of those were served. Later, after the party was over and the sun was coming up, Barberet and his staff would demolish the wedding cake, cutting hunks of it off the sides and eating as much as possible, right down to the wires.

At 1:00 A.M., with no signs of the party slowing down, Melania slipped off to her room for an outfit change, reemerging in a body-hugging Vera Wang gown—white, of course—with detailed ruching at the bodice and a flowing Grecian-style hem. She had taken down her massive beehive hairdo and let her natural waves tumble past her shoulders. In lieu of the veil, she had put on a floral crown made of white roses. The costume change was significant enough to switch Melania from formal Palm Beach bride to tropical party-vibes bride. Her nutmeg-colored skin dark against the white of the dress, smile as big as could be, she danced with guests outside on the patio, which had been transformed into a nightclub-like space, with colored lights and dance floor. Melania had removed all of her diamonds from the wedding, stripping off the sparkling bracelets and massive necklace. She was, it appeared, very much having fun. Trump, not one to dance to modern music, stayed mostly on the periphery, talking to his VIP guests, discussing the success of *The Apprentice*, and asking everyone if they thought Melania was the most beautiful bride they had ever seen. ("Of course, Donald.")

At 4:00 A.M., the party finally wrapped, and legend has it Trump actually carried his bride over the threshold to their suite. The event had gone off without a hitch, exactly as Melania anticipated. She was now Mrs. Donald Trump, the only title she ever imagined she would have. Never in a million years, and especially not that night as she slipped into her bed at Mar-a-Lago, with its high-thread-count sheets and fragrant roses on the nightstand, did she believe she would one day be first lady of the United States.

9

———

Family First, First Family

"Sometimes I just think, 'Oh my God, this is my baby. I have a baby.' There's nothing like it."

—MELANIA TRUMP

From the day she had him, Barron Trump became Melania's world, her most prized possession and the barometer by which she would make decisions for the rest of her life.

When Melania got pregnant, it made the cover of the *New York Post*. "Trump Baby: Melania Due in Spring" screamed the headline, as though everyone in Gotham was on a first-name basis with Melania Trump. She called in to Martha Stewart's talk show the day the news broke. Martha, as she is wont to do, was candid, promptly declaring that she had an inkling Melania was with child because Melania looked fat in an appearance on her program the week before. "You looked just too wholesome . . . and plump."

Melania also gave an interview to *People* magazine, recalling the moment she told Trump "he was going to be a father." Of course, he'd been a father already for more than two decades. "At first he needed to take it in. He was very surprised. And then he was very happy." Trump corrects his wife, saying he was more surprised the doing it actually worked as fast as it did. "I expected we were going to have children, so I wasn't totally surprised," he says. "But I was surprised by the speed of it. It happened very quickly." Always quick to plug his successes.

As a present for getting pregnant, Trump bought Melania a snazzy silver Mercedes-Benz SLR McLaren sports car, which he had delivered to her at Trump Tower complete with a big red bow on top. Not exactly a family car—there's no space for a car seat—but then again Trump's never been one for sentimentality. It was a splurge, however; the sticker price is somewhere around $550,000.

Trump also did a solo interview about Melania's pregnancy, again centered on the concept of timing, only with a much more sinister bent. "I think I'll give her a week," he jokes to Howard Stern about how much time Melania will have to get her body back after the baby. His wife, listening at home, is then five months pregnant. "I've seen 'em all types. I've seen beautiful women that for the rest of their lives have become a horror," says Trump, talking about the miracle of childbirth and what it may or may not do to a woman's physique. "You know, I mean it's been a very tough life for them, okay? They gain, like, 250 pounds. It's like a disaster." He reassures Stern that Melania isn't going to be like that. No way. Any listener would be cringing by now, internally begging him to shut up, just don't make it worse, be quiet. But he doesn't. "I mean monster in the most positive way," he goes on. "She has gotten very, very large—in all the right places." Ten years later, *New York Post* columnist Andrea Peyser will disavow Trump and his presidential candidacy because in her eyes he's a total creep and she's had it. One of the incidents she cites as proof happened two months after Melania had Barron, when Peyser visits the triplex for an interview. She is being nice and cordial when she compliments Melania, standing nearby in five-inch stilettos, for having lost all her baby weight. "Trump corrected me: 'She's *almost* lost all the baby weight.'"

And if she does get cellulite? Trump pledges he will, valiantly, stay in the marriage. "I will. I will love her so much, you have no idea. I'm a very loyal person. I will love her so much." It's the first time the word "love" has been uttered by Trump in an interview when talking about Melania. Sadly, it may also prove to be untrue, at least the loyal part. More than a decade later, two women will come forward and say they had affairs with Trump shortly after Melania gave birth. Former *Playboy* model Karen McDougal claims she had a ten-month affair with Trump in June 2006. And porn star Stephanie Clifford, aka Stormy Daniels, says she had a one-night fling with him the following month. Trump denies both allegations.

For Melania, the pregnancy simply provided another opportunity to ignore the outside world and focus on her independence. She got to work dismantling parts of the 67th floor of the triplex—specifically, a few of the guest rooms—being careful not to disturb the decades-old gold facade the public had gotten used to seeing during interviews, reality television episodes, and photo shoots. Melania builds out a nursery suited for a new Trump baby, since the last to live there was Tiffany, more than a decade earlier. She spends most of her days resting or visits with her sister, Ines. Never married and with no children, Ines, an artist, has also moved to New York City, living in a Trump-owned building on Park Avenue, in an apartment said to be worth $2 million, a handful of blocks from Trump Tower. Amalija visited often, and both she and Viktor planned to spend even more time in Manhattan, with a grandchild coming and because Melania asked that they be actively involved in helping care for the child. Ultimately, Viktor and Amalija have spent so much time with Barron, watching him, looking after him, staying with him when his parents travel, that he is fluent in Slovenian. Those who have spent time with him say that he has a slight Slovenian accent.

By this time in her pregnancy, Melania was not yet a United States citizen (she became one four months after Barron was born), but she had had her green card since 2001, when she sponsored herself, controversially, on the basis of being a model of "extraordinary ability." Once a citizen, she was able to sponsor her parents to obtain green cards and, ultimately in summer 2018, U.S. citizenship. The type of family visa process that the Knavses and Melania used is specifically the kind that Trump and his administration are trying to repeal, calling "chain migration" harmful to the United States. But, apparently, it's okay for his in-laws.

While having a baby for Melania meant gathering up her Slovenian support system, for Trump the pregnancy was a chance to boast about his virility. At red carpet appearances over several months, he's photographed with his hand on Melania's growing stomach or actually pointing to it with a big grin as if to say, "See? I DID THAT." Melania, next to him, is smiling in practically every picture during this time period, beaming, actually, that at thirty-five she is finally getting what she had hoped for: a child. The sense of family instilled in Melania from a young age and her close relationship with her parents and sister made her want to be a mother. Additionally, having a child with Trump would mean the child would be well cared for financially and afforded privilege and prestige, necessities in the life she wanted for her offspring. Again, in her decision to tie herself to Trump, the wait was worth it to fulfill that goal. If the paramount goal was to settle down and only settle down, could she have married someone and had a child earlier in life? Sure. But could she have given that child the life she envisioned for them, and herself, if she had settled? Probably not.

But getting pregnant, with Trump's or anyone's baby, didn't mean Melania packed up her tendency for glamour; that she started knitting booties for the cover of *Pregnancy* magazine. On the contrary. In the April issue of *Vogue,* where just over a year before she appeared on the cover in her wedding gown, there is Melania, seven months pregnant, in a gold OMO Norma Kamali string bikini and Christian Louboutin stilettos, with a gold silk Carolina Herrera coat opened wide to expose her body and long legs. Shot by Annie Leibovitz, who in 1991 photographed the iconic *Vanity Fair* magazine cover of a naked Demi Moore clutching her very pregnant belly, the two-page Melania spread similarly showcased Melania's stomach and was featured, ironically, in *Vogue*'s annual "shape" issue. The headline read "Golden Girl."

"I think it's very sexy for a woman to be pregnant," says Melania in the story. "I think it's beautiful, carrying a baby inside"—something her husband might disagree with. But in this image, he's not the focus; he's on the left-hand page of the spread, sitting in the driver's seat of the Mercedes he bought for his wife months before, the gull-wing doors of the half-million-dollar sports car open, like he's waiting for Melania to walk on over and hop inside. She would, maybe, but she's too busy posing on the back steps of the Trump jet, parked at the airport in West Palm Beach. Melania also tells *Vogue* that she will be a "strict, but not too strict" parent and that she intends to be "very grounded" bringing up her child. Read into the irony of the accompanying photo of her getting onto her private jet what you will.

For her baby shower, thrown by her friends Audrey Gruss, a Manhattan philanthropist and socialite, and Pamela Gross, at the time editor of New York society magazine *Avenue,* Melania and guests take over the FAO Schwarz store on Fifth Avenue. However, though there were toys and baby gifts to be bought all around, none were purchased for baby Trump. Instead, Melania insisted that the things guests bought at the shower go to charity. The surplus of toys was later delivered to New York Presbyterian Hospital. It's a gesture of kindness that friends say is a hallmark of Melania's personality, and an early indicator of her soft spot for sick children. Since becoming first lady, her most genuine—and lengthy—hospital visits have been quiet, under-the-radar stops to see ill children, often in the ICU. Donating the gifts and money from her baby shower, and doing so without calling *Page Six*, while not Trumpian, are very much in alignment with Melania's independent streak.

On March 20, nine days early, Melania went into labor. After eight hours, Barron William Trump was born, weighing 8.5 pounds and measuring 21 inches long. The name is unique, but not entirely out of left field. In the 1980s, reporters got used to speaking with a John Barron (or, sometimes, Baron) when they wanted to get a quote or a statement from Donald Trump. Barron, they were told, was a spokesman for the Trump Organization. He was also Donald Trump.

Trump used to pretend to be his own PR guy, John Barron/Baron, to pump his own stories and triumphs, plant his name in the paper, and bloat his identity—and sometimes his wealth. In 1984, Jonathan Greenberg was reporting the fabled Forbes 400, the annual ranking of the richest people in America. Greenberg was put on the phone with John Barron, a Trump Organization "official," who went into deep and rambling detail about Trump's assets and why they were worth more than the magazine had ranked Trump the previous year. When he ultimately went back and listened to the recorded "Barron" interviews, Greenberg said he was "amazed" at the time he "didn't see through the ruse." Trump had changed the cadence of his voice, said Greenberg, and deepened his New York accent, but it was him.

Whether Melania knew about the John Barron ruse when she and Trump named their only child is unclear. Even more unclear is what she might think now that she knows the origin of the name and its history with Trump's misrepresentations.

Unlike when Marla delivered Tiffany, Trump was thrilled when Melania told him it would be fine to wait outside and not be in the delivery room while she was pushing. Marla was in labor for twelve hours and had opted for natural childbirth. As with most things with Marla, it was dramatic. Trump was by her side for most of it, agonizing as she screamed out in pain and praying as she was surrounded by a breathing coach (who performed reflexology), her mother, and a doctor. Trump, a famous germophobe, found the whole thing very, very uncomfortable, to put it mildly.

With Melania, twenty minutes after Barron was born, Trump wasn't in scrubs, he was on the phone announcing the news of his fifth child by calling in to *Imus in the Morning*, Don Imus's radio program. "I continue to stay young, right?" fifty-nine-year-old Trump says, managing to make the birth of his new son about himself. "I produce children; I stay young." He also took a call from Regis Philbin, who habitually referred to Trump as the Trumpster on his live morning television program. "She gave me a nice son," Trump told Regis of Melania's efforts.

On her personal Web site, now defunct, Melania said, "Donald and I are very happy and excited. We can't wait to take our new little Trump to his new home."

Melania was soon on the interview circuit herself. Just two weeks after the birth of Barron, she was on *The View,* chatting with the ladies about her "very, very easy" childbirth and answering with a laugh as to whether she had an epidural ("Of course!"). At the time, remember, *The View* was very friendly turf—this was prepolitics. Nowadays, Melania is one of the show's favorite targets. The hosts frequently lambaste her with accusations of everything from being complicit in her husband's policies to having a body double.

But back then she was the model mother. Melania told *The View* audience that Trump was up in the morning with Barron, reading the newspaper "with him" in the bedroom. When Barron soiled his diaper, she said, Trump always said, "Time to see Mommy!"

"He's not like a crybaby. He's calm and it's fantastic," Melania told *People* magazine in a story titled "Billion Dollar Baby," done shortly after her *View* appearance. Posing with the baby and Trump, wearing a suit and holding little Barron, Melania is definitely not wearing what most new mothers wear three weeks after they give birth. She's dressed in a black satin dress with a neckline so deep that to call it plunging would be an understatement. Diamond earrings dangle from her earlobes, and her hair is piled up in an elaborate chignon. This is how Melania does motherhood.

Both Trump and Melania are staring straight into the camera, neither one smiling, neither one looking down at Barron, who is asleep on Trump's lap. In one of the photos in the story, Melania holds Barron in one arm and, with the other hand, pushes a gold baby carriage, complete with gold spoke wheels and a mini crystal chandelier hanging from the top. It was a baby gift, and a play on Trump's love of gold, from Ellen DeGeneres. "It's fun. It makes you laugh," says Melania.

After she becomes first lady of the United States, political opponents will use this image of Melania in her golden apartment, pushing her golden pram, as an example of how out of touch the Trumps are and how ridiculous their lifestyle is that they actually had a carriage like this for their newborn. All very valid criticism, though no one mentions the gifter was DeGeneres.

Melania spends every minute she can with her new baby, even though there is a nurse to mind Barron when Melania needs sleep. "I feed him, I change him, I play with him," she says. Trump revels in his hands-offness. "Some women want the husband to do half the chores. That's not Melania—fortunately for me."

She does an interview on television's *Access Hollywood*—ironically, the same program on which, less than a year before, her husband was recorded bragging about his ability to get any woman he wants. "Hello, *Access*," Melania coos to the camera, holding little Barron. The host (not Bush) gets a tour of the baby's nursery, where Trump proudly shows off a humongous stuffed puppy dog, flopped on the ground in the corner of the room. It was a gift from Barbara Walters, Trump confirms. Gayle King's baby gift is another huge stuffed animal, this time a green frog. The walk-through of the penthouse baby zone continues to the bathroom, which is basically just a bathroom, the only sign that it's maybe for a tiny baby is a rubber ducky perched on the white marble bathtub.

As they pass the changing table, a converted Louis XIV desk, the interviewer asks Melania if her husband changes diapers. It's an ongoing issue, the diapers, and whether he changes them, as though the visual of an almost-sixty-year-old billionaire wiping poop from his baby's bottom will change the course of history.

Melania, never one to be fake, says clearly, "No, he doesn't," but quickly follows with, "and I'm okay with it." She talks a bit more about how special the penthouse view is for Barron (he's not even eight weeks old and has probably just spotted his feet) and how she has enjoyed decorating the Trump Tower penthouse for her new son. It's Melania's moment, but Trump, as he often does, changes the topic of conversation to his real princess: Ivanka. "When Ivanka was growing up, Ivanka grew up in this room," he says, awkwardly, Melania staring at him. There's a slight pause and Trump goes on about the decor of the nursery. "We just change it from woman to man." Huh.

Barron soon became Melania's reason for staying off the social radar in New York, then her reason for avoiding her husband's presidential campaign, and, ultimately, her reason for not moving into the White House after she became first lady of the United States. And even when she does eventually move to D.C., he is her reason for adopting a light work schedule and generally refraining from trips that take longer than one day, so she can be home when Barron gets back from after-school soccer practice.

She had convinced Trump that he should have another child, a fifth, and he went along with it, but he was not shy about the fact that he wouldn't be involved in hands-on parenting the kid. He talked about it every chance he got, as if to pound into Melania's mind that she was going to be on her own with this parenting thing.

"If you have the money, having children is great," Trump said to Larry King in 2005, his new bride seated right beside him, not yet pregnant. "I'm not going to be doing the diapers. I'm not going to be making the food. I may never see the kid."

He said it again in an interview with Howard Stern. "It's not like I'm going to be walking the kids down Central Park." For reference, minutes before he expounded on fatherhood, Stern tested Trump's marital commitment, too, posing a scenario in which Melania is horribly disfigured in an accident. He asks Trump if he would stay with her if she was unreasonably jacked up. "Well, how do the breasts look?" Trump asks. "The breasts are okay," says Stern of this imaginary world where Melania is mangled beyond recognition but her boobs survive. "Yeah, of course I stay," says Trump. "Because that's important."

"What about when Melania gets stretched out? Big belly, fat ass from carrying a baby?" Stern, as he does, goes on. "No, no, I will totally love it," says Trump, with surprising reassurance. Stern ribs him that he won't; that's not him. Trump says he will love her, no matter what, but then he says, "Besides that, she's listening right now."

Being so hands-on may make her a great mother, but Melania is not the complete picture of domesticity. She has people to clean the triplex, she has some part-time child help, and she definitely doesn't cook. In a particularly weird segment on Martha Stewart's television talk show, she and Trump and Martha make meatloaf sandwiches, which Martha at least claims are Trump's favorite. Trump is wearing his usual bulky suit and tie, but with a white apron over it, tied at his waistline. Melania has smartly eschewed the apron, instead making her sandwich in a cashmere belted V neck sweater, again so open at the décolletage that for a second one wonders if her breasts might actually be on the menu.

"No, I don't eat onion," she snaps at Martha when she tries to layer the sandwich with toppings. She okays pickles, gingerly placing them on top of the meatloaf with her manicured fingers, her massive diamond rings getting into the shot. When Martha puts the slab of meatloaf on Trump's sandwich, she uses her hands, a no-no for the notorious germophobe. He shrugs it off, giving her the all clear. "It's fine, what am I going to catch from you?" She's clean. proceed.

Melania then makes a joke at Trump's expense, saying now that he knows how to make a sandwich, he can make one for her when she asks. Martha smiles. Trump doesn't.

They still went out after the baby was born, but not as much, and when they did, it was sometimes with Barron in tow. Melania liked to dress him up sort of in the style of a posh European schoolboy, shorts and knee-high socks, with button-down shirts, Peter Pan collars, and tiny camel hair or cashmere suit jackets. He's a beautiful little boy, with big blue eyes and curly blond hair. Trump could be seen bouncing Barron on his knee at the US Open, Melania took him to a red carpet hospital fund-raiser, they all went to Mar-a-Lago with regularity, but, as can happen when a baby comes into a family, the focus shifted away from the spouse to the child.

For the most part, Melania disappeared from the spotlight and into motherhood, spending days with the baby and her parents, speaking Slovenian, staying in. Trump, when it served, occasionally used

120   Kate Bennett

Barron as a publicity prop, which isn't so unusual considering how often he has put his older children on *The Apprentice,* cobranding his business endeavors with his family. Around Barron's first birthday, Trump gets a star on the Hollywood Walk of Fame—one that, later when he is president, will be vandalized so often there is an ordinance passed to have it removed—and the family travels to Los Angeles for the ceremony. In remarks in front of the gathered crowd, Trump thanks his supporters and all his kids and then asks to hold the baby. Melania passes him over. Holding his youngest son, Trump says, "See? That's Barron. He's strong, he's smart, he's tough, he's vicious, he's violent." It's funny if only because Barron is so cute, grasping at the microphone on the podium like any baby would. Then Trump gets serious about his son for a second. "And most importantly, hopefully, he's smart, cuz smart is really the ingredient. So, Barron, good luck."

When he was a toddler, Barron and his mother made what was by then a rare appearance on *The Celebrity Apprentice,* in a segment filmed at the Trump Tower triplex. Trump greets the contestants, saying of his home, "some people say it's the greatest apartment in the world." He tells Barron, who is in his mother's arms, to say hello to the group and adds, "Barron, hopefully, someday, will be a great entrepreneur."

"What do you want to do when you grow up?" Melania coos to the baby boy. "Bid-ness!" he says. It's well rehearsed but still adorable, and everyone laughs.

"He's doing well, just eighteen months old, and he's doing really well," says Trump, always so desperate to make sure everyone can tell that his progeny is smart.

Once she became the Republican candidate's wife, and ultimately first lady, the things Melania used to love to do she could no longer do. It was challenging to spend time with her husband and her son. She didn't feel comfortable visiting with her small group of friends. She felt strange and out of place watching Barron's baseball games in Central Park with the other moms; she couldn't just decide to jet off to one of her other homes at a moment's notice; she had trouble shopping in her favorite stores, like Barney's or Bergdorf Goodman, without feeling as if she had lost some of her treasured privacy.

Nor could she document her activities in the way she had grown accustomed, posting with regularity on Twitter and Instagram. She revealed just enough to paint a picture of a posh and happy lifestyle, blurring out details of places using a filter or shooting photos off-center to hide exact locations and avoid providing too much detail in the background. She was sharing, yes, but she was doing so with signature mystery.

Granted, nothing about her previous life was all that exciting or titillating in the large-scale world of Trump flash and cash. In fact, Melania's social media feeds, some of the photos from which still exist on her Facebook page and her personal Twitter page, perhaps most authentically illustrate Melania Trump BWH ("before White House"). And it's all sort of milquetoast, but wealthy milquetoast. Her Facebook profile pic is a classic Melania beauty shot, nonsmiling, of course. Her cover photo—the larger image of a profile page—is a supertight close-up of her cobalt blue eyes.

Melania's Facebook mobile uploads, images she has snapped on her phone and posted to social media, reveal she likes to travel, eat well, observe flowers (there is an abundance of tightly cropped pictures of blossoms), and skip around between her homes (one can seasonally keep track of which house she is at using the color of leaves outside or the presence of snow or sand as indicators).

One of the most shared photos from her social media account is a selfie, with Melania holding her iPhone, facing the mirror in her personal bathroom in the Trump Tower penthouse (a deep porcelain bathtub with a pink shower cap resting on the faucet are in the background), wearing a navy blazer and white jeans, unsmiling in her huge sunglasses. The caption reads: "Bye! I'm off to my #summer residence #countryside #weekend." Some might call it tone-deaf; Melania would probably just shrug.

To read into these glamour shots is an exercise in futility. Like most women on social media, she's mostly just chronicling her life for her friends, and that picture of her ponytail, captioned "Thursday," is probably just that: a picture of her ponytail on a Thursday.

She has a few of Barron and Trump together, where she refers to them as "my two boys." "I always thought she should write a guide for parents on raising children," one of Melania's closest girlfriends tells me. Melania is the "other mom friend" she calls or texts when this friend needs help. "She gives the best, most spot-on advice."

The friend adds that Melania is great at keeping things down-to-earth for her son, but she is still the mother of a Trump, and Trump life is not down-to-earth. Like the time Melania revealed she had taken her young son to . . . wait for it . . . the grocery store. "He had a lot of fun and it's a new experience for a child, you cannot shelter the child." By keeping him from the grocery store. "We went because I want to show him [the] supermarket. He had a fun time, he was putting everything in the shopping cart, 'we need this, we need cereal,' we need so many stuff," Melania says. She was also asked if she, Mrs. Donald Trump, ever has to go to the market, to which she answers, yes, once she did.

Social media also reveals a bit more of Ines Knauss, Melania's older sister, who, like Melania, dropped Knavs to go by Knauss. The two are exceptionally close, but little is known about Ines. A pencil sketch on paper of two women talking from August 2014, captioned "art of gossip #courtesy of #artist ines knauss," on Melania's Instagram page, shows an example of Ines's work. Ines has her own Instagram account, which she keeps fairly current even today. It feels more like a Melania fan page, however, than a social media account of her own. She posts flashback pics of the two of them as little girls in Slovenia or old photos of herself or her parents. People who know Melania best say Ines is her most important confidante and advice giver.

One of the most famous photos from Melania's social media feed is her asking an existential question about a white beluga whale, head peeking through the surface of the ocean. In 2012 it goes viral: "What is she thinking?" reads the caption. Of course, the image will again make the rounds as a meme once Melania becomes first lady, mostly because it's such a bizarre question, but also because it's what most people in the country want to know about Melania.

Another of her posts that went viral is a video clip of a family drive with Donald and Barron. It remains on her Facebook page and shows her vantage point from the back seat, Rolls-Royce wings on the hood visible up front, with Trump driving and Barron riding shotgun. Taylor Swift's "Blank Space" blares from the radio as the trio drives along in silence for a solid seventeen seconds: "Fun night with my two boys DJT & BWT [heart emoji]."

The photos also show a real love that Melania has for her husband. "Date night with my [heart emoji] DJT." Despite the gauzy filters, the shots paint the clearest picture of what Melania felt like sharing about her marriage. "Isn't he gorgeous?" is the caption of a picture of Trump.

In 2011 Melania (ironically) does an interview with Billy Bush for *Access Hollywood,* where she talks about, of all things, Trump's legs. "He has beautiful legs. He has a gorgeous legs. Beautiful legs, long, beautiful legs." She puts her thumb and fingers apart and drags her arm up and down, indicating how lithe and trim she thinks her husband's legs are.

The rewards for her adoration, or maybe they're just gifts out of the blue, come with regularity for Melania. She shows off her expensive bags and jewelry and furs and clothes. Of course, it's just a sampling. In real life, as the kids say, she has amassed hundreds of thousands of dollars in Hermès Birkin bags alone, with at least ten of them at her disposal, the most expensive a crocodile-skin Birkin that retails (after a significant waiting list for potential buyers) for about $60,000. It's difficult for many to believe, but Melania is actually not personally a heavy spender. She's careful with money, and though she does get a healthy amount for her upkeep and clothes and such, she's not the type to spend wildly on five-figure Birkin bags on her own. Trump likes to ask what she wants and then he typically gifts them to her. She treats them with care and actually uses them, unlike many women who can afford them but keep them, museum-like, on the shelves of their walk-in closets.

One of her Instagram pictures is simply a photo of a large Chanel shopping bag, captioned, "Nice surprise." There are also yearly throwback shots to her wedding day on January 21, the couple's anniversary, something Melania will no longer reference or acknowledge on social media once she enters the White House and becomes first lady. Whether driven by privacy—she doesn't want to share her personal dates with an invasive public, now that she has her whole life on display—or by lack of emotional connection, as of this writing Melania has not wished a happy anniversary to her husband, nor he to her, in a public way, during their time in the White House.

Memories, private events, personal mementos are all incredibly special to Melania, and she fiercely guards them. In part, she does this because she had such important and memorable times as a child herself, traveling with her parents in Europe, going on ski trips with them, taking coastal vacations. As tightly knit as the Knavses were, so is this Trump threesome: she, Barron, and Trump.

In her study and her private office in Trump Tower, Melania has volumes of photo albums and scrapbooks. She has always been purposeful about documenting her life. Friends say she doesn't keep a personal diary, but she has for decades made meticulous, chronological albums of each year of Barron's life, and her own, with Trump. Each leather-bound album is embossed with the dates in gold on the front. Some showcase travel; others, holidays.

She may be the third Mrs. Donald Trump, and her son the fifth Trump child, but Melania wants nothing about her experiences to resemble anyone else's, which is why she so thoroughly keeps track of memories and experiences. Hers might feel like a chapter in her husband's book of life stories, but Melania is hell-bent on not becoming a footnote.

10

Just Melania

"I like beautiful stuff. I live the life."

—MELANIA TRUMP

The years Melania spent between having Barron in 2006 and emerging on the public stage as the wife of a prominent presidential candidate in 2015 are not well documented. Unlike Ivana, who tried her hand at running Trump properties once her kids were in school, and Marla, who was still trying to break into acting, Melania had very little motivation to do much of anything in the professional sense. She told friends she was quite happy at home doing mundane things, taking care of her son, spending time with her small circle of friends, and dabbling a bit in the charity circuit. She wasn't interested in modeling or acting after she got married, although she did one gig playing a Bride of Frankensteinesque character in an Aflac commercial. A mad scientist swaps her brain with the Aflac duck, and then the duck speaks with a sultry Melania voice about insurance—and she barks the duck's "Aflac!" at the end, screaming when she realizes she has duck feet.

In 2010, having decided the family business of real estate wasn't for her, and neither was playing a duck-footed bride, Melania started having discussions with Trump about what she should "do" now that their son was old enough not to need her constant attention. Trump was smack in the middle of a career high: *The Apprentice* had spun off into *The Celebrity Apprentice,* and it was still ratings gold. He wasn't necessarily interested in his wife having a career, since he'd been burned by it with the first two wives. But he also knows that Melania has been bored, a common malaise that many mothers, even wealthy Park Avenue (or Fifth Avenue, in this case) trophy wives, face once their child is out of diapers and they suddenly remember the career path they were on before being sidetracked by husband and baby.

Unfortunately, Melania's career had been modeling, a job that has a definite shelf date, and at forty, hers had long expired. Barron was four, old enough for her to start working on something, anything. She's always liked designing and she's always liked jewels—she combines the two and, boom, she's a jewelry designer.

As a Trump, that she didn't already have a brand with her name on it was sort of strange anyway. Interestingly, however, Melania decided to call her line Melania Timepieces and Jewelry. Notably absent was the Trump part, the part that her husband thinks is worth its weight in gold. Melania, apparently, did not. Even the watches she designs have a simple M on the face, not MT. A few times, when reporters interviewed her about her line and accidentally referred to it as Melania Trump Timepieces and Jewelry, she was quick to correct: "Just Melania."

As such, she fashioned the line after her own lifestyle and based it on the three cities she said she loved most: New York and Palm Beach, where she had homes, and Paris, where she lived as a model— albeit in a tiny apartment with a Swedish roommate, surviving on tuna sandwiches and exercising by running up and down the staircase. The Paris part of her jewelry line was far more aspirational than the reality of her life in Paris in those days. The New York jewelry was contemporary; the Palm Beach, sporty. The hook? Every piece was less than two hundred dollars, a steal in the land of Trump.

She took it very seriously, making promotional videos set to classical music, which show her sketching the designs from the golden desk in her home office. "I have many roles in my life: mother, wife, daughter, sister—and I design for those kind of women," Melania says in one video, just after white letters spell out her name across the screen in curlicues. "I want women across the country to feel glamorous, elegant, chic, and happy when they wear my jewelry." There is a lot of "me," "my," and "I" in this business undertaking. Melania insists that the line does not use the word Trump anywhere. She is clear that the aspirational element of her business is all about her own life, not her husband's. When she is inevitably asked about Trump's role in the undertaking, Melania is annoyed, telling one interviewer, "He's very busy with his own stuff. I don't want to bother [him] with this." During another TV spot to promote the line, the reporter wants to know which piece is Trump's favorite. "I didn't ask him," Melania replies.

Melania designs multiple collections over several years, doing the main selling herself on QVC, usually at odd hours, flying privately on the Trump jet to the television shopping network's Pennsylvania headquarters, hawking the line late on Sunday nights, early Monday mornings.

The pieces continually sell out, mostly because Melania's breezy statements about how and why and when to wear them ("with a sarong, when you're running around"), though ridiculous, feel, oddly, genuinely authentic. Part of Melania's charm is her ability to put people at ease, to make them feel welcome. Here she was on QVC, the great middle-class shopping milieu, extending the world of the rich to the masses and giving them a how-to. And it felt, well, legitimate.

A couple of years later, she attempts the launch of another Melania (no Trump, please) product, the Melania Caviar Complexe C6 Collection, a skincare line based on a lotion concocted with caviar. The bottle design is very Melania, white and gold, with elegant script displaying her first name—again, not a Trump in sight. She does, however, use the tried-and-true Trump style of promotion, going on talk shows like *The View*. During one of her appearances on the lady-chat show, she famously announced that she slathered the caviar cream all over Barron after his nightly bath.

Perhaps the best marketing for the skin care line came from Trump's *Celebrity Apprentice,* an episode of which was devoted to the team task of creating an advertising plan for the boss's wife's newest side hustle. On the show, Melania visits each team as it prepares for the big ad-campaign pitch; one of the team leaders is Dennis Rodman, who asks Melania if he can go to her personal bathroom to get a more intimate look at her beauty routine. The other team is even creepier. Gary Busey apparently takes a liking to Melania: "Have you ever had your genitalia so excited that it spins like a Ferris wheel on a carnival ride?" asks Busey, looking into the camera. (Um, no.) "That's how beautiful she is."

Amazingly, Busey and his team do not lose the challenge—that distinction goes to Rodman's crew, who make it through the entire presentation of their advertising campaign without realizing they have spelled Melania's name Milania—with an *i.*

The misspelling should have been a harbinger of things to come for the skincare line. It never got off the ground, despite all the hoopla, because of a complicated lawsuit with the backers and producers of the product. Melania's partners' company devolves into a series of nasty suits, one aimed at her, which she fights and wins. She testified that she spent time promoting the product, only to have no product for her customers to buy. Exonerated but not satisfied, Melania fights back ten times harder, in the same way as she will later describe how her husband goes after his enemies, countersuing the defunct company for $50 million in potential lost royalties and damage to her name brand. She scores there too, settling out of court.

Though the jewelry line was a success, and presumably the skincare line would have been too, Melania ultimately decided to let both businesses die a quiet death. They kept her too busy to focus on Barron and her motherly duties.

She folds the line, and little is heard about it again until Melania becomes first lady and her official biography on the White House

Web site lists her accomplishments, one part stating: "Melania is also a successful entrepreneur. In April 2010, Melania Trump launched her own jewelry collection, 'Melania TM, Timepieces & Jewelry,' on QVC."

People freaked out. Accused of promoting her business—which didn't even exist anymore—on her official White House page, an updated version was soon posted, excluding the name of the jewelry line and the part about QVC.

"It is not uncommon for the White House to note the accomplishments of the first lady in her official biography," said a *Washington Post* story about the incident, "but Trump's decision to include a detailed list of her media appearances and branded retail goods is unusual."

To be honest, the charge isn't fair, considering her job *was* to make media appearances and be in the pages of magazines as a model, and she actually did launch a line of branded retail goods. It was unusual, but it wasn't untrue. Melania didn't have a law degree, like her predecessor Michelle Obama, nor did she have Laura Bush's experience as a political wife, taking part in policy programs and charitable initiatives, visiting with victims of natural disasters and the downtrodden. She had none of the accomplishments that Hillary Clinton had as a governor's wife and a partner at a law firm.

Melania Trump's professional accomplishments were unlike any first lady's before her, but they were very much aligned with being a sexpot model who married a mogul and had time and money on her hands to try her hand at a business endeavor. *Sports Illustrated, GQ, FHM* spreads, and a jewelry line—QVC had discontinued selling the Melania jewelry line long before she went into the White House, so there was no need to clutch pearls over using the White House Web site to "promote" a business. It was just that her business wasn't what the people expected, or preferred, from their first lady. Today, Melania's official White House bio has been further scrubbed and now has zero mention of her jewelry line or her magazine appearances.

But Melania still found a way to make her own income, even in the White House. A control freak when it comes to her image, with an extreme dislike of people making money off her, Melania owns the licensing agreements to most of her private photo sessions. She has a "rights-managed" license with Getty Images, something that many celebrities have, which allows her to be compensated for the use of photos she poses for with professional photographers. It's clever, and also wily. The agreement also allows for her to decide which news outlet can use the images. Anyone who reaches out to Getty to license the photos must be approved by a Trump representative—who is typically the first lady herself—and if she doesn't like the person/story/outlet, she can just say no. It's pretty genius, actually. And lucrative. In spring 2018, the Office of Government Ethics released its annual financial disclosure for the president for the previous year. Melania received between $100,000 and $1,000,000 from Getty for licensed photos of herself, with many sources thinking it was closer to seven figures.

She may have given herself over to the public to a great degree when her husband won the presidency, but Melania was still going to know which images of her, her home, and her son were being released, who was publishing them, and where.

Her new role left her with few avenues to exert independence, but Melania would manage to find them. As for the vast and foreign White House itself, Melania would move in only when she felt good and ready. Like most things Melania, she would confront it, but on her own terms.

11

The White House

"There are prison elements to it. But it's a really nice prison."

—MICHELLE OBAMA

At about the year and a half mark, all first ladies start to go a little crazy. That's when they realize they're trapped, says a former Secret Service agent who has watched it happen to the three he guarded during his tenure: "There's no way to avoid that feeling." The eighteen acres of grounds, the thirty thousand square feet and four floors of the White House's private residence, begin to feel claustrophobic.

The president, at least, is allowed to walk to the Oval Office, get a bit of fresh air when he wants to walk along the breezeway from the East to the West Wing, a journey that, depending on his clip, can take five to seven minutes from the residence to the Oval Office and is about the length of a football field. The first lady, not so much. Her offices are just downstairs from the residence, in the East Wing, about a minute away. (The exception is Hillary Clinton, who while first lady managed to keep the East Wing space as well as commandeer offices in the Executive Office Building and an office for herself in the West Wing. In 1993, Bill Clinton's press secretary, Dee Dee Myers, told the media that Mrs. Clinton was given an office in the West Wing "because the president wanted her to be there to work.")

In all, there are 132 rooms in the White House, 35 bathrooms, 147 windows, 28 fireplaces, 8 staircases, and 3 elevators. Some of those rooms, about 35 of them, are private and just for the first family and their guests. Still, live there a while, and the walls, while plentiful, start to close in. Michelle Obama once said, "There are prison elements to it. But it's a really nice prison." Harry S. Truman called it "this great white jail."

There are eyes on you everywhere, and you have no control over things you once had control over in your own home, your own penthouse, your own country house, your own beach house—for Melania, the list is long. You don't control the air—the Secret Service regulates the temperature and the oxygen levels (that thermostat is a dummy). You don't control the electricity—the Secret Service dictates which lights must remain on or off. You don't control the food—the Secret Service can have a say in that, too, for safety. You don't even control if you can open the window to get fresh air—the Secret Service won't allow it. Let's say you do put a lock on your door, as Trump insisted be put on his own bedroom—the Secret Service will put up a stink, but ultimately say it's all right—only because they can breach the door whenever they need to. But if you think you can live without your every step being monitored, you're fooling yourself. "When you're first lady, you lose the spontaneity of your life," says the agent.

It used to be a far less protected situation for first ladies. Before September 11, 2001, they were barely a blip on the Secret Service's radar and were able to do most things without a lot of agents. There was maybe one Suburban and two chase cars—it was ad hoc at best. From Jacqueline Kennedy to 9/11, not a lot changed. But when the planes struck the Twin Towers, shit got real. Laura Bush, who had a fairly intense travel schedule, suddenly found herself in meetings about global threat levels when she wanted to go somewhere. There was a slow creep up in manpower. One vehicle went to three, then to five, then to nine. By the time Michelle Obama became first lady, the entire FLOTUS Secret Service manual was reorganized and updated. Now she had to be in an armored vehicle, all events would need magnetometers, and tactical teams were standard. Her motorcade for scheduled events grew to at least ten vehicles and often included a communications vehicle, as well as a military aide and a member of the White House medical team.

At present, first ladies are always considered to be potential targets for an enemy. That means life, as they once knew it, is forever altered as soon as their husband wins the election. They may not be POTUS, but they're the most POTUS adjacent, which places them in a particularly perilous position.

At one point in the not-too-long-ago history of the Secret Service, getting the FLOTUS assignment as an agent used to be so plum that the standard code, FLD, which stands for "first lady detail," morphed into "fine living and dining." The life of a first lady usually meant less stress for an agent—much less to do in terms of crowd control and logistics. Less in the way of levels to break through. The views were often better, too. While the president would be stuck at a G20 summit for several days, for example, in decked-out hotel meeting centers, having bilaterals and trilaterals all day long, the first lady would often be touring the host country, seeing the sights, taking in cultural phenomena. In Taormina, Sicily, in May 2017, Trump's first Group of Seven (G7) summit, he sat with leaders for an expanded session, talking trade and defense and global wellness (all issues he tires of quickly when talk doesn't match his philosophical and political ideals). Melania, meanwhile, tweeted a picture of the blue waters off the Sicilian coastline from her helicopter, captioning the image, "On my way to lunch & mtgs as part of #G7. Taormina-> Catnia #Italy." The president was talking global economy with world leaders, and Melania was sightseeing in Sicily, wearing an outfit that cost just shy of the U.S. median household income. (On the ground, she hopped out of her protected vehicle wearing a Dolce and Gabbana jacket with silk floral appliqués—which had a retail price tag of $51,500.) She looked like something out of a Fellini film, letting the wind catch her hair as she stood on the balcony of Catania's city hall next to other leaders' spouses, looking nonplussed in their bland dresses with boat-necks and three-quarter sleeves. Odds are, lined up next to Melania, they were questioning every choice they had made getting dressed that morning.

Melania got used to the Secret Service presence more easily than most first ladies, mainly because her husband always had his own pri-vate entourage of security, led by the ever-present Keith Schiller, who for almost two decades was Trump's top bodyguard. She already lived in a world of limousines and chartered planes and VIP entrances, of people to get her to and from, and while it wasn't her personal pref-erence to have extras hanging around, Melania was accustomed to the upsides of being guarded. When Trump became a candidate with viability, she was given more protection; when he became the Repub-lican nominee, even more so; and once he was president, even when she was still living in New York, she had agents all over the place, outside every door.

The downside to Melania's not moving into the White House when the president did and, instead, staying in New York City while Barron finished the school year was that Melania's Secret Service agents were on a rotating shift cycle, which for most of them meant spending two weeks with her and then leaving to guard someone else, returning six weeks later for two more weeks, and then repeating the cycle. The rotation was part of the Secret Service's protocol, and it bothered most of the agents simply because it didn't necessarily make logical sense.

Only Melania's lead agent at the time, a woman named Mindy O'Donnell, was a consistent presence. O'Donnell, by many accounts, wasn't particularly well liked by others in the Secret Service. Some colleagues questioned how close she was getting to Melania, her main asset; there were rumors that O'Donnell was using the same hairstylist as Melania, a no-no in the Secret Service because there is supposed to be a boundary between the personal life of the agent and the personal affinities of the protected. Other agents on the FLOTUS detail chuckled about O'Donnell's shoes, which were almost always a chunky heel, higher than what other female agents wore, and certainly less practical. "The lead agent's main job is to protect the asset from danger, and if that means physically picking the asset up and carrying them to safety, that has to happen," said one former agent who worked with O'Donnell. "We were always left scratching our heads at the visual of how she would be able to carry the first lady and run in those ridiculous high heels."

O'Donnell would be replaced in 2018, after a few non-Melania-detail-related conflicts arose. Changes at the helm of an assignment are fairly normal after about a year and a half into the lead agent's tenure. Melania's new lead agent was a former college lacrosse champion who came up in the Secret Service ranks, serving in the New York field office during 9/11 and the months after. A team leader on the Counter Assault Team before his promotion to the president's detail and, eventually, FLD, he's the one who was quick to catch Melania when she visited an elephant orphanage in Kenya in October 2018, during her first solo trip abroad, to Africa. One of the baby elephants she was feeding with a giant bottle of milk was excited and gave her a friendly nudge, knocking her backward off her footing; in a flash, the agent had his arms up to prevent a fall.

It's a tricky relationship between a government asset as important as the first lady and her security detail. Building a rapport with the protectee is not frowned upon. In fact, the brief eye contact, the "good morning" or "good evening" twice a day, the familiar face outside the front door—those things can dramatically build trust.

"It put her at a disadvantage," says the agent of Melania's constantly rotating detail of agents while she still lived in New York. "We're not going to talk to her, that's not our job, but she will need to talk to us, especially if she wants to understand how best to use us to her advantage."

"That two seconds of banter creates trust, and that makes a relationship," says another agent with expertise guarding first ladies.

Melania will realize, or won't, as the case may be, that wheeling and dealing with the Secret Service about what she can and cannot do is a useful and common practice. When Laura Bush would push back on stringent guidelines for a solo trip, for example, she could more easily achieve what she needed because she had that open dialogue with her lead agents. Same with Michelle Obama, who used to like the "freedom" of walking the dogs on the South Lawn of the White House until she realized it meant tourists and pedestrians had to be cleared from the fence line all around the perimeter. She stopped doing it, so as not to unduly bother anyone. However, Michelle got savvy and learned that she could work with the Secret Service to determine the best times of day to walk Bo and Sunny to minimize the impact on civilians and still get her few minutes of fresh air. "You really don't know what you don't know until you're here," said Michelle of how different life is inside the White House gates.

Later in her tenure, Michelle, whose Secret Service code name was Renaissance, got so good at finagling private time (or so frustrated with not having any) that she was able to keep a routine exercise-class schedule without too much disruption. She went to her boutique fitness spots, SoulCycle for spin class and Solidcore for an amplified Pilates-style workout, with little to no disruption. Her agents would spin alongside her or a few rows behind, or they would wait outside the door while she had one-on-one classes. Michelle even once had an itch to do some shopping and walk around a mall, "just like a normal person," she told her detail's operations leader. It was a bit of a horse trade getting the negotiation settled—she'd have to forgo fancy clothes and makeup and keep her hair in a ponytail, under a baseball cap, and not tell anyone she was going to do it. For a couple of hours one random weekday, Michelle Obama was able to cruise around Pentagon City Mall in nearby Northern Virginia, and not a soul knew who she was.

This is the sort of stuff Melania hasn't quite figured out how to accomplish—if she even wants to. She is able to sneak off to New York City, which she does with regularity, mostly for fittings with her stylist, Hervé Pierre, at her Trump Tower penthouse, and for hair color appointments. Her longtime hairstylist, Mordechai Alvow, tends to her locks in private these days, also at the penthouse. One time in 2018, Melania flew on a government 757 down to Mar-a-Lago for an overnight, and no one would have known had a CNN reporter (me) not gotten wind of it and broken the story. After making a few calls, it was confirmed that Melania had indeed slipped down to Florida for a quick trip, the purpose of which her office said was "personal." The president's schedule can't be "personal," as his movements must be revealed and put on public record. Hers do not. He must have a protective press pool—the small group of rotating members of the White House press corps who are there to document or be on standby for the president's every move—with him during all of his movements. She does not have to. She can deploy the "it's personal" button and travel without having to really tell anyone if she doesn't feel like it.

But simply put, Melania Trump's life for nearly three years very much isn't her own, and that has been the most difficult aspect of being first lady for her to wrestle with. When Melania went from being Mrs. Trump to Muse, her Secret Service code name, which like those of her husband (Mogul) and others in her family were chosen from a list provided by the White House Military Office, she became a thing more than a person. Her life, her privacy, and her motives were now open to questioning and speculation by millions and millions of people—no longer her own to control. And the White House executive residence was not *her* house, though she would hire an interior decorator to try making the mood and vibe more familiar. "It's hard to explain how big it is, but then also how small at the same time," says someone who has worked closely with first families. "Living in the White House is brutal."

Working there was something else Melania had to get used to. She had been without a "job" for several years, having dismantled her QVC jewelry and watch line. Now here she was with the most thankless job in a president's administration. Not only is the job undefined, it is unpaid—yet it places a level of expectation on the jobholder that is higher than for any other member of the administration, except for the president.

To think about it fairly, Melania had gone from the comfort and privacy of essentially being a wealthy, stay-at-home soccer mom with a somewhat regular schedule of evening social events and travel to her different homes around the country to overseeing the 55,000 square foot "People's House," a large operation.

There are approximately one hundred staffers who run everything at the White House behind the scenes. There's the floral department, the lead of which had to "audition" in front of Michelle Obama in a sort of *American Idol* format, creating with other contenders what she thought were her best floral arrangements until the "winner" was announced. Hedieh Ghaffarian became chief floral designer in 2015, and Melania has kept her around, pleased with the work Ghaffarian and her small team churn out from the White House flower shop, a space in the basement, not far from the kitchen. Each first lady articulates her overall style, Melania included. For Laura Bush, florals and greenery were tailored and sculpted; Michelle Obama liked a more natural garden style, sort of wild and filled with colorful flowers. For Melania, it's clean, chic, and generally monochromatic. Ghaffarian has at least two full-time staff members on the floral team, one of whom has been there for more than two decades. It might seem like a lot for flowers, but the team is responsible not only for the White House (East Wing, West Wing, and residence) but also Camp David (when there are visitors) and Blair House (where foreign dignitaries stay).

Then there are the ushers and butlers and housekeeping staff, all of whom are overseen by the chief usher, Timothy Harleth, who previously worked at the Trump International Hotel in Washington—keeping it in the family, so to speak. Harleth replaced Angella Reid, a holdover from the Obama years who was not particularly well liked by the household staff. Reid, on the job for six years when she was asked to leave, was strict and foreboding. In the spring of 2017, about a month before she moved full-time into the White House, Melania had her fired. It made news for a variety of reasons, not the least of which is that the role of chief usher is one typically held for many years by the same person, often until retirement. Since 1900, there had only been nine chief ushers when Reid was fired.

Her dismissal might have earned Melania scorn from the media (Reid was the first female and second African American chief usher in the history of the role), but the move actually made her popular inside the White House.

As Melania was in Washington more and more ahead of her move, she had gotten to know the staff of the executive residence quite well. No stranger to "help," as it were (she was a Trump, after all), Melania immediately earned a reputation for being kind and warm to the staff. One evening, having settled dinner and clean-up and preparation for the next day, Melania decided to let one of the regular residence butlers go home early for the night. She was, after all, mistress of the house, and whatever she desired was to be followed. The butler, surprised but grateful, departed. The following night, Melania repeated the same routine, getting word to the butler that he could head out early, since he was no longer needed and she could handle whatever she might want by herself. So she was surprised when she walked into the private kitchen later that night and found him still there. She asked him why, since she had dismissed him earlier. Reluctantly, the butler shared that Reid found out about his early departure the previous evening and admonished him, docking his pay for the hours he was given off by the first lady. Not wanting to face Reid again and be punished for accepting the kind gesture from Melania, he had stayed on that evening.

Though not the only reason Melania fired Reid—she had heard enough stories to understand that the chief usher was not well liked or well respected by the staff—the incident with the butler was certainly the straw that broke the camel's back. "I think it's best if the White House explains," is what Reid told *The Washington Post* when asked for comment on her dismissal. Of course, the White House didn't give a reason; it only said that it wished Reid the best.

Besides the chief usher and the butlers, there are maids and cooks, maintenance workers and groundskeepers, though the latter are technically employed by the National Park Service, since the land on which the White House sits, all eighteen acres of it, is a national park. The White House itself is vast, as noted earlier, spreading across six floors, plus two hidden mezzanine levels. It is like Downton Abbey, only more modern and on steroids.

For a first lady, overseeing the operational aspects of the White House and working with its staff, most of whom have stayed on for years and years, unaffected by administration changes, can be challenging in that the role inside the house is not political. A person I spoke with who used to work in the White House in a senior management role and who is still on speaking terms with the current household staff tells me they "rave" about Melania as a boss, and do the same about Trump. Staff members, whether Hispanic or African American, or white, for that matter, have a personal relationship with the Trumps, and how they as bosses handle that responsibility is what makes them likable or not likable.

"We love to live in Washington; we have a very busy life. It's exciting, as well," Melania told me when I interviewed her in China, on the Great Wall, just a week or so before a private media lunch she held back at the White House. Our brief chat was her first solo, on-camera interview since becoming first lady, ironically on CNN, the network nemesis of her husband. She was friendly during our encounter, and when she arrived at our hastily set up shooting area, on a small terrace at the base of the funicular that takes people up to the Mutianyu section of the Great Wall, she was somewhat breathless, having walked a few flights of steps to greet us. Since I had taken the same route about an hour before, I was familiar with the climb and the altitude's effect. "Would you like a minute to catch your breath before we start?" I asked. She smiled, and laughed for a second, relieved, I think, that I had noticed and made the offer.

During our one-on-one, I also asked what had been the most challenging part of the new gig so far. She paused, gave it a moment of thought, and said something that, while simple, spoke volumes about how her life of leisure had been upended. "It's a lot of things that we need to take care of and a lot of responsibilities." Sure, this sounds canned, even maybe disingenuous, but I think she was being truthful. Melania, I am certain, was ill prepared for what she encountered when she moved to the White House. She had no one to speak with in detail about it beforehand. Who was she going to call? Barbara Bush? Her husband had just spent the campaign calling Bush's son names. Michelle Obama? Not a fan. Hillary Clinton? In essence, she entered the biggest job of her life without anyone telling her how to do said job or what said job would really consist of.

The White House hosts hundreds of events every year, from lunches for world leaders and teas for their spouses to State Dinners to the Congressional Ball to public events like the Easter Egg Roll and holiday tours. Melania, by several accounts, is consumed with the mistress-of-the-house White House experience. "There's so much to do here," she reiterated at lunch.

But the "much" part for Melania is about picking the white roses or the cream ones, determining which tablecloths should be used at an event, or if the dessert that day should be a cranberry and honeycrisp apple crostata with vanilla bean ice cream (it was) or a chocolate cream pie with a scoop of vanilla ice cream (a Trump favorite).

"But what does she do?" people ask when I say I cover the first lady for my job. It's a good question, and a fair one, and difficult to answer with "she does a lot of stuff around the house."

Melania seems to like the hands-on approach to being the female head of household, and it's something she has done for many years, organizing and overseeing decorations and details from Bedminster to Mar-a-Lago. She is almost intimidatingly comfortable in the traditional role of wife and mother and always has been—there's not one person who would say Melania was secretly harboring some ambitious aspiration to be a CEO or a successful entrepreneur.

Melania has few tangible job skills beyond being a warm and con-summate hostess—unapologetically, this is her wheelhouse. As such, she's very much involved in the minutiae, even though she doesn't necessarily have to be. At Christmastime, when the White House dec-orations were unveiled—a pretty big to-do around those parts—a press release noted the wreaths hanging in each of the White House's 147 windows were "designed by the first lady herself with signature style." Yet they appeared to be your average wreaths with big red bows. Pressed on what made them "signature," Stephanie Grisham, at a media preview of the holiday decor, said she would get back to the reporter who asked and hurried off to check with one of the dec-orators on Melania's staff. "They're made from white pine," she an-nounced on return. Ah.

When Michelle Obama was in her first term, someone who worked for her said she was more stringent about the details than she was later on, having tastings for important meals, often inviting her mother, Marian Robinson, who lived with the Obama family but had her own space on the third floor of the residence. Michelle and her mother and the social secretary would settle in at a table set up in the Yellow Oval Room, also part of the residence, and spend hours trying all the food. (Mrs. Robinson enjoyed the wine pairings at the tastings, which a staff member tells me made for a good time by the end of the meal.) Michelle was vocal about what she liked and what she didn't like, but there were always plenty of options to choose from. However, by her second term, she was much less hands-on and more willing to experiment with food and florals and decoration.

Melania has yet to branch out significantly in her tastes, often sticking meticulously to white flowers, menus featuring Dover sole, and shades of ivory for decor. The one time she did stray off that course was her second holiday in the White House.

Melania revealed via a tweet in July that she was already working on the Christmas decor for the 2018 season, complete with a photograph of her going over pictures of ideas and mood boards. "There is still a lot of work to be done," she tweeted, five months ahead of the reveal, "but I hope everyone will enjoy our final holiday vision for the People's House."

Most didn't. She was eviscerated for lining the East Colonnade with bright red "trees" made from thousands of cranberries. The Twitterverse said the trees reminded them of blood, or the dystopian *The Handmaid's Tale*. Media outlets had psychologists analyze why Melania chose to use red (the White House clearly stated in the press release about the decorations that the red was taken from the "pales," the red stripes in the presidential seal, which stand for valor and bravery). Also, well, it's Christmas. The trees were red; the carpet was green. It's not rocket science. But, man, did Melania take a beating on those red trees. Yet the choice was classic Melania: she didn't want to go with precedent; she wanted to step out of the box. Melania is one of few creatives who has ever been first lady—she actually has a background in design and fashion—so for her to apply a new and independent aesthetic to something as traditional and expected as White House holiday decorations was much more of a statement than the red trees themselves.

Jeremy Bernard, who was social secretary for four years under the Obamas, said it's not uncommon for a first lady to get criticized for the holiday decorations. "You didn't have enough Santas, or you had too many Santas. Or, it wasn't at all religious, or it was too religious," says Bernard, who agrees with me that the attacks on Melania over something as innocuous as holiday decorations were ridiculous. "You couldn't win." So meticulous have the rules for holiday decorations become, staff must ensure that every decoration is made in the United States, and every state must be represented; someone from the White House counsel's office used to walk Bernard through every aspect of the displays.

When Melania finally addressed red tree–gate, she was refreshingly unapologetic. "We are in twenty-first century and everybody has a different taste. I think they look fantastic," she told an audience a week after they went up.

Being physically careful with the decorations is just as important as being aesthetically careful, as Michelle Obama learned in 2014 when one of the large garlands hung in the State Dining Room crashed to the ground, almost taking out the portrait of Abraham Lincoln and the volunteer holiday decorators who were standing underneath it. Large chunks of historic pilasters went with it; the hooks the carpenters had been using to hang decorations for decades apparently gave way. Since then, garland has never been hung above the Lincoln portrait, or any portrait for that matter.

Despite the pounding she took in the press for staying in New York City for the five months from inauguration until Barron finished his year at Columbia Grammar and Preparatory in Manhattan, Melania has told those close to her she never even considered not doing it. Barron was and continues to be her first priority, and, whether the public liked it or not, she intended to keep it that way. She also admitted the plan had a bit of reverse psychology to it, something she smartly gamed out ahead of the move. As weekend visits to the White House increased through late winter, and as her son got more acquainted with the actual cool stuff about the place—the pool, the bowling alley, the movie theater, the Secret Service guys with their gear and their toys—Barron was more comfortable with the idea. By the time the cherry blossoms were on the trees in D.C. and before his school year in New York was out, he was ready. "Melania is one of those rare people who know on a cellular level that the only way to achieve what is expected of her and what she expects of herself is with patience and purpose," one of her close friends explains to me when I ask her about Melania's anxiety level during that period, when she had to shift from her old life to her new one. "She just always seems to know there is no rushing."

Melania virtually ignored the flood of criticism that came her way for staying in New York City, despite the headlines about the hundreds of thousands of dollars it cost taxpayers for Secret Service protection and the actual inconveniences posed to New Yorkers, plenty of whom were sick and tired of making way for Trump-generated motorcades and barricades and protesters.

Pundits in general had a field day with speculation about Melania's not moving to the White House, something that had never been done before. She didn't want to be first lady, they said. She considered herself too good for Washington, people whispered. And, the most fun gossip of all, she flat out didn't want to be around her husband. It's certainly quite feasible Melania wasn't in a particular hurry to fling open the curtains on her private life to the rest of the world, but the idea that she never intended to move to Washington is patently false. She was picking where furniture should go from diagrams of the White House private residence and working with the White House Historical Association to make sure she followed the correct guidelines of what was movable and what wasn't long before her moving trucks arrived.

None of the Melania-won't-move-here theories proved true, of course, and Grisham said as much when asked. "She plans to move to Washington as soon as her son finishes his school year," she repeated, ad nauseam, to the press. But used to the fudged deadlines of her husband (his tag line would become "Let's see what happens," about everything from North Korean nukes to whether he would fire his chief of staff), the media didn't believe her. Yet by this point one thing should have been clear to observers of Melania Trump and Donald Trump: she actually does what she says she will do, and in the approximate time frame she says she will do it. He does not. It's part of the vast disparity of the East Wing and the West Wing. Melania's statements are few and far between, but accurate.

Still, Democrats and anti-Trumpers were in disbelief over the idea that a first lady wasn't moved in when her husband took office. "This isn't how it's done!" they cried, completely missing the error of their ways, the very one that plagued them throughout the election season. Comparing Trump to a paradigm of normalcy or to what had come before was an exercise in futility. They took the decision as evidence that Melania was intimidated by her new position, afraid to assume the historically relevant title of first lady, cowed by the process, when they should have seen it as the first sign that Melania has an independent streak on par with, or possibly stronger than, that of her most recent predecessors.

To that point, Michelle Obama, lest people forget, also toyed with the idea of not moving directly to the White House after inauguration and, instead, waiting until her young daughters, Sasha and Malia, finished their school year in Chicago. She went so far as to ask her husband's aides if she even *could* delay moving in, an idea that was ultimately shot down in favor of "wanting her family to be together," as Obama adviser Valerie Jarrett later said, according to one interview. But it is interesting that Michelle, too, seemed willing to disregard public perception and to at least explore the possibility. It reveals what must be a common trepidation for first ladies about giving up their "old" lives for the White House. First ladies, to be honest, have a more emotionally all-consuming adjustment to make as mothers and protectors, while their husbands are off and running to manage the country.

Melania approved the erection of a full-size soccer goal, with net, to be set up in the Jacqueline Kennedy Garden south of the East Colonnade. For members of the press, who sometimes sit in vans along the south driveway, waiting for a motorcade to load up with the president or first lady, seeing the goal a few feet away is jarring. It feels remarkably out of place, like, "What's this sports thing doing here?" That a tween boy lives in the house is forgettable in the swirl of the news cycle that his father creates at breakneck speed on a daily basis. The goal is actually a testament to the way Melania has devoted herself to keeping his life and his world private.

During the Obama years there was a sense of family, cultivated in a way, sure, with plenty of references to Sasha and Malia by their parents, always a handful of "Dad" jokes from the president; we never forgot the girls were there, even if we didn't always see them. When Donald Trump moved in, one of the very first things he ordered was the removal of the swing set Obama had set up near the Oval Office. So much for kid play.

12

A Most Independent First Lady

"Any channel she wants."

—STEPHANIE GRISHAM

It was, and still is, a tricky thing, Melania's relationship with the media. As the most popular Trump family member, a year into her tenure in the White House she had enjoyed relatively strong poll numbers without doing pretty much *anything*. She hadn't announced an official platform, she hadn't yet taken a major solo trip, she hadn't given a major speech lasting more than two minutes since the campaign, and she spent the first six months as first lady not even living in the White House. All things considered, that she was polling well was a remarkable feat.

(In January 2018, after a run of headlines about Trump's alleged cheating scandals, Melania had a 47 percent favorable rating in a CNN poll; Trump, just 40 percent. The same time one year before, just after the inauguration, she was only at 36 percent, with a whopping 23 percent saying they had no opinion of her, a stunning admission considering Trump had just been sworn in as president of the United States. By comparison, at that same point in her tenure, Hillary Clinton had an approval rating of over 50 percent; Laura Bush, first rated in a

Gallup poll in 2003, was in the mid-70s for approval—insanely high; and, right after Barack Obama took office, Michelle Obama was polling at 72 percent. Trump, a fervent watcher of poll numbers, obsessed with likability, both his own and that of his adversaries and allies, addressed a black-tie dinner at the White House in 2017, praising his wife. "The star of the Trump family," he said, adding, "they love her out there, I'll tell you. We walked all over Florida. We walked all over Texas, and they're loving Melania."

Imagine what those numbers could be if Melania actually said something of major importance on a regular basis. Or if Americans were more freely able to know her—if she used the press in the way her predecessors had, doing regular interviews? In all her time as first lady, Melania has only twice come to the back of the plane during a trip to talk off the record with the traveling press pool, a fairly common and somewhat traditional practice for first ladies past. The first time happened when we were flying home from Canada after her first solo trip; she went to Prince Harry's Invictus Games opening ceremony as a representative of the United States. The second time was when we were on our way to Africa, her first major international trip by herself. As the only reporter who is consistently part of Melania's press pool, I always get a kick out of listening to other reporters on the plane who haven't been on the beat ask each other if they think "she" will come back to the press area and talk to us. "Probably." "Yeah, I mean, why wouldn't she?" "She will." I give it a few minutes and then I weigh in: "She won't. She only has twice in almost three years. Trust me, she won't." I hate to burst the bubble, but like her husband, Melania doesn't do things the "normal" way.

Melania's argument against talking to the media? Essentially, "Why should I?" To be fair, it holds some weight. Opening herself to that type of scrutiny is not only something she doesn't want to do but something she feels she doesn't need to do. Like Trump, she is naturally, quite intensely, wary of the media—simply put, she doesn't like us. She is a bit like Jackie Kennedy, who was also not a big fan of the press but who understood the part it plays in building a narrative.

Kennedy helped craft her persona by manipulating the desire of the public to know more about her. She understood that remaining somewhat mysterious to the American public would compel them to always be curious about her. It was smart. And it worked.

Almost a year into her tenure as first lady, Melania decided to invite a handful of members of the media to get to know her in her new habitat. A select group of ten representatives, in pairs from each major television network—one bureau chief, and one reporter—had been asked to lunch, an off-the-record confab with Melania.

At this point Melania wasn't eager to throw herself to the wolves (as she saw the press), but without throwing us the occasional bone, she risked having the mainstream media craft its own narrative, and Melania at least wanted to help control it. The White House luncheon was a small step in that direction, a chance for her to see that reporters don't actually have scales under their clothes and for us to see, conversely, that neither does she.

A long table was set in the Blue Room, which is on the main floor of the White House, flanked by the Red Room and the Green Room and smack in the middle of Cross Hall, marked on opposite ends by the State Dining Room and the East Room. Throughout history, the Blue Room has been one of the most common locations for receptions and meetings, and Melania, since moving in, has taken a liking to it as a place to host friends and dignitary spouses. She often has a small table set for tea or a light lunch when she and the spouse of a visiting leader are paired up while the heads of state meet in the Oval Office.

Like the Oval Office, the Blue Room is curved; it's the middle of the building structure of the White House, directly above another popular space, the Diplomatic Reception Room, and directly below the Yellow Oval Room, a grand drawing room that is part of the first family's private residence.

With its floor-to-ceiling french doors that open to the South Portico, the original room was destroyed in the White House fire of 1814 but brought back to life by James Madison three years later. Madison, a Francophile, had commissioned a furniture set from a French designer and textiles from France for the upholstery. But the color scheme for Madison was mostly red, and it stayed red through John Adams, until Andrew Jackson moved in and swapped out the red motif for green. It wasn't until 1837, and Martin Van Buren, that the room became the Blue Room, and while presidents and first ladies renovated and redecorated through the years, the room remains predominantly blue in its decor, with blue upholstered chairs, replicas of the Madison-commissioned originals, and a gigantic blue oval rug with gold detail in the middle of the room.

For her media luncheon, Melania instructed her social secretary, Anna Cristina Niceta Lloyd (who goes by Rickie Niceta), that she would like the table to be set with the official Clinton china. Ironically, with its swirly gold border and gold White House model etched in the center of each plate, the Clinton china is the most Trumpian-looking of the official White House china sets. It's a lot of gold and curlicues. Melania uses it often. One of the perks of living in the White House is having every set of official presidential china at your disposal, and each has its own style and feel. The Clintons' is tasteful if not a touch gaudy. As of this writing, Melania has yet to reveal the design of the official Trump china, but she is working closely on the project.

The luncheon table was also set with loads of fragrant white flowers, Melania's favorite, mostly cream and white orchids and freesia that lined the middle of the table from one end to the other in small silver bowls and even smaller silver julep cups.

After several minutes, in walked Melania Trump. At five foot eleven, she is a formidable presence. Dressed in a fitted gray sweater and black slacks, her signature 4.7-inch Christian Louboutin pumps added even more height to her stature. It should be said, Melania enters almost every room with a signature wave, a two-handed deal that resembles what a toddler does when she first learns how. Arms out in front, elbows bent upward at ninety degrees, palms facing forward, raise and lower fingers, raise and lower fingers, raise and lower fingers. It's a friendly gesture and far more comfortable for putting others at ease than, say, Hillary Clinton's perfunctory side-to-side wave or Michelle Obama's full-forearm windshield wiper.

She smiled almost immediately, which quickly helped melt the formality of the occasion. The most common misperception about Melania is that she is cold, when she is frankly the opposite. Melania in person hits all the senses. "She's quite possibly the most beautiful woman I've ever seen," whispered one of the network guys to me after the lunch was over. He was glassy-eyed, almost in a daze, like he'd just lunched with a mermaid.

While she might not have been a supermodel, in real life Melania is uncommonly beautiful. In photographs, her eyes tend to look squinty, but in person they're wider, and an almost otherworldly cobalt blue. Her skin? Luminous. Faux tanned, but not orange. Makeup? Flawless. Heavy around the eyes with liner, lashes for days. Smile? Hypnotic.

Then there's the way she smells. She has a distinct, noticeable fragrance, even to those who generally don't notice such things. It's unique, so when it hits the nose, reporters know to get out our notepads and photographers know to put their fingers on the shutter button—you've got about two seconds of smell warning before she enters the room. Melania's perfume is of unknown provenance, and apparently as confidential as a state secret. It may very well be off-label, custom-made—a mix of jasmine and lily and something more exotic, like oolong tea, cinnamon, maybe?

Her voice ("Hello, everyone") is neither too high nor too low, and like most people for whom English is not a first language, it lilts upward at the end of sentences, as though each phrase is a question, and it often is, because she adds, "yes?" to the end of most of them. "Let's have a nice lunch, yes?"

The people at the table were entranced; everyone nodded.

A White House butler offered white wine to guests, about half of whom accepted. But at Melania's seat—she had placed herself at the chair closest to the door, by the way, facing the South Lawn—there was no wine. Instead, a tall glass of Diet Coke, no ice, appeared at her setting—so very European. Yet unlike her husband, who chugs the stuff all day, Melania barely took a sip. She also hardly touched the first course, a squash bisque served with shallot oil and pumpkin seed crisps. Like most models, it was clear somewhere along the way that Melania had mastered the fine art of looking like she was eating without actually eating. It's a skill that involves maneuvering utensils around a plate or bowl, engaging the food, but not actually bringing the fork or spoon to your mouth more than two or three times.

"Ask me anything," Melania said, the words every journalist hopes to hear from a subject but rarely does.

By the time the main course of potato-crusted Dover sole arrived, Melania had divulged more personal information than any members of the media had gotten from her in the eight months since her husband was sworn in. She was friendly and kind, open and real, and she had all of the fabled one-on-one charm and sensitivity that her husband is alleged to have when he's in a similar situation. ("I actually like the guy," admit some lawmakers, previously sworn enemies.)

When she is asked if the speculation that she wasn't going to move to Washington ever prompted her to consider changing course and moving sooner, she smiles and says simply, "No."

"I love living here," Melania, seated to my left, says when I ask her whether the rumors are true that she feels like a prisoner and is miserable inside 1600 Pennsylvania Avenue. "I don't get it. All that 'free Melania, free Melania.' Why would I be unhappy here?" She gestured to her surroundings, the fabled opulence of the Blue Room, adding how she marveled at the history of the place, the grandeur and importance of what the building and the home represented.

Meanwhile, I was trying to hide my deep satisfaction at the surreal moment of having just witnessed Melania make a "free Melania" reference. In that quick flash of savvy, it was clear that even if she wasn't an active participant in her press coverage, she definitely followed it—and her memes (and, as I would come to learn, perhaps guide it as much as she could behind the scenes).

Melania went on to talk about Barron and being a mother, and it all sounded so abnormally . . . normal. The life she described was not at all how the general public assumes the Trump family lives. For Melania, things like homework, play dates, and soccer practice were all paramount concerns, as with most parents of a child on the cusp of his teenage years. Making a home for Barron in the White House had taken Melania's full efforts, and she was finally at a place where she felt comfortable, and where order was restored.

She even talked about how the family had considered getting a dog when they moved down to Washington and had gone so far as to investigate a few different breeds. Ultimately, they decided that a dog might be too much to handle for the time being and that anything but a small one wouldn't work, because at some point they would have to move back to Manhattan, and how fair would it be to keep a big dog in an apartment? The journalists, most in their late thirties to late forties, and most with kids of their own around the same age as Barron, nodded in agreement: Melania had just managed to make them think of themselves as her peers, up against the same "Mom/Dad, can we get a puppy?" conundrum that she was. *Melania, she's just like us!*

Soon the luncheon approached its second hour, a time limit virtually unheard of in the tightly controlled world of presidents and first ladies. Melania was asked about daily life with her husband, and her answers felt, well, normal. The picture of marriage that Melania laid out wasn't that dissimilar to most couples, especially those who have been together for just shy of twenty years, as have the Trumps, who met in September 1998. In the evenings, they talk about the day, what's going on with their child, any upcoming travel. Though she may have begun her tenure as first lady not wanting to delve into weightier matters, or the West Wing, she has become more involved, often talking to her husband about whom she trusts and whom she does not and about what the television networks are saying about him (networks other than Fox News, which is his preferred channel).

In one infamous example of his Foxaholic nature, *The New York Times* reported a story about Trump's "raging" at his staff for not tuning Melania Trump's television aboard Air Force One to Fox News. It was set to CNN, which made him angry. I asked Melania's spokeswoman if the story was true (apparently *The New York Times* had not requested comment from the East Wing before running its piece). Stephanie Grisham told me the entire story was ridiculous considering the actual "work" Melania was doing on behalf of children and families. But she closed her rant to me by saying, "Seems kind of silly to worry about what channel she watches on TV (any channel she wants, by the way) or if she heard some recording on the news." Naturally, that response, "any channel she wants," became its own newsworthy tidbit, another assertion of her independence or, as some saw it, a snippet of resistance.

It should have come as zero surprise, even to the president, that Melania was monitoring other outlets besides Fox News. She has a deep capacity to remember which reporters are saying what about her husband and to take the temperature on the issues of the day. She regularly gives Trump her opinions, whether he wants to listen to them or not, but she does not nag. Her political leanings are similar to those of her husband—she is conservative. But when she disagrees, she says so. Melania was critical of the zero-tolerance policy of separating children from their families at the United States border. She said she was "blindsided" by the way it was handled and "heartbroken." Yet when Trump tweeted that four female congresswomen of color should "go back" to the "totally broken and crime-infested places from which they came," even though three of the four were born in the United States, Melania was silent. Several days after the tweets, the story still had legs, and Trump was asked how his wife felt about what he said. "[Melania] feels very strongly about our country," he said, adding that she thought the congresswomen's feelings about America (which Trump viewed as overtly negative) were "horrible."

The irony is that the only member of the four elected congresswomen not born in the United States, Ilhan Omar of Minnesota, actually became a citizen before Melania Trump did. Omar, from Somalia, became a United States citizen in 2000, when she was seventeen years old; Melania became a citizen in 2006, when she was thirty-six.

Melania's knowledge of national and global affairs does, like her husband's, come mostly from watching television news and reading stories online from newspapers and other outlets. She is not versed in the writings of political thinkers, nor has she delved deeply into the history of America. But talk to her about current events and she's more knowledgeable than your average Joe or Jane. "She keeps up with absolutely everything going on in politics," says one of her close personal friends.

Of her ability to let her husband make his own decisions about how he handles the job, and his Twitter account, and to avoid being rattled when he is erratic about both, Melania to this day chalks it up to her firm belief that a leopard can't change its spots. "I've always been that way. I take people the way they are," she once said. "You could work your whole life to change them and they never will. What's the point? They need to be who they are"—words of advice that pretty much everyone from those on Capitol Hill to those in the State Department, the media, and the West Wing, present and future, might want to let sink in.

As for what she does each day, that's still evolving. Her public schedule remains relatively light compared with her most recent predecessors. That's not to say she doesn't have a lot that comes across her desk—she must make decisions about everything from event decoration and planning to what the theme of Halloween should be. There are an inordinate number of minutiae in the upkeep and preservation of the White House, all of which falls in her purview, and all of which she is hands-on about. She meets with people and keeps up with correspondence—all of which *she* does; she doesn't delegate to her staff. There is nothing Melania hates more than someone speaking for her if she knows she can do so herself. It's part of the reason her team is so small. She simply doesn't want anyone else doing the talking.

Melania also frequently takes time off away from the White House, spending most of her non-Washington days at Mar-a-Lago, Trump's Palm Beach resort compound, where Melania hosts important holidays for the family: Thanksgiving, Christmas, New Year's Eve, and Easter. In between, she flits back and forth between D.C. and Florida several times for long weekends, sometimes alone, sometimes with Barron, and on occasion with the president, who also enjoys time off at Mar-a-Lago to golf at his nearby resort. Melania must fly on a government jet, per security protocols, so the taxpayer expense for her jaunts is now well into the hundreds of thousands of dollars. Though less engaged in the general "work" of most first ladies, Melania has ceaselessly focused on her job as a mother, and she maintains that regularly scheduling time away from Washington, doing the things that she has done with her son since he was born, is just as important as, say, developing a policy base for her platform. This is not an exaggeration. For most first ladies, the compulsion, whether they had worked in full-time careers before the White House or not, has been to treat the role as a job. Melania has made it something else. Yes, she works at being first lady, she does the ceremonial parts of the gig, but there's also the sense with her that it feels almost like it's part-time. She has events, but only when she wants to have them, usually one to three a week, none lasting more than an hour, though typically they are far shorter. And she's sparse on the extracurriculars. She doesn't do the talk shows, she doesn't make YouTube videos (like Michelle), she isn't very interested in bolstering administration policy (like Hillary), nor has she participated in many interviews for television or magazines.

It's that strange and unprecedented dichotomy that is Melania Trump. Should she be attacked for not being more consistently and devotedly dedicated to her "job" as first lady? Or should she be praised for always doing what she thinks is best and right for her, even if it means having way less of a public profile than her predecessors? After all, what kind of job is it that expects total passion and commitment but does not allow the jobholder to express true, personal convictions? For Melania, the role needed a cause, and so she conjured up Be Best, her platform for "helping children" that has three facets: overall well-being, social media kindness and safety, and care for children affected by the nation's opioid crisis. It's a lot, to put it mildly. And she hasn't made it as impactful as the platforms of her predecessors; it doesn't roll off the tongue like, say, Just Say No or Let Girls Learn. Not that Melania cares all that much—she's just fine with keeping the initiative as it is and holding an event or two per month, mostly centered on kids. Maybe she's learned the frustrating secret of being a first lady: no matter what you do or how you do it, you will inevitably be belittled. The inherent sexism of the role limits first ladies' work to ornamental initiatives at the periphery of the national consciousness. Lady Bird Johnson, for example, had the forethought to think about the environment with her highway beautification project, but while she toiled to get an actual act passed in support of it in 1965, focusing on the conservation of scenic highways and securing federal funding, most thought she just wanted to plant pretty flowers.

A first lady isn't necessarily responsible for anything—the description of the role is what each one makes of it. You can take a position on something or you can skip doing so altogether. Just look at Melania and cyberbullying. She knew that she would get blasted for including cyberbullying in her overall Be Best program (most Americans think that's *all* it is), but she did it anyway. Her husband even told her it would be a bad idea. Trump was not unaware that his personal habit of trashing people on Twitter would open his wife up to a ton of backlash for taking up the cause. He warned her against doing it. She did it anyway and has faced the consequences.

She has meetings with her team most days, and she plots her next moves, trips, events, and outfits. She works to incorporate Be Best into programs that already exist, not ones that she has created from scratch. Be Best does not so much involve building something from the ground up—like Just Say No, literacy programs in schools, health and nutrition guidelines for kids—but having Melania endorse companies, programs, hospitals, and initiatives that are already in place. It's a much easier way of doing things and, some would argue, smarter and more fiscally responsible. Partnering with programs in the Department of Health and Human Services, Department of Education, and Office of the National Drug Policy Council also keeps her staff to a minimum.

At twelve, Melania's East Wing team is by far the smallest since Rosalynn Carter. Two of her recent predecessors had as many as twenty to thirty staffers on hand in the East Wing. Michelle Obama was the administrative head of a hospital before she became first lady; Hillary Clinton was a partner in a law firm. Both women had success leading large teams and directing strategy. Melania hasn't had, nor has she requested, the sort of resources demanded by her predecessors to accomplish their lofty goals. Michelle Obama wanted to change school lunch programs and incorporate exercise programs into schools. Barbara Bush wanted to make sure every American learned how to read, and she got funding for her Foundation for Family Literacy. Hillary Clinton was so driven to make her "cause," healthcare reform, succeed that she demanded a West Wing office so that she could have access to the infrastructure of the administration.

Unless something dramatic happens with Be Best, Melania's legacy won't be as a legendary champion of her three-pronged platform. I mean, can you name its three entities without going back a few paragraphs to check? And if people do recall the initiative long after her tenure as first lady is over, they will likely remember it for how the anti-cyberbullying stance was in marked opposition to the Twitter habits of her husband. Being Melania, she probably understands this. That she picked something to rally around that brought with it added complications because of her husband, thus making the fight against it more difficult, says a lot about who she is. Because, like Trump, Melania relishes a good "come at me" challenge. Go after her, if you will. She doesn't really seem to care.

13

Cordial, Not Close

"Why Men Want to Marry Melanias and Raise Ivankas"

—JILL FILIPOVIC, OPINION IN *THE NEW YORK TIMES*

From the very beginning of his relationship with Melania, Trump had made clear that Ivanka was daughter dearest. If she wanted to appear with them at an event or on *The Apprentice* or on the red carpet for a movie premiere or a Fashion Week function, well, he had two arms, one to grasp Melania and one to grasp Ivanka. There are endless shots of the three of them together in the early 2000s, posed just that way. Whether he intended to or not, Trump set up his daughter and his third wife to compete. Both are beautiful, tall former models, and both are inextricably tied to the same man.

During the campaign for Trump's presidency, even though Melania stayed out of the way, the media liked to gin up stories about stepmother and stepdaughter. (*The New York Times* ran a piece titled "Why Men Want to Marry Melanias and Raise Ivankas.") A lot of it was Trump's own fault for talking about one whenever he talked about the other. To this day, more often than not, if he mentions Ivanka, he quickly follows by mentioning Melania and vice versa. "Ivanka has been so great. And Melania has also been so great."

For a time, the two women had enjoyed a comfortable, if not warm, alliance. But the White House has not been good for the relationship between Melania Trump and Ivanka Trump. "Cordial, not close," is how it was described to me by someone who has spent ample time around both women.

At the start of Trump's presidency, Melania and Ivanka were equally popular with the public, according to polling. Both were curious accoutrements to the Donald Trump administration, glamazons about to be a part of American political history. Now the stock of Daddy's favorite child has dropped and continues to do so as more time passes in Washington. Melania, however, remains the most liked member of the Trump family and the administration. Some would argue that's not a difficult achievement, considering the company she finds herself in.

In the beginning of her White House tenure, before her stepmother moved in, Ivanka had free rein. Unlike Melania, Ivanka had been an active and prizewinning surrogate for her father: glamorous and personable, she had filled in on the trail when Melania had abstained. Ivanka was the de facto spouse.

When Ivanka arrived at the White House, she took liberties because of what she had achieved, perhaps deservedly so. She was able to walk the hallways of the West Wing, but it was also fine for her to take the occasional dip into the East Wing. Without Melania there, she had the virtual run of the place, which must have been exciting and alluring.

Ivanka was all too happy to take at least a pass at the role of first lady, subbing in for Melania when she was still in New York living at Trump Tower. Like her father, and as a Trump, she wanted it all and didn't see that as absurd or understand why she couldn't have it. She wished to be taken seriously as a political adviser, a career woman, a real estate executive, a brand developer, an influencer, a working mom, and a devoted wife. And she tried her hand at being all of the above and then some. And Trump let her do as she pleased, as he had basically done since she was born.

In February 2017, just one month after her dad was in office, Ivanka posted on her Instagram a picture of herself in the Oval Office seated at the Resolute desk, her father, the president, at her right and the Canadian prime minister Justin Trudeau at her left. Both men were standing. "A great discussion with two world leaders about the importance of women having a seat at the table!" Ivanka captioned the post, with emojis of the American and Canadian flags.

It was an empty statement, meant only to showcase that she got these two world leaders to stand over her—and Dad let her sit at his desk. It felt demoralizing for the men, props in her social media she-nanigans. When you've stared at the picture long enough, you recognize its utter absurdity. It was cringe-worthy.

Melania would never post something like that. No sooner would Melania make a joke about being a woman seated at the table in a setting as revered as the Oval Office than she would do cartwheels across the South Lawn. Not only is she private, she isn't prone to social media "moments" meant for clicks.

Ivanka also featured her three kids, particularly the two older ones, Arabella and Joseph, in her Instagram feed. After the family arrived in Washington, D.C., she documented the various family field trips she took them on around town: to museums and the zoo, sports games and parks. One day she brought Arabella, six at the time, to the Supreme Court to watch a case be argued. And she did it all with a smile and a blowout, almost always wearing something from her eponymous label. It was like "D.C." Ivanka was the En-joli woman from the old commercials, doing it all because she's a "wooo-man." It wasn't unusual for her hungry fans to peep in on every part of her day if they followed her social media feeds: Morning workout! White House time! Crafts with the kids after school! Dinner!

Posting such frequent and private details is, again, something Melania would never do. For Melania, the goal was to make Barron virtually disappear, not place him in the virtual world for strangers' eyes to gaze upon.

Melania was smart enough to know that using her son in her social media feeds might make her more relatable as a mother to the rest of America or that having a staffer snap a photo of him in the White House with his dad (the way they used to for *People* magazine or *The Apprentice*) would likely help Trump project the softness he needed. But she wasn't about to do it. "Sacrificing her son's privacy to look well rounded on social media for strangers? No way. Not Melania," says a friend. But Ivanka was all in. Kids, job, White House—nothing was off-limits.

"Taking a call in the White House with my personal assistant, Theodore" was the caption of one shot of Ivanka in a White House hallway holding her youngest son. Marketing 101 was Ivanka's wheelhouse. She fancied herself a big part of the reason why her father had won the White House, and she'd earned that right, endlessly campaigning, even while heavily pregnant, and rarely taking a day off from spreading the MAGA message across the country. If she wanted to walk around like she owned the place and have her kids hold their grandfather's hand as they strolled the South Lawn to the helicopter, she was going to do it.

In January 2017, as Trump took the oath of office on Inauguration Day and placed his hand on the bible, held by Melania, Ivanka, in a bright white suit by Oscar de la Renta, positioned herself in a very Ivanka way—right in front of the podium, with the microphone at her chest level, the seal of the president of the United States clearly visible. From an angle, especially in almost every front-facing photograph after the fact, Ivanka, standing where she was, looked to be the president, or *a* president, about to speak to her people. Don Jr. was off to the side, behind Melania and Barron; Eric to Ivanka's other side; and Tiffany, always Tiffany, farthest away from her dad.

Heading to the parade that same weekend, Ivanka posted from inside the limo, her kids sitting in protective booster seats. It was all very wannabe Kennedy, but was she trying too hard? A lot of people thought so. Arriving in D.C. days before, she stepped off a government plane in an all-green outfit, also Oscar de la Renta, baby Theodore in one arm, guiding Arabella with her other. Ivanka strode from the plane first, Barron, Tiffany, and Melania's parents behind her. She was saying that she had arrived, here to lead the Trump family, next gen.

Ivanka posted shots from inside the White House that weekend to her millions of followers, tweeting a video of barefoot little Theodore having his first crawl in the State Dining Room, Ivanka seated cozily on the rug, added as part of the Obama renovation of the room a year before. She looked at home, which would have been fine, had the home not been the people's house, and had Melania not been its actual mistress.

As soon as the official public events of the inaugural weekend were over, Melania and Barron hopped a jet back to New York, not even sticking around to stay the night in the White House. Melania had soured on the festivities early, according to one account—the focus, the pressure, the overwhelming need to be "on" was just too much for her and her son. Entry into the presidential bubble was not something she wanted to drink from a fire hose. Ivanka, on the other hand, didn't want the weekend to end.

But that is who Ivanka is: from birth groomed to find a marketable way to connect and sell a brand to the public. Born in 1981 to Donald Trump and his first wife, Ivana Trump, young Ivanka was the apple of her dad's eye. She was driven and ambitious, and she stayed out of trouble, for the most part, attending New York City's posh private day school Chapin before heading to bucolic Wallingford, Connecticut, for boarding school at Choate Rosemary Hall, a favorite of the millionaire set. Ivanka had paid attention to both her mother's and her father's drive and competitiveness, which rubbed off on her, clearly: she worked as a model in her teenage years and later entered elite Georgetown University before transferring to the University of Pennsylvania's Wharton School of Business, Trump's alma mater. While other heiresses with family names that are part of the pop culture vernacular opted to exploit their wealth for fame (remember Paris Hilton?), Ivanka turned her sights on business and adopted a lower social profile. She partied and shopped and dated around and about Manhattan, but she did so without much in the way of accompanying scandal. As she grew into a swanlike beauty of five foot eleven, she weathered the tabloid stories about her parents' divorce and did so with more responsibility and self-awareness than most girls her age probably would, given her background. She didn't use her family's wealth and her exposure to the tabloid headlines as an excuse to devolve into a poor little rich girl, partying too hard, acting out, and so forth. She kept it together, and did so remarkably well.

It was no surprise that eventually she joined the family business and used the family name to spin off her own fashion and jewelry lines, get book deals, and attract social media followers. By the time she got to Washington, Ivanka was married to another wealthy heir from a New York real estate family, Jared Kushner, and was the mother of two small children.

She would promote, promote, promote—her Instagram feed becoming an unofficial advertisement for her brand, which she had stepped away from to be in the White House (and which would fold for good several months later) and her new book, titled *Women Who Work*. What Ivanka failed to recognize was something that, like her father, she just couldn't fathom: she rubbed a majority of people the wrong way. Instead of finding her strong and amazing, they found her cloying and ubiquitous.

In the family's first interview after Donald Trump was elected, Ivanka insisted—with her father's blessing—that she be seated in the front "row" of the family. After Trump was interviewed by Lesley Stahl alone and then with Melania, the *60 Minutes* crew set up the chairs in the living room of the triplex with Trump, Melania, and Ivanka in front and Tiffany, Don Jr., and Eric in back. Trump liked when his daughter was on equal footing with his wife, and Melania, in a red, tulip-sleeve Antonio Berardi dress, let it happen—she knew to pick her battles, and she had gotten used to Ivanka wanting to have equal billing. It didn't particularly bother her.

During the interview, Melania was her usual self, calm and measured, telling Stahl that she was prepared to lose her independence.
"You won't be able to walk down the street," Stahl said, trying perhaps to stir up some emotion. "I didn't do that for two years already,"
answered Melania. "It will just continue. It's another level, but it will
continue." She was measured and practical, and the audience couldn't
tell if she was happy about losing her identity or furious about it.

That interview would also be the first time that Melania addressed
what would become the Achilles' heel of her Be Best campaign—
stopping cyberbullying. Her husband is the biggest cyberbully on the
planet. How can you tell kids to be nice online when your husband is
such a jerk? asked Stahl—not quite in those exact words, but something to that effect. "So, you never say to him, 'Come on' [when he
tweets bad things]?"

Melania: "I did."

Trump: "She does."

Stahl's not buying it, and she keeps at Melania—it's revelatory,
because clearly Stahl thinks there's no way this woman who has been
such a passive participant throughout the campaign has the balls to tell
her husband she thinks he should shut up when he tweets something
horrible. "If he does something that you think crossed a line, will you
tell him?"

Melania: "Yes. I tell him all the time."

Stahl: "All the time?"

Melania: "All the time."

Ivanka doesn't get these questions. During her sit-down, she used
all the "Ivanka" adjectives that she has become known for using—
"We had enormous pride, joy. It's incredibly exciting. And we're very
grateful for the opportunity. And we take that opportunity very seriously," she said when asked what it was like to watch her father win
the election. She also denied that she would join the administration.
Sort of. "No, I'm going to be a daughter. But I've said throughout
the campaign that I am very passionate about certain issues and that
I want to fight for them. Wage equality, childcare. These are things

that are very important for me. I'm very passionate about education. Really promoting more opportunities for women. So, you know, there are a lot of things that I feel deeply, strongly about. But not in a formal administrative capacity." Hmm.

Funny how when Melania told Stahl about her antibullying agenda, she received pushback, getting questions about her husband and his behavior. Yet when Ivanka, with all of her breathy adjectives, said she wanted to promote women, Stahl didn't ask her about the charges being levied against her father from a number of women, who accused him of sexual misconduct. Melania had already been labeled the vapid-model trophy wife; Ivanka, the savvy career mom.

Later that same evening, a press release went out to the media: "Style Alert," it said, Ivanka was wearing "her favorite bangle from the Metropolis Collection" from her Ivanka Trump Fine Jewelry line on *60 Minutes,* and it can be yours for a mere $10,800. The release was not only in poor taste, it also highlighted the nebulous legal vortex that Ivanka and her various fashion and jewelry lines had slipped into, where she was sort of using her father's election to sell her wares, but also sort of maybe not? Ivanka had tried something similar after her RNC speech, tweeting a link from her personal Twitter account: "Shop Ivanka's look from her #RNC speech."

It was, yet again, something Melania would never do.

But Ivanka was convinced she could also, on top of everything else, become a style influencer. Unprompted, she showed her gown for an inaugural gala on her Instagram feed (a white Oscar de la Renta dress with a big black obi-style sash), from inside a chinoiserie-wallpapered bedroom at Blair House before she left for the party. Melania, on the other hand, made people wait to see her gown, only caring that the public saw her body-hugging, head-to-toe nude sequined Reem Acra gown if they happened upon it via a press photo after the fact. Melania had already taken a page from Jackie Kennedy's book, in that she understood, as did Jackie, that the more there is mystery, the more they, the public, want to know. Jackie would dole out bits and pieces of her life, her children, the White House, but she was never effusive about a desire to be an open book. Melania felt the same. She knew that crumbs were an effective tool to lure favor, and if she used them all at once, she was blowing a valuable commodity. Ivanka, on the other hand, was eager for everyone to see how fabulous everything was right away, as quickly and intimately as possible.

During the day, Ivanka stepped in front of as many cameras as she could in the White House, at cabinet meetings, during dignitary visits, at roundtables, and inside the Oval Office. Often, she wore sleeveless tops and floral dresses, while other female staffers stuck to de rigueur navy suits. Ivanka was at the greatest job in the world, America! Or, possibly, going to a garden party.

Meanwhile, up in New York, Melania was hiding from paparazzi, who were desperate for a glimpse of the new first lady. The dynamic between stepmother and stepdaughter was growing more distant. Melania was looking at Ivanka's behavior in Washington, not quite with surprise but, rather, with acceptance. As she knew to be true of Ivanka's father, Melania knew that trying to change someone or expect different behavior from them was a fruitless endeavor. Ivanka had always craved the spotlight; Melania had wandered into it. Ivanka saw the presidency as her chance to achieve her own ambitions; Melania saw it as something tangential to her life, which was primarily being a mother.

Before Melania even moved to the White House, Ivanka had posted more than a hundred photos of her children on her social media accounts. Melania had almost zero (well, there was one old one of her and Barron that she posted in honor of Mother's Day 2017). Melania stealthily settled in at the White House on June 11, 2017, only announcing it via a photo on her @FLOTUS Twitter account that showed candles lit on a table in the executive residence and the view through a window over the Truman Balcony that looked out onto the South Lawn; the caption read, "Looking forward to the memories we'll make in our new home! #Movingday." A few days after that, Ivanka, thirsty as ever and happy to show she's still there, too, posted a photo of Arabella, hand uplifted, in the White House China Room, with the caption, "Raise your hand if you're ready for the weekend?!"

Behind the scenes, Melania had made it clear from New York that Ivanka was not to have an office in the East Wing, because the East Wing, when she ultimately did arrive, was to be her territory and hers alone. A stickler for tradition, Melania wasn't about to bend the rules for Ivanka's unprecedented role in the administration, which was publicly becoming part adviser, part first family representative, and, quite honestly, part first lady. An office in the East Wing wasn't something Ivanka necessarily wanted anyway; she was really much more about having full run of the White House, east, west, north, and south, but people who know her assume it was Ivanka who had leaked the possibility to the press. Melania was already redecorating the space, picking new paint and furniture for the official Office of the First Lady, a suite of offices on the second floor of the East Wing, first established as the home base of the first lady by Rosalynn Carter in 1978.

Meanwhile, Ivanka was busy trying to create the model of what a first daughter is, since there hadn't really been anyone like her, in her role as family member and presidential adviser, in modern White House history. If she hurried, she could possibly establish herself as the most essential woman in her father's administration, someone with political influence who was also a celebrity hybrid of sorts and who could potentially parlay her time in the White House into a spin-off series, to use television vernacular.

It is a poorly kept secret that Ivanka harbors her own political ambitions. Trump has already endorsed her. "If she ever wanted to run for president, I think she'd be very, very hard to beat," he said in a recent interview. Ivanka's portfolio of political interests was initially affordable childcare and federal maternity leave. Now she's more focused on women's economic empowerment and promoting STEM for young women. She has claimed an area, particularly female-centric policy issues, that has traditionally been the purview of a first lady. Her initiatives were destined to cross over with those of Melania. And cross over they did, in a big way.

In spring 2019, Ivanka took one of her first solo international trips . . . to Africa. Africa was coincidentally the continent Melania visited in fall 2018 on her first major solo international trip. Melania partnered with USAID during her visit, stopping in four countries: Ghana, Malawi, Kenya, and Egypt. She was joined by USAID administrator Mark Green. Ivanka, too, partnered with USAID and was joined by Green while visiting Ethiopia and the Ivory Coast. Melania's trip was centered on helping children and delivering more financial support in the form of USAID programs. Ivanka's trip was focused on women's entrepreneurship and newly announced efforts to support female empowerment.

The trips were, according to a source, a little too close for comfort for Melania, who thought Ivanka was infringing on her turf. The competition between the two feels almost unfair to inflate, just because they are women—catfight!—an all too common and unjust way to paint female relationships. But according to many sources, it's a real thing.

Ivanka and Melania would clash over the Africa trip. Melania took off with some fanfare, getting as many headlines about her visit as she could muster in the light of Trump's usual usurping of the news cycle. The trip was a big deal for the first lady. Most of the first solo international trips of first ladies get coverage in the press. Patricia Nixon was the first first lady to make a solo visit to Africa, in 1972. Hillary Clinton's first solo trip was also to Africa; she went for two weeks, taking Chelsea Clinton with her on a six-country tour. Michelle Obama's first solo international trip was to Mexico. Melania would be carrying on a long-standing tradition of an American first lady spreading goodwill and, typically, the message of her formal platform around the globe. She spent her first full day in Ghana helping at a children's hospital, holding babies, visiting with mothers, and passing out supplies.

Meanwhile, back home, Ivanka Trump was doing something she normally doesn't do: visiting hurricane survivors, holding babies, and passing out supplies. And the reason she normally doesn't do these things is that normally Melania does. Ivanka not only stepped onto Melania's turf but also went so far as to have a video made—which included footage of her high-fiving an African American toddler in her arms—and posted it to her Instagram with instrumental music.

With the help of a White House staff videographer, Ivanka now has these videos made regularly. Often, she is speaking directly into the camera, explaining to the audience why whatever policy issue she is championing is so important, why she is passionate or "incredibly excited" about it. Sometimes she does a voice-over about a cause while video footage shows her laughing with students, walking through an automotive factory, taking photos with fans, or speaking at a podium. For her Africa trips, the videos would often incorporate slow motion to show her walking alongside the leaders of Ethiopia, learning how coffee is made, or dancing with locals. To put the videos in context, it would be like Obama's top aide, Valerie Jarrett, making a video of her accomplishments after each domestic trip, speech, or policy announcement. Or Karl Rove posting for the public in slow motion each time he shook hands with a leader or had a meeting with the head of General Motors.

So not only was Ivanka stepping into Melania's area but the videos felt very much in the same vein as those done by Melania, who had found success months before with minivideo journals of her own events and visits to places that included shots of her with children edited together with a soundtrack of upbeat classical music. She shared them on her Twitter and Instagram accounts, and the views were often well into the hundreds of thousands.

By several accounts, Melania was not happy about it. Ahead of the trip, the East Wing had delicately asked the West Wing to give Melania a wide berth during the five days she was in Africa and to try not to have the president (or Ivanka) do anything that might distract or draw attention from the activities Melania was doing while abroad. It was an ask that was not made with expectation it would actually work, and it was one Melania's staff had rarely made before, but given the newsiness of the West Wing, they felt it was best to have the discussion and provide the information and the dates and make the formal request. From what I gather, no one on Melania's team had high hopes that anyone would be able to control the news cycle based on Trump—unfortunately, with Trump, the news runs hot to liquid lava, so Melania is typically not covered in a way that would allow her to request a predesignated focus. Ivanka was the one they didn't think they needed to worry about.

"Her office let the West Wing know about the dates of Melania's Africa trip well in advance of her going," said someone with knowledge of the events. "It was fair. And she knew it wouldn't necessarily stop the president from making news, but she didn't think Ivanka would do something like that." Trump's then–chief of staff, John Kelly, was alerted to the striking similarities of Ivanka's activities back home, and he stepped in to chide Ivanka's staff for their choice of timing. Months later, after Kelly, like most, unceremoniously left the White House, having fallen out of favor with Trump and his daughter and son-in-law, Jared Kushner, he would give an interview, saying Trump's family "were an influence that has to be dealt with," before clarifying, "by no means do I mean Mrs. Trump—the first lady is a wonderful person."

To be fair, both Ivanka and Melania have tried very hard to like each other and achieve more than mere toleration. And for many years it worked. Melania didn't have to try all that hard not to care when Ivanka would accompany her and Donald Trump to events, essentially third-wheeling on a date, and Ivanka would grin and bear it when Melania's exotic beauty and glamour would outshine hers.

Ivanka's chief concern with her father and his girlfriends had always been whether they were with him for his money, which, of course, they often were. She wasn't, however, concerned that they would siphon away her portion of the inheritance, even if she had genuine concern for her father. Ivanka was eleven when her parents divorced, and after the Marla Maples incident, tween and teenage Ivanka was intensely protective of her father. She had seen up close the type of woman to whom he was typically attracted, and many of them were truly only with him for a hit of the limelight, or in the hopes of getting a rent-free Trump apartment.

She didn't feel that way about Melania, which took some of the heat off the relationship. Also, Melania was age-appropriate in Ivanka's eyes, even though she was twenty-six years younger than her father and only eleven years older than herself. Ivanka would joke when her dad was single that as long as his girlfriends never got any younger than her oldest brother, she was okay with it—but added in a flash of deadpan that Don Jr. was already in his twenties, so options were thinning out. She also got the feeling that this one was sticking around. While they were dating, Melania didn't appear to mind being a tourist in a Donald Trump world, and Ivanka admired that about her. She saw, as did her dad, that Melania was genuinely charmed by him, strikingly independent, and low on the drama.

But Trump's ascendancy to the White House has let Ivanka's ambition run rampant, seemingly without any check. To set herself apart, staff at the White House say Ivanka always likes to enter the room last at events, and she must always sit in the front row. I've personally seen her several times work a room like nobody's business, pressing flesh with all of the charm and flattery that Washington types feed off. She's keenly aware that she has an effect on people in person. She makes them feel as if she may be flirting with them but, at the same time, is laser-focused on what they are saying and the intellectual exchange. She's one part friendly vixen, one part hyperastute businesswoman. She gives everyone she talks to her full attention, often touching them in a familiar way, something a little more than a handshake, maybe a squeeze on the arm for you, senator, a laugh and a tap on the shoulder for you, congressman.

Also, before many of the traditional "first lady" events, like the Easter Egg Roll, the lighting of the national Christmas tree, the Thanksgiving turkey pardon, and, really, any other ceremonial event where Melania will be entering last because she is accompanied by the president, Ivanka makes sure to get face time in beforehand. She's not a sneak-to-her-seat-at-the-last-minute person. The night before the

Thanksgiving turkey pardon in 2018, a story had broke about Ivanka's unauthorized use of a personal e-mail account for work matters—an attention-getting headline considering her father's constant hammering of Hillary Clinton's personal e-mail habits. There was buzz in the press area about whether Ivanka would show for the pardon. I had no doubt she would. Sure enough, just as the rest of the guests were seated twenty rows deep in the Rose Garden and the media, sequestered in the far back section, had their cameras focused and their live shots up in the control room, in walked Ivanka with her three kids in tow. And in case anyone missed her, she wore a large velvet headband with gold polka dots. She walked boldly in front of the entire audience over to the two turkeys, awaiting their ceremonial pardon, treating her children to an up-close and personal meet and greet with Peas and Carrots. The president and Melania came out several minutes after Ivanka had taken her seat—in the front row.

Of course, Ivanka has been busted a few times trying to assume the spotlight. Who can forget how she managed to sneak a spot at the table (without yet having a title or a security clearance) next to Angela Merkel on the German chancellor's first visit to the Trump White House? Or, better still, when Ivanka plopped down in her father's designated seat with other world leaders at the 2017 G20 summit? In a pink dress with big bows on the sleeves, Ivanka casually sat in her dad's chair, right between the president of China and the prime minister of Great Britain. She had been sitting in the back, far too many rows back, apparently. When Trump got up to briefly step out, Ivanka walked the several feet down to the front and stepped in. She was crucified for it. Brian Fallon, Hillary Clinton's former campaign spokesman, put it this way: "I'm sure Republicans would have taken it in stride if Chelsea Clinton was deputized to perform head of state duties."

The microscope on Ivanka can actually be unfair. "If she weren't my daughter, it would be so much easier for her. Might be the only bad thing going, if you want to know the truth," said Trump. But the scrutiny is also the result of her place in the administration. In holding

herself apart from the rest of the administration, using her relationship as presidential offspring in tandem with her job as presidential
adviser, Ivanka has created overlaps that have resulted in stinging
criticism. (Bob Woodward, in his West Wing tell-all, *Fear*, recounted
a fight between Ivanka and Steve Bannon. "'You're nothing but a
fucking staffer,' said Bannon during one shouting match. 'I'm not a
staffer! I'll never be a staffer. I'm the first daughter—and I'm never
going to be a staffer!'" she yelled back.)

Ivanka's stunningly poor sense of optics and fondness in interviews for using words the wrong way has given rise to a whole new
bevy of critics, mostly media and elites who saw her as, well, fake. "The
presidency of the United States is an incredible thing, you have an
ability to effectuate change at the highest levels. There are issues I am
deeply passionate about," she said to a fashion magazine during
the campaign. "Well, obviously, I'm a huge advocate for women and
women's issues, like child care. The cost of child care is incredibly
onerous. It's not sustainable or appropriate."

Melania noted all these gaffes—and did the opposite.

At the start of Trump's administration, and even at the nascent be-
ginnings of his presidential campaign, Ivanka and Melania appeared
to have quite positive feelings for one another. Ivanka said in an interview, "Melania is very smart, she's very warm, she's got an incredible
heart. She's always been very charitable and there are many organiza-
tions that she's worked with. Not just for a season but over the course
of many years and decades in some cases."

"I'll leave it to her to put forth what her platform will be but I
know that she'll be a very powerful and impactful first woman," said
Ivanka in another interview, careful not to step on toes. "I know that
anything she sets her mind to she does with her full heart so I have no
doubt that when she decides which platform she's going to prioritize,
she'll be incredibly effective in that regard."

In *People* magazine, Ivanka backed up Melania's campaign strategy, or lack thereof, saying, "It's pretty uncommon for wives of candidates to not be on the campaign trail every day. And she made a

decision I totally respect. . . . My father's traveling so frequently, and she is an unbelievably consistent, loving and reliable figure in Barron's life. . . . She takes [Barron] to school every day, picks him up every day. It's a really remarkable thing and she's a great inspiration to me as I raise my own children in terms of family first and having the right priorities." When Ivanka and Jared moved into their multimillion-dollar, eight-thousand-square-foot rental mansion in D.C.'s posh Kalorama neighborhood, they brought with them their two live-in nannies. That's not to say Ivanka isn't a hands-on mom; she is, but she has consistent help doing the day-to-day stuff that most working moms don't have time or the money to do.

However, the tide is shifting in the White House, with Ivanka's realization, halfway through her father's first term, that Melania is gaining steam. Ivanka Trump's ubiquitous presence, TMI social media posts, and general Ivanka-ness haven't helped her surpass her stepmother's popularity. In the Trump orbit and beyond, in the sweet spot of the GOP base, people like the first lady, and it's frustrating for Ivanka. And even those who loathe Trump, either for his politics or just because, are invariably intrigued by his wife.

Without so much as a few words here and there, her stepmother has managed to become not only likable to the public but influential in the West Wing. In June 2018, when the border crisis was peaking and families were being torn apart, it was Melania behind the scenes who got in Trump's ear to put a stop to it. "She was very involved with telling him it was wrong and had to end, fast," a senior White House staffer tells me. "This wasn't something she sat back about. She was all over it."

Melania was the first Trump family member to release a statement about the issue, which is important not just because the country was reeling from images of babies being taken from their parents but also because she was exhibiting feelings on a policy issue, something she had never done before so forcefully. "Mrs. Trump hates to see children separated from their families and hopes both sides of the aisle can finally come together to achieve successful immigration reform.

She believes we need to be a country that follows all laws, but also a country that governs with heart." It was clearly meant to stake claim to the topic, as well as to indicate that, whatever the president did or did not do, she was going to call it like she saw it. First ladies are usually hamstrung when it comes to issues like this—they are expected to be there to bolster compassion and sympathy for an administration, but there is politically little they can actually *do* to effect change.

In fact, ever since images of separated families had begun to flood the news, Melania had been having intense talks with her husband in the residence each evening, telling him how upsetting it was and how poorly it would reflect on him if he neglected such an emotionally charged issue. "She told him he had to do more," a White House aide says. "Whether he did it with Congress, or whether he did it on his own, it needed to stop, period."

But it was Ivanka who got a lot of the credit when Trump finally signed the executive order ending his own policy of separating families for detainment at the border. There was a coordinated communications office effort to get Ivanka some *good* press on this topic. She desperately needed it because days earlier she had posted a tone-deaf photo on her social media feeds. As the rest of the country was starting to hear stories about children of illegal immigrants being taken from their parents to god knows where for god knows how long, Ivanka put up a picture of herself holding her two-year-old son, Theodore, in his jammies, nuzzling him, with the caption, "my heart." It was terrible, terrible timing. She was lambasted on cable news talk shows and on social media. "Isn't it just the best to snuggle your little one—knowing exactly where they are, safe in your arms? It's the best. The BEST. Right, Ivanka? Right?" tweeted actor Patton Oswalt sarcastically. "How lucky you are to live in a bubble" was another tweet. It was just one of several photos Ivanka shared during the period when immigrant family separations consumed headlines. Another shot showed a fun afternoon "date" with her daughter while Ivanka frolicked outdoors; one showed little Joseph in his car seat, clutching a hockey stick on the way home from his first NHL game, mom raving about how much he loved it, and the popcorn! "When you have babies being taken away from their mothers, you have to ask why the counselor to the president, who was brought in to help the president perhaps create good policies surrounding women, parental leave, and domestic policies is so tone deaf," said MSNBC's Mika Brzezinski, who once considered herself Ivanka's close friend.

Ivanka had to act fast to dispel the bad press and quickly change the narrative, a trick she'd learned from her years in business and from being the daughter of Donald Trump.

That Ivanka was instrumental in helping shut down the policy, doing anything she could to use her congressional connections to find a legislative solution, was very much just the sort of story that would help reverse the negativity. In news accounts, members of Congress said that Trump had identified Ivanka as the one who helped him see the light, and the urgency, of changing what was happening, not necessarily Melania.

The next day, Trump signed the executive order ostensibly ending the zero-tolerance policy of separating families at the border, but he did so after getting an earful from Melania the evening beforehand, asking him why Ivanka was getting credit for this and not her. As Trump spoke to the media in the Oval Office after signing the order, it was clear he had gotten the message. "Ivanka feels very strongly about it," but also, next breath, "my wife feels very strongly about it," said Trump, careful, after the dressing-down he had gotten the night before, to interject Melania.

It still wasn't enough.

The next day, I was on a plane with Melania, her team, and a handful of other press members. We didn't know exactly where we were headed, but we were told that we were going to the border—and were unable to report it until we landed, ultimately, in McAllen, Texas. "I'm headed down to Texas" is what Melania told the president, apparently two days before, which is not a time frame that is generally workable to move a political principal around the country. It typically takes at least a week for the Secret Service and an advance team to

Melania attending a Michael Kors runway show at New York Fashion Week, February 2007. Melania would later go on to wear many of Kors's designs as first lady, notably a $10,000 sequined suit to President Trump's first joint address to Congress. *(Mark Peterson/Redux)*

Melania delivers her most pivotal public speech at the Republican National Convention in Cleveland, Ohio, July 2016. Parts of her speech were taken from a speech previously delivered by former first lady Michelle Obama. *(Mark Reinstein/Alamy Stock Photo)*

Melania Trump, then Melanija Knavs, attends the birthday party of her childhood friend Diana Kosar in the small town of Sevnica, Slovenia. Melania is seated first from right, her sister, Ines, first from left. *(Tadej Znidarcic/Redux)*

Seven-year-old Melania *(first row, second from right)* participates in a fashion show for clothing manufacturer Jutranjka, where her mother, Amalija Knavs, was a pattern maker, in 1977. *(Tadej Znidarcic/ Redux)*

Shots of Melania's first professional modeling images, taken by Slovenian photographer Stane Jerko, who discovered Melania on the streets of Ljubljana, Slovenia, when she was sixteen years old. *(Nicola Zolin/Redux)*

Melania Knauss and Donald Trump attending a New York Knicks basketball game in March 1999, about six months after the two met at a Fashion Week party in Manhattan. *(John Keating/Newsday RM via Getty Images)*

Donald Trump kisses daughter Ivanka while holding tight to Melania, on the red carpet at the Costume Institute Gala at the Metropolitan Museum of Art on April 26, 2004. The date is significant because it is Melania's thirty-fourth birthday, and earlier that evening, Trump had proposed to her, as noted by the large diamond engagement ring Melania wears in this image. *(Evan Agostini/Getty Images)*

Donald Trump and Melania pose playfully at a charity event at the Waldorf-Astoria Hotel in New York City in April 2005, three months after their lavish Palm Beach, Florida, wedding. *(Laura Cavanaugh/UPI/Alamy Stock Photo)*

Melania joins Trump at a New York Mets baseball game at Shea Stadium in 2001 with his daughter Tiffany, who at the time was seven years old. *(Howard Earl Simmons/New York Daily News Archive via Getty Images)*

Melania and her father, Viktor Knavs, in a 2007 photograph taken at Mar-a-Lago, Trump's private club and Florida residence. Both of Melania's parents spend several weeks a year at Mar-a-Lago. *(Media Punch Inc/Alamy Stock Photo)*

Melania plays with Barron Trump, almost two, at a Halloween party in New York City, 2007. *(A Scott/Patrick McMullan via Getty Images)*

Melania holds Barron Trump at the ceremony unveiling Donald Trump's star on the Hollywood Walk of Fame, January 2007. *(Tsuni/USA/Alamy Stock Photo)*

First lady Melania attends Donald Trump's State of the Union Address, January 2018. Amid headlines about Trump's alleged infidelities, Melania took a separate motorcade to the address, breaking with the long-standing tradition of the first couple riding together from the White House to the U.S. Capitol. Her choice to wear a white pantsuit that evening also raised eyebrows. *(Patsy Lynch/Alamy Stock Photo)*

Melania wearing the infamous pussy bow blouse to a presidential debate in October 2016, which some observers thought could be a reference to the phrase used by her husband on the *Access Hollywood* tape. Behind are her stepchildren Ivanka, Eric, and Donald Trump, Jr. *(Scott Olson/Getty Images)*

President Donald Trump applauds as Melania introduces him at a rally in Miami, Florida, in February 2019. The appearance is one of few Melania has made at Trump's frequent rallies. *(T. J. Kirkpatrick/The New York Times/Redux)*

Sitting in on a meeting with Trump and the prime minister of the Czech Republic in the Oval Office, Melania, wearing a green leather trench coat, ignores the media frenzy. March 2019. *(White House Photo/Alamy Stock Photo)*

Walking past the Pyramids of Giza in Egypt on the last stop of her first solo international trip as first lady in October 2018. Melania's outfit caught a lot of press for its similarities to other iconic looks, from a villain in an Indiana Jones movie to Diane Keaton in *Annie Hall*. (*Saul Loeb/AFP/Getty Images*)

Wearing a white hat, custom-made by her personal couturier, Hervé Pierre, Melania stands beside French first lady Brigitte Macron at White House ceremonies for the official state visit of the leader of France, Emmanuel Macron, April 24, 2018. (*Alex Edelman/Zuma Wire/Alamy Stock Photo*)

Another "hat" moment from Melania, this time at Buckingham Palace with Queen Elizabeth and the Duchess of Cornwall, June 2019. (*Victoria Jones/Alamy Stock Photo*)

On safari at Nairobi National Park, Melania rode with a guide. She would be chastised by critics for having worn the pristine white pith helmet, a common symbol of European Colonial rule. (*Doug Mills/The New York Times/Redux*)

Melania as first lady of the United States often makes trips to children's hospitals to visit with young patients as part of her Be Best initiative. Here, she greets four-year-old Essence Overton, at Monroe Carell Jr. Children's Hospital at Vanderbilt University in Nashville, Tennessee, July 2018. (*Saul Loeb/AFP/ Getty Images*)

Melania announces her Be Best initiative, aimed at helping children, in the White House Rose Garden, May 7, 2018. Exactly one week after the announcement, Melania would enter the hospital for a kidney operation. (*Pat Benic/UPI/Alamy Stock Photo*)

Melania holds a baby during a stop at the Nest Orphanage in Nairobi, Kenya, part of her solo international trip, October 2018. Melania traveled to four African nations in six days: Ghana, Malawi, Kenya, and Egypt. (*Doug Mills/The New York Times/Redux*)

Melania takes her first dance as first lady of the United States on January 20, 2017, at the Freedom Inaugural Ball. Before they began to dance to the song "My Way," Trump introduced Melania, saying, "My number one supporter, Melania. What she puts up with—ugh." *(Aaron B. Bernstein/Getty Images)*

clear a trip for the first lady, and even that's very tight. There must be coordination for the actual travel, as well as with local law enforcement. Ingress and egress points need to be dedicated, with backup plans; different motorcade routes must be established; and everyone on the ground who will interact with the first lady needs to be vetted and checked. It's not an easy or fast undertaking. Forty-eight hours of notice wasn't common, nor was it easy to accommodate.

But this wasn't an ask—she was going. Initially, Trump tried to talk her out of it, saying it wasn't the right time to keep this story top of the headlines, but he got onboard as soon as he saw how determined she was about it. Fighting with Melania when she wanted something never got him anywhere. She said that whether or not he signed the executive order (this was the night before he did), she was going to go. "This was one hundred percent her idea," Grisham told me.

Melania was the first and, for quite some time, only Trump family member or senior administration figure to actually visit the border facilities and tour them. Unfortunately, much of her trip was overshadowed by the jacket. You know, THE jacket. That army-green parka with the words "*I really don't care do u?*" printed on the back in bold white lettering. Because of that ridiculous statement jacket she decided to wear onto the plane at Andrews Air Force Base on her way to McAllen, the entire trip was negated. No one wanted to talk about Melania's well-intentioned reasoning for going, what she saw while she was there, what she learned about the border patrol's family-intake process or the facility where many of the children were taken when they were separated.

None of that mattered because Melania had worn that $39 jacket from Zara—coincidentally, or not, the fast-fashion brand favored by Ivanka, who during that period had been wearing lots of pieces from Zara on an almost daily basis. Melania, to my knowledge, hadn't worn Zara before, and a $39 anything wasn't ever her price point. I don't believe coincidences exist when it comes to Melania Trump. Having covered her for as long as I have, each thing she does has meaning to it, even the clothing she wears.

To me, and I was asked about the jacket over and over again—I literally had friends from high school texting me "what did it mean?"—it felt personal. In my Melania-trained brain, I was almost certain the connection was to Ivanka and Zara and the way Ivanka had tried to take credit for getting Trump to soften his stance on immigration policy. I believed, and still do, that the jacket was a facetious jab at Ivanka and her near-constant attempts to attach herself to positive administration talking points.

There are many reporters, myself included, who have been contacted about how Ivanka tried to push for this or was instrumental in accomplishing that. It's become sort of a running joke in the newsroom that whenever there is a story about Trump's signing something (or almost signing something), Ivanka must have been behind it. Or if Trump does something controversial and Ivanka tries to stay quiet about it, she typically pops up somehow as being opposed to it once the media has called her out for said quietness. Trump pulled out of the Paris Climate Accord? "An administration official" says Ivanka tried to lobby her father to stay in it. Trump lets a crowd at a rally chant "Send them back!" about four minority congresswomen? "An administration official" says Ivanka spoke with her father the morning after the rally to dissuade him from supporting the rhetoric. There are other examples of "anonymous sources" defending Ivanka's public silence on hot-button issues. So when "a source close to Ivanka" tried to feed the fire that it was she, the first daughter, and not the first lady who had helped convince her father to sign the executive order to prevent the zero-tolerance child-separation policy, Melania flared.

In all honesty, when we left Andrews Air Force Base, we, the traveling press with Melania that day, didn't notice the jacket. We only have a couple of minutes to set up under the wing of her plane before she rolls up and steps from her SUV to board. In those moments, the pool TV camera, the three or four photographers from the wire services, and any other reporters, like myself, need to be ready to capture her and report. And then once she walks up the steps to the plane and goes inside, we have seconds to scramble to the back steps, climb up with all our equipment, and get onboard before the plane begins its taxi. Traveling via government airways is nothing like a commercial flight, which might be obvious, but every time I get on Melania's plane, I am surprised by how little time there is between when I sit and buckle up to when we're barreling down the runway for takeoff.

So that day, none of us really noticed right away the words on the back of her jacket. I saw some lettering but just assumed it was a "fashion" moment, as when Louis Vuitton launched a line of its iconic bags and clothes graffitied by the artist Stephen Sprouse. I actually asked Stephanie Grisham when I noticed the writing out of the corner of my eye, "What does her jacket say?" But she didn't answer me, and with the engine of the plane whirring just feet away from us, likely didn't hear me to begin with.

When we landed back at Andrews Air Force Base later that day, the press, as we normally do, gathered under the wing of the plane to catch a shot of Melania getting off via her front stairs and climbing into her SUV. Then we all loaded into our press vans and the lot of us motorcaded the fifteen-minute drive back to the White House.

On the flight home, once the wire photographers had a chance to edit their photos and send them back to their editors for distribution to awaiting media outlets, the story about the jacket was the hot topic of the moment. How could the first lady of the United States have gone to visit children and families at the border wearing messaging literally signaling she doesn't care?

The reporters assembling under the wing when we got back were placing odds that Melania would not be wearing the jacket again. It's important to note that when we landed in Texas, she had changed into a completely different outfit, as she regularly does, and there was no sign of the offending jacket the entire trip. She didn't wear it on the ground in Texas, which to me was evidence the messaging was not meant for greater public display. I would say fifty percent of the time Melania travels, she will wear something different on the plane from what she wears on the ground—usually, I'm assuming, for comfort. So while the other reporters wondered what she would wear, whether she would keep on what she had in Texas, the "inoffensive" look, or whether she could put back on her travel clothes, with the jacket, I knew better.

I'd been covering the first lady since the week before Inauguration Day, the only full-time reporter dedicated solely to Melania Trump. I was aware of Melania's stubborn streak, one of the things that binds her to her husband: when she gets attacked, she attacks back. I had a feeling she would be reading the news reports on the plane home in her front cabin the way the rest of us were in the back, and if there's one thing Melania hates, it's being tsk-tsked by the press.

She's Melania; she wasn't going to cower from a hot news story.

I said out loud, to no one in particular, as my colleagues weighed whether she would or wouldn't have it on, "Just watch. She's going to be wearing it."

The words were no sooner out of my mouth than the door to the plane opened and Melania stepped out and down the stairs, wearing her white jeans, white Stan Smith Adidas sneakers, sunglasses, and, yep, the jacket.

I can't say with any reportable certainty that she wore that jacket to send a message to Ivanka to quit taking credit, but Melania's message was surely conveyed loud and clear to the intended receiver. As I've said before, there are no coincidences with Melania Trump.

14

The Firing Squad

"You don't fuck with the first lady."
—ANONYMOUS WHITE HOUSE STAFFER

The jacket fiasco aside, Melania's independence has most often served her well. When Grisham, months prior and not too long into Melania's tenure, first told me in an on-the-record statement that Melania was independent and did what she felt like doing because she thought it right and not because she was helping bolster the West Wing, it was fairly groundbreaking. I can't even recall what exactly I was asking her about that first time because there were so many instances of Melania's being radically different in how she behaved—not acting in tandem with the West Wing, as her most immediate predecessor had been. If she is aligned with Trump in practice and theory, she will stick by him—but if she is not, she or Grisham will happily say that she is not.

One of the most glaring examples of Melania's being, well, Melania would come several months after Jacket Gate, when Melania called for the ouster of one of her husband's senior staffers—because she, Melania, did not like her, nor did she trust her.

In November 2018, Grisham made a statement on behalf of her

boss that was unlike any public statement issued by a first lady before: "It is the position of the Office of the First Lady that (Mira Ricardel) no longer deserves the honor of serving in this White House." In a swift sentence, Melania, via her spokeswoman, had trod upon staffing decisions in the West Wing, a matter she had never involved herself in before. She was telling not only the president that she didn't like one of his senior employees but the rest of the world, too.

It was a jaw-dropper.

Ricardel was deputy national security adviser, a position that on its surface had nothing to do with Melania's East Wing world. But Ricardel did have something to do with Melania's team—she had a dustup with Grisham before Melania's Africa trip the month before, and it had spilled out into the open in an extraordinary and unprecedented way with the release of this statement.

I should preface this story by saying none of the several people I spoke to about this incident, many of whom had professional relationships with Ricardel, had anything nice to say about her. Her reputation as a team player was not good, and she was known to backstab. She was technically a member of John Bolton's national security team, and when Trump hired Bolton as national security adviser in March, he brought Ricardel with him as a top aide shortly thereafter. With Grisham's statement, her time in the West Wing didn't last more than six months.

The whole thing began when the first lady was planning her trip to Africa, her first major solo international trip. Seats on Melania's plane were scarce—there were staff to consider, Secret Service, tactical teams, advance staff, military office personnel, and the press. Melania doesn't fly on a 747 like her husband typically does for long trips; her plane is a smaller 757, designated a C-32 due to its military status, with fewer seats and a tighter layout for the interior cabins. Ricardel wanted a say as to which members of her own staff were to be on the plane; she didn't feel that they should fly commercial. While it wasn't necessarily unusual that someone from the national security team would be on a trip like this, the first lady's staff at the last minute determined one of Ricardel's National Security Council staffers' seats would be pulled to make room for a journalist. Ricardel flipped when she got the news.

As a result, Ricardel decided to withhold resources from the NSC for Melania's trip, making it more difficult for operations to run smoothly. It was a petty move and clearly meant as a form of sabotage. Melania's staff members were denied basic logistical information on the trip, details of which were confidential for security reasons but that only served to emphasize how detrimental Ricardel's retribution was. The trip lasted six days and included stops in Ghana, Malawi, Kenya, and Egypt, countries that lack the modern infrastructure allowing a high-level dignitary to smoothly get around. Melania's staff members also weren't given promised policy documents or helpful communication strategies, which, again, in countries like the ones they were visiting caused headaches and delays. Ricardel was behind it all—just because of a seat on a plane.

When Melania found out about what had happened, she was furious. Her staff works hard for her, and she knows it, which doesn't go unappreciated. She values what they have given up to work for her (Grisham's young son lives in Arizona with her ex-husband; Melania's chief of staff Lindsay Reynolds's, three children reside in Ohio with her husband, and she flies back most weekends to be with them). Melania adores her staff, and they rely on her not only to be fair with them but also to have their backs. Grisham and the rest of the staff didn't need to press the issue any further—Melania listened, took it in, and believed them. Ask anyone in the White House, and they will tell you the first lady is ferociously devoted to her team—the ones you ask who work in the West Wing will say it wistfully, in a way that says they wished their boss was the same. "You don't fuck with the first lady," someone who works in the White House told me. When Ricardel decided to retaliate, she basically signed her own exit papers from the Trump administration.

Ricardel didn't stop her vengeance even when she got home, doubling down instead. She spread stories about Melania's staff's behavior on the trip to Africa, saying they were partying too hard and making themselves look bad as representatives of the White House. That was the final straw. If there's something that inflames Melania's quiet demeanor, it's rumors about her that aren't true. Since the days of the campaign, she's been quite forthright about how she hates people who make things up about her. "Only I have my story," she once said, "only I know the truth." Melania's tight-knit staff is intensely loyal to her, and she has made it clear that loyalty is a two-way deal.

Melania went right to the president, telling him about Ricardel's behavior, what had happened on the trip, and how she was leaking nasty and untrue rumors about the East Wing. Trump tried to calm her, telling her he would take care of it. However, Ricardel technically fell under Bolton, and Trump wasn't all that interested in telling his new national security adviser what to do with his staff. The whole thing felt dramatic and uncomfortable. When he told Bolton that Melania wanted him to do something about Ricardel, Bolton responded that she was a trusted aide and he wanted to keep her on. Trump let it go.

But Melania didn't.

As Ricardel stayed on and the stories and friction continued, Melania again spoke to her husband, insisting he do something about this bad apple in his West Wing. Ricardel was also infuriating others with her leaks to the press about other administration officials she apparently had it in for, ones she crossed paths with on a daily basis, including then–chief of staff John Kelly. A White House official confirmed that Ricardel "liked to pick fights" and that her "personality isn't for everyone." Ironically, Ricardel and Melania had never met in person; Melania was acting only on what she had been told. But that was enough for her.

When Trump once again didn't move fast enough for the first lady's liking and Ricardel was clearly still employed, Melania and Grisham crafted the statement, which was released to the public. They didn't give the West Wing a warning it was coming—even the president was blindsided.

By the following day, Ricardel was packing her office in boxes, essentially fired by the president, who had no other choice. To keep her on would be to publicly ignore this powerful pronouncement from his wife. He couldn't do that. It was negotiating power that really only Melania had.

"That was something," one Melania observer said of the whole debacle.

It's not unusual for a first lady to weigh in on staffers she doesn't like. Nancy Reagan's famous distaste for Ronald Reagan's chief of staff, Don Regan, led to his firing in 1987. Nancy, who always looked out first and foremost for the well-being of her husband, had a frosty relationship with Regan, but it boiled over after a screaming match on the phone about whether the president should participate in a press conference. Nancy thought he should not; Regan believed he should. In the end, as with Melania, the president sided with his wife.

The only big difference between Nancy and Melania was that Nancy carried out her mission behind closed doors; Melania did hers in a very public way. It was the first time that Melania exercised her power as first lady, and people both in the White House and outside it took notice. Most everyone who had taken a surface pass at Melania's personality deemed her quiet and uninvolved, more interested in her clothes and privacy than matters of state and country. With the Ricardel episode, it was clear they were wrong.

Not only did Melania have power and influence with the president, she perhaps had more of both than anyone else in the entire White House. Melania's team was small, but it was mighty. And Melania's go-to mouthpiece, Stephanie Grisham, was as fearless as her boss— and the president was about to take notice.

15

The East Wing,
the White House's Tightest Ship

"We are all very, very loyal to her."

—STEPHANIE GRISHAM

Stephanie Grisham came into Trump world early. She worked in GOP politics in her home state of Arizona for years, and for a time jumped onto Mitt Romney's campaign in 2012. But when she offered to help the nascent Donald Trump campaign with a speech he did in Phoenix, wrangling press and acting as a conduit between Trump staff and local media, Grisham caught the Trump bug. She decided that day: I'm going to work for him.

By mid-2015 she was onboard officially, working with the media as Trump traversed the country, building momentum, picking off his fellow Republican contenders until he was the only one, and, ultimately, beating Hillary Clinton to become president. Grisham in the meantime earned her stripes with the Trump campaign press-embed reporters. She was well liked and tenacious. There's a story told about her that on one late night when there was a hiccup with the press plane, Grisham served the media warm chocolate chip cookies and milk. It's true.

Grisham was rewarded with a role in the White House, getting the title of deputy press secretary, working under Sean Spicer, who was then the press secretary, though not for long (he lasted just six months). But in February 2017, barely into her West Wing tenure, Grisham caught the eye of the first lady. Melania had gotten some heat for not being there to greet the Japanese prime minister, Shinzō Abe, and his wife, Akie Abe, when they arrived in Washington, D.C., for a visit with Trump at the White House. Typically, a first lady is around to entertain a visiting spouse accompanying her husband on an official visit. It's not a rule per se, but it's definitely recommended protocol. Melania was MIA for Mrs. Abe, who toured Washington by herself. (It should be noted that Melania has since gotten quite good at being present for leader visits, and she's adept at hosting other spouses for tea or lunch in the Red, Blue, or Green Room while the heads of state hold meetings in the Oval Office.) Melania did meet the Abes at Andrews Air Force Base for the ride on Air Force One down to Mar-a-Lago, where the Japanese leader would stay for the weekend at Trump's invitation, but the story of the first lady of the United States missing the first opportunity to host a fellow first lady was already out there—mostly because I reported it. I will add here that the blowback to my pointing out Melania's faux pas triggered the only call I have ever gotten from Air Force One, which is kind of scary and enthralling at the same time. I was chewed out by Katie Walsh, Spicer and Reince Priebus's top comms deputy, who tried to spin me that it was fine and that Melania was with Mrs. Abe on the plane and would remain with her for the duration of the weekend, and so I should correct the language of my previous piece. I did not.

It was Grisham who stepped in on the ground to help Melania with Mrs. Abe for that weekend in Palm Beach. As usual, Trump's team had overlooked the first lady's needs in terms of communications, press releases, and official statements on the visit, so Grisham gathered a press pool for the ladies' visit to a local Japanese garden. Grisham hopped in and Melania was grateful for it. One month later, she tapped her as East Wing communications director, and Grisham happily left the discombobulated West Wing chaos of Spicer and Steve Bannon and Priebus and Ivanka and Jared et al. and moved down the long hallway into a spacious office on the second floor of the East Wing, right next door to the office of her new boss. In her office to this day hangs a framed clip about Grisham's hire in *The Washington Post*, autographed in big black marker by the president, saying how proud he is of her.

Grisham is literally Melania's first line of defense. She's her guard dog, her mouthpiece, and, at times, her confidante. The two communicate throughout the day, sometimes in person, often on the phone, and frequently by text, which Melania does oftentimes with emoji— conveying her happiness, disappointment, or surprise.

Grisham has always been emphatic about how real and "down to earth" Melania actually is, once telling me, "You meet her, and she's the one saying, 'Can I get you a Coke? Do you want a coffee? Are you comfortable? Is it warm enough?'" It's a side that Grisham and I often go ten rounds about because Grisham rarely lets the public see it. There's a tendency for Grisham to want it both ways about her boss. She'll complain that we (CNN/media at large) don't tell the real story about who Melania is and only focus on the more salacious headlines (not true, by the way), but then Grisham guards the first lady and her privacy like a bulldog, which, let's face it, makes it a challenge to showcase who she "really" is. Grisham also says Melania is very funny, and one of their favorite pastimes is to "laugh" at the rumors and false stories about the first lady. I find that puzzling, but I think it's also an indication, again, of just how little Melania cares what people think and how little effort she and Grisham put into correcting the record. "I've learned from her that we don't have to tell everybody everything. We just don't. And it works out fine," Grisham told me.

While the slings and arrows fly in the West Wing, with massive numbers of staff departures and feuding factions, the East Wing is indeed quite drama-free. Melania's chief of staff, Reynolds, who worked in the George W. Bush administration in the White House Visitors

Office and therefore had some experience in the White House, is so quiet and unassuming that when I first saw her, carrying Melania's Birkin bag and toting a long coat over her arm, I assumed she was one of her personal assistants, but then I learned that (a) Melania doesn't have personal assistants and (b) holy shit, that woman is her chief of staff. Reynolds is from Ohio, where she was once a schoolteacher and also at one point ran an upscale events company with two friends. She is simple in her look: minimal makeup, bland but very chic style, a tight strawberry blond bob often tucked behind her ears. A mother of three young children, she spends most weekends, with Melania's blessing, back home with them and her husband in Ohio. But she is the one in the East Wing to convey Melania's schedule to her, explain her options for trips and events, inform her of the people who have reached out, address her correspondence requests, and take care of her day-to-day responsibilities. To give you an indication of just how quiet Reynolds is (ghostlike is not a stretch), I have been on the FLOTUS beat for almost three years now, and, besides a nod of hello here and there, I have never had a full conversation with her, despite my requests for an interview.

Also on the East Wing team is Melania's social secretary, Rickie Lloyd. Melania's hiring of Rickie was textbook Melania. Though she had been given numerous suggestions for whom to tap as her social secretary, a crucially important job in any White House since the social secretary oversees every event, from a two-person luncheon with the president in the Oval Office to the Easter Egg Roll for thousands to a state dinner, Melania didn't want to listen to the advice of people she didn't know—especially Washington people, whom she *really* didn't know. The job is also essential in that the person holding it (and there has been a White House social secretary since 1901, when Theodore Roosevelt created the role) must oversee and work in tandem with the massive White House residence staff.

So, instead of taking anyone's word for whom she should pick, as she and Trump dined inside the Capitol building on Inauguration Day at the traditional luncheon with Congress, just minutes after her husband had taken the oath of office, Melania took note of how smoothly things were flowing for this meal of tradition and importance, with hundreds of the most VIP of VIP guests. The courses were tasty and served in a timely manner, the dishware was flawless, the flowers impeccable, and the details, from linens to place cards, were very much to her liking. That was all Rickie, who at the time was an executive with Design Cuisine, a posh Washington catering company that handles all the "best" events and dinner parties. If you were on the social circuit in D.C., you knew Rickie. After several interviews—one of which was held in New York City in Melania's home office at Trump Tower—Rickie was hired. It also didn't hurt that Rickie was married to Thomas Lloyd, a grandson of Bunny Mellon, the wealthy American benefactor whose friendship and influence with Jackie Kennedy resulted in the creation and design of the White House Rose Garden.

A prim and proper middle-aged beauty whose hemlines never rise above her knee and whose brown hair is often pulled back under a headband, an Hermès scarf around her neck, Rickie can often be spotted in the background of most events, never stepping into the spotlight occupied by her boss and always creating the environment requested by Melania. For Halloween, Melania said she wanted "spooky," and Rickie made it so. For her first state dinner (for France) as first lady, Melania wanted white and gold and tasteful, and Rickie did just that, using cream linens and ivory floral arrangements, gilded china, and tall white-tapered candles.

The three women, Grisham, Reynolds, and Niceta, are essentially the core of Melania's staff; the other five or so members fan out from there. Grisham, for instance, has a communications assistant, Annie LeHardy, a young woman she hired from the West Wing's press office, who travels with the press and oversees all the crucial media movements when Melania has events. Annie has taken on more responsibility since Grisham became Trump's press secretary and White House communications director in July 2019. She's still (also) Melania's chief spokeswoman. It's a lot.

The new role was offered to Grisham at Melania's urging. She was keenly aware that her husband needed someone like Grisham—or, it turns out, Grisham herself—to combat his negative press and to defend him. Trump knew Grisham was loyal; with the exception of his social media director, Dan Scavino, no one in the West Wing had been there as long as she had. Also, Grisham had been in the room many times with Trump and Melania, she had witnessed their inter-actions, their movements, their conversations, and nothing escaped her—she was like a vault. Trump could not say the same about so many other members of his staff, whose leaks from the West Wing were so frequent and plentiful it made the place look more like a sieve than a tightly functioning office, the most powerful one in the land. Trump hated that. He liked Grisham, and he knew that if Melania recommended that he hire her, he should hire her. In their marriage, what Melania wanted, Melania often got.

For her part, Grisham has wanted to be White House press secretary since as long as she knew what the job was, at least for the bulk of her two-decades-long career. Many young people know they want to be a doctor, a lawyer, a scientist, a ballerina—Grisham wanted to be a press sec.

It should be noted that Trump boasts about his business acumen, but so far he has not been able to build a properly functioning West Wing communications shop, or a soup-to-nuts staff. People come and go, leaks abound, nominees are scuttled after embarrassing informa-tion turns up in their background checks. Melania, on the other hand, who is known for being arm candy, is the one who has built a highly successful East Wing. Her appointees have not only stayed, they've stayed loyal, which is quite a feat in a shark tank like Washington, D.C.

16

The Marriage

"It's not always pleasant, of course, but I know what is right and what is wrong and what is true and not true."

—MELANIA TRUMP

It is tradition, as are most things inside the White House, that the president of the United States rides in the same vehicle as the first lady of the United States on the evening he delivers what is arguably one of the most important speeches in politics. It's not necessarily written in stone, but it is how it has always been. But less than an hour before President Trump was set to depart the White House for the two-and-a-half-mile trip to the U.S. Capitol Building to deliver his very first State of the Union address to Congress, the staff got word: she's not riding with him.

That night, as the message made its way from Melania down through her staff to his staff to the Secret Service, residence staff, and on, no one said a word. Too nervous to chatter on about the lord and lady of the house's marital tension, the silence as the White House prepped for Melania's solo departure was deafening. It fell to Reynolds, Melania's chief of staff, to share the news with Trump's chief of staff at the time, John Kelly. Everything about this was uncomfortable, but no one had the nerve to speak up or ask questions—it was what Melania wanted, and therefore it would be done.

Normally, when the first couple arrives at the Capitol, together, the first lady veers into an anteroom to wait until the speech is about to begin before taking her seat with guests in the gallery. The president glad-hands on arrival, chatting with congressmen and senators, the vice president, the speaker of the House. He does the "work" of laying out his thoughts and plans for the country he oversees; the first lady is there, as she often is, in a supporting role, to back up his words, supply the human side (again, as expected), and generally look pretty, smile, and wave.

Not exactly heavy lifting for Melania. The only problem was, on January 30, 2018, the night the State of the Union was to be delivered, she didn't much feel like supporting her husband.

The Trumps hadn't been seen together in public since December 31. On January 12, *The Wall Street Journal* broke the story that a porn star named Stormy Daniels (real name: Stephanie Clifford) had been paid $130,000 in October 2016 by Michael Cohen, Trump's longtime lawyer and fixer, to sign a contract pledging to keep her mouth shut about an affair she alleges that she had with Donald Trump in July 2006, which would have been eighteen months after he and Melania got married and four months after Melania gave birth to Barron. It was a bombshell of a scoop, with all sorts of complex legal implications for the president, but it was a gut punch to the first lady.

It was the biggest speech of Trump's tenure so far, his first State of the Union, but CNN's coverage led with my breaking news that Melania had driven separately from her husband, with video of her motorcade speeding up Pennsylvania Avenue toward the Capitol. Several minutes later, there was live video of the president, getting into the Beast, alone. It was a stark portrait of the lonely, chastened, most powerful man in the world. With one swift last-minute decision, Melania had delivered a punishing blow to the potency of the president on one of his most important nights.

Her spokeswoman, Grisham, told me that the reason Melania went separately to the Capitol was so she could spend more "quality time" with the fifteen special guests she had invited to attend the speech in her box in the gallery.

Another part of the evening's tradition is that first ladies host guests in their box who are typically referred to during the president's speech. That night, Melania was hosting a marine who had been injured in battle, a family who had lost a family member to an MS-13 gang member, one of the founders of the rescue group the Cajun Navy, and a New Mexico police officer who, with his wife, adopted a baby from parents who were addicted to opioids.

Grisham's reasoning was fair, but it's also fair to point out the fact Melania had already broken with tradition once that evening by hosting a private reception for all the guests at the White House on her own—another independent move that had nothing to do with Trump's separate meet and greets for guests in the Oval Office, which Melania did not attend. However, according to Grisham, the first lady felt the need to host a separate event, one that offered more "personal" exposure to the honorees of the evening. It was odd, and an excessive flex of her doing something by herself, no question—especially since, once she and the guests arrived at the Capitol, they had *another* private reception (the third!), this time with Melania and Karen Pence in an anteroom near the Capitol gallery. That evening, the special guests of the president and first lady were more like children of divorced parents, shuttled between two events marking the same achievement, only one was with Mom and one with Dad.

Melania had steeled herself against all sorts of stories of infidelity involving her husband through the almost two decades they had been together and had weathered them in the way she best knew: she ignored them, publicly at least. She knew well the man she married: that he was no arbiter of moral fortitude, that he had a shoddy track record with fidelity. But the past few weeks that Melania had endured were so publicly scathing and deeply humiliating that she was angry with him more because of what he had exposed to the world than because of what he was alleged to have done with Daniels.

One source who knows Melania well said to me, "She's not locked herself in a golden bedroom somewhere to cry her eyes out that he was possibly unfaithful, if that's what anyone might be thinking."

"To be with a man as my husband is, you need to know who you are," Melania has said. "You need to have a very independent life as well, and supporting him." But that night, she didn't really feel all that much like supporting him. In fact, the two hadn't been spotted together publicly for a month; they were last seen walking into the annual New Year's Eve party at Mar-a-Lago, Melania wearing a sparkly pink sequin dress, with an expression that was neither sparkly nor festive.

There was nothing pink or feminine about her look at the State of the Union. When she was announced entering the gallery, she stood atop the stairs, giving her open-close hand wave, wearing a bright white Christian Dior pantsuit with matching white button-down shirt. It smacked of suffragette symbolism and, yes, possibly resistance, maybe even a nod to Hillary Clinton's favored ubiquitous menswear. Whatever she was trying to say with that suit, and she was trying to say something, it had a message, and the message had nothing to do with supporting Trump.

The white suit was just one small act of defiance, perhaps, but is something to analyze in the greater orbit of Melania moments, especially those moments in the first months of 2018, when story after salacious story about her husband's alleged affairs filled the headlines.

On January 20, ten days before the State of the Union, Melania posted a photo on her Twitter and Instagram accounts marking the one-year anniversary of her husband's becoming president. The photo and the caption were striking: neither had anything to do with Donald Trump: "This has been a year filled with many wonderful moments. I've enjoyed the people I've been lucky enough to meet throughout our great country & the world!" were the words that accompanied a picture of her from Inauguration Day 2017, smiling in her baby blue Ralph Lauren suit and matching leather gloves, arm in arm with a tall, handsome-looking military escort, hat positioned low, covering his eye, who was definitely not her husband. With this simple post, Melania was saying something about her mood, her year, and her emotional state. She was marking the one-year anniversary of her own role, no one else's. She was telling everyone, I can and will, if I need to, do this by myself.

Two days later, January 22, neither she nor Trump would publicly acknowledge another anniversary, this one more personal to the couple: their thirteenth wedding anniversary. The absence of a post or a tweet was even more conspicuous to a country coming off eight years of the mushy anniversary messages of love between Barack and Michelle Obama. Trump and Melania were crickets.

And then, later that same evening, I reported that Melania was canceling her trip to Davos, Switzerland, to join the president while he attended the World Economic Forum. I made sure the story was accurate, double- and triple-checking sources, because just the week before I had reported, with White House confirmation, that Melania *would* be going to Davos and that, per her spokeswoman, she would be there to show support for her husband, as she had done on his previous international trips up to that point. Not so much anymore, apparently.

Before my story on Melania's trip cancellation went live, I asked Grisham to comment on the reason, and she said simply that the decision was based on "scheduling and logistical issues." I pressed more, laying it on thick, asking if the first lady would be disappointed that she wouldn't be present to watch as her husband spread his message of making America great again abroad to a powerful mix of business and financial leaders and to take in another important milestone of the Trump presidency? She paused and reiterated: "scheduling and logistical issues." I had offered her the opportunity to answer a different way, and she didn't.

By January 26, as Trump was returning from the Davos trip, Grisham tried to put out the growing fire of speculation about the state of the first couple's marriage—over the weekend it had reached satire status in a skit on *Saturday Night Live*. "BREAKING: The laundry list of salacious & flat-out false reporting about Mrs. Trump by tabloid publications and TV shows has seeped into 'mainstream media' reporting. She is focused on her family & role as FLOTUS— not the unrealistic scenarios being peddled daily by the fake news," Grisham tweeted.

She was yelling into the wind. The story wasn't extinguishable. In many ways, however, I understood what Grisham was saying, as I watched and read and listened to other reporters from different out- lets and networks than my own catapult their version of events into the thick soup of gossip and innuendo about the Trump marriage. We are a nation built in many ways on popular culture, and we have a popular culture president.

Everyone was hearing something, about the prenup, about her moving back to New York, about her trying to sell her jewelry, about how she's interviewing divorce lawyers. And a personal favorite, one that made the rounds among my sources for months and months, and which some people still believe to this today: Melania was living not at the White House but, instead, at a home occupied by her parents and her son in Potomac, Maryland. And on and on. All I could do was dig, and report, and dig, and report—and I honestly couldn't find substantial evidence of any of those things, including the house, which had then reached urban legend status. Believe me, it wasn't for lack of trying.

January was rough. Melania was starting to emerge from the Daniels saga, but doing so slowly, having not quite found it in her to completely rejoin the program. "Not good," was how I was told things were when I checked in with White House sources on her mood. While outwardly her willingness to accompany her husband on a day trip to Cincinnati, Ohio, a week after the State of the Union to champion his new economic plan signaled support, Melania actu- ally used the occasion not to be present for her husband's speech but to create an agenda of her own.

When Air Force One landed in Ohio, she didn't hold his hand while walking down the steps, instead keeping her arms at her sides, her trusty coat-over-shoulders move concealing her hands. At the foot of the stairs down from Air Force One, the couple split up; she sped off in her own motorcade, bound for Cincinnati Children's Hospital to visit with medical experts and ill children. He went to his speech. Though they met back at the plane for the flight home later that day, Melania arrived first, sequestering herself aboard Air Force One until he got there.

"This isn't a couple who is joined at the hip" was a familiar refrain from someone who knows both of the Trumps and had witnessed them spending periods of time apart and still very much functioning in their brand of marriage. "She never feels like she has to do whatever it is he is doing. It's not like that. That's not their marriage; that's never been their relationship."

"I have my own mind. I am my own person, and I think my husband likes that about me," Melania has said. But with each public fray, Trump appeared in the doghouse, something he was maybe accepting but definitely not liking.

On the Saturday night before Valentine's Day, the first couple went to dinner together at the BLT Prime by David Burke steakhouse inside the Trump International Hotel in Washington, the only restaurant they have ever gone to for "date night" since moving to D.C. It was a sign that perhaps Melania's iciness was thawing. They chatted with each other, talked to the chef, to the staff; Trump had his usual: shrimp cocktail, boneless New York steak, and french fries. Melania ordered her favorite fish: Dover sole.

By Valentine's Day, she had resumed her somewhat normal first lady public schedule, visiting sick children at the National Institutes of Health's Children's Inn in Bethesda, Maryland, about a thirty-minute motorcade ride from the White House. I covered that appearance and spent most of the time just a few feet from the first lady. Melania seemed happy to me, but then again, she almost always lights up around kids. It's one of the few times she lets her guard down, when that Slovenian stoicism melts away.

Unfortunately, the warmth and happiness that Melania exudes

when she is around children is not something the public necessarily gets to see, because her husband usually sucks up all the oxygen in the daily news cycle. Also, at this point, she hadn't fully formed an official platform or agenda and rarely made remarks at these events and visits, making television coverage difficult to obtain. It's left to those of us members of the press who cover the first lady's events, usually me and five to ten other people, to tell the story of her events and visits as best we can, good or bad.

Melania genuinely enjoys spending time around children. Her whole demeanor changes. She laughs, she hugs, she gets down on the floor and plays or works her fingers around arts and crafts or other projects, as she did that day, making Valentine's cookies with a little girl named Lucie, who at nine years old had already made twenty-nine visits to the Children's Inn so she could receive treatment and be studied for the rare immunodeficiency disease from which she suffers. "Do you like to play and run around with your friends?" Melania asked her, as the two rolled out dough and sprinkled heart shapes with colored sugar. Clearly relaxed, enjoying herself, Melania visited another group of young patients, passing out White House–branded Valentine's cards of her own, printed with red and pink hearts. One young man in the room gave Melania a pair of black Children's Inn sunglasses, to which the first lady, known for wearing her giant shades on most occasions, said, "These are very fashionable. I love sunglasses."

At the end of her visit, Melania was presented with a painting of a colorful heart and the words "Happy Valentine's Day, Mrs. Trump." I watched her face as she looked at it. We all did. There had been no recognition from her husband so far that day about how much he loved her or how special she was. Here, these sick little kids, unaware of the soap opera story line Melania had endured during the past few weeks, had taken time to paint a piece of artwork for her, a big red heart smack dab in the middle of it.

Whatever the gesture meant to her in the broader context of her current state of emotional affairs, she was clearly moved, her voice quavered slightly as she thanked the children and staff. "I will treasure all of this," Melania said, accepting her painting from the kids. Her new friend Lucie rushed in for a hug.

Melania and Trump would not publicly acknowledge the holiday. My requests to the White House communications departments in both the East Wing and West Wing as to how the first couple planned to celebrate went unanswered.

Two days later, as the dust appeared to be possibly settling on Stormy Daniels, another cheating scandal emerged. This time, the other woman was Karen McDougal, a former *Playboy* playmate whom Trump was alleged to have seen for several months in 2006 and 2007, even spending time in Melania's New York City home when she wasn't there. Again, Trump denied the affair. The story broke in a *New Yorker* piece written by Ronan Farrow; the tale of the tryst was detailed and explicit, and the damage in terms of humiliation and emotional toll would be far more intense for Melania than the one-night fling Daniels had alleged.

That same afternoon as the McDougal story came out, Melania and Trump were slated to go to Mar-a-Lago for the weekend, but as the press gathered in their usual post to watch them depart the South Lawn on Marine One, a regular occurrence not only for the Trumps as they left for a trip but also for most modern first couples for the last two decades, only Trump emerged from the White House.

Surprise. Melania had once again taken a separate mode of transport, leaving Trump alone for a walk of shame across the lawn and a solo ride on Marine One to Andrews Air Force Base in nearby Maryland.

"It was easier to meet at the plane at Andrews" was the reason Grisham gave me when I asked why Melania had opted not to take the helicopter with her husband, and she did not explain further how driving eighteen minutes on the road with the added staff and expense of law enforcement escorts in the motorcade was "easier" than taking a four-minute helicopter ride above traffic. Also, according to my calendar, she had no public schedule of events that day, so there was nothing she was rushing to or from to make the plane. In that moment—again, purely visual, not verbally spelled out—it was apparent that Melania was not keen to do the couples' walk across the lawn of the White House that day, or maybe ever again.

It's an iconic first-couple moment, the walk to Marine One. Those of us remember when Hillary Clinton and Bill Clinton walked toward the massive chopper after news of the Monica Lewinsky scandal emerged, Chelsea Clinton walking between them, her hands linked on one side to Mom and the other side to Dad. Jackie Kennedy, through her husband's long-rumored affairs, became, like Melania, adept at manipulating images to portray her solitude, her loneliness. She wasn't a fan of putting Caroline and John Jr. in front of the cameras, but she would on occasion make sure there were plenty of shots of the three of them alone, without the president, to shore up public sympathy.

Being first lady is a symbolic role; it's not made to include the complicated gray areas of reality or private emotions or personal woe. The first lady's job is to be a wife—devoted but not overly so. She's supposed to be supportive but not cloying. She is expected to accompany but not get in the way. She's the partner, but she should also have her own agenda. When you think about it, it's sort of a massive burden, a fight between what you want the public to see and what you are going through in private. The persona she must carry with her always is a weight; one can only assume it gets even heavier when, emotionally, the last thing she wants to do is pretend everything is fine, when she really can't stand to be in the same room as her spouse.

That Melania defied the normal expectation, that she didn't get in the motorcade with him, that she didn't go with him on a trip, that she wouldn't fake a walk together across the lawn—all of that makes her incredibly modern. Melania Trump is the first first lady to put her hand up and say, no, I'm not going to do this, even if I'm "supposed to."

While the media went gaga over another public snub, I kept thinking to myself: Why shouldn't Melania be able to be pissed? Should she maybe even be applauded for not doing the doting-political-wife thing that America has witnessed so many times after a man in a position of power has done some abhorrent thing? Isn't the fact that she is humiliated and angry and annoyed that—again—she's faced with this a sufficient explanation for why she doesn't want to spend one-on-one time with him for the cameras?

"For all the talk of progressiveness in Washington, political insiders have a preset and admittedly chauvinistic viewpoint for what the role of the first lady should be," a former staffer tells me, "so when someone like Melania Trump threatens to smash that narrative, they try to tear her down." The fact that she refused the grip-and-grin with Trump, holding his hand while the cameras were on them, likely dropping it when they were out of sight, felt utterly authentic. For a first lady that people complain is too icy, too removed behind her sunglasses, she was being remarkably candid and transparent. But for whatever reason—she's the unsmiling model, the vapid trophy wife, the woman who married "him"—the public has trouble connecting Melania Trump with the idea of authenticity. They can't see past the narrative they want to believe, that has been spun along political and partisan lines.

Upon landing in Florida for that long weekend, after his solo walk of shame and her private motorcade, Melania put duty ahead of her feelings. The Parkland school massacre had happened just before the trip, and the Trumps went to local hospitals to meet with victims, doctors, and first responders. At those sorts of visits, and there have been plenty of them, sadly, Trump is often softer and more vulnerable than he is outside of tragedy. This side of her husband is something Melania has always been attracted to, says a close personal friend; she is drawn to his sweetness. At Mar-a-Lago, after their afternoon hospital visit, the Trumps sat together, the two of them alone on a bench outside one of the ballrooms, where a preplanned, disco-themed event was taking place. They were huddled together, laughing quietly, looking cozy after a day that had begun with brutal headlines and separate transportation. It appeared to end with bonding. By Sunday night they were back in Washington at the White House, she in a glamorous and sexy black lace gown, he in a tuxedo, as they strode into the State Dining Room to host the Governors' Ball, together.

The roller-coaster ride of their relationship continued throughout that spring, but Melania carried on, as she typically did in her marriage to Trump, going about her business and her schedule, not worrying about his, focusing on Barron and keeping him protected from the headlines as best she could. Trump's moods, and the drama of the legal issues conjoined with Daniels and the Russia investigation, his record-breaking staff turnover in the West Wing, and his blistering attacks on enemies, weren't anywhere near the top of her list of concerns. "Melania is in no way codependent on anyone, her husband included," one of her close personal friends tells me. She soldiered on, relying on that friend and a small handful of other confidants, many of them still in New York City.

On March 22, another bombshell. Karen McDougal's interview with Anderson Cooper aired on CNN. The former *Playboy* model was trying to fight a catch-and-kill deal she had made with American Media Inc., the publisher of the *National Enquirer*, which purchased the story of her alleged affair with Trump for $150,000 and then spiked it when he ran for president.

To Cooper, McDougal revealed details of what she says was a ten-month tryst with Trump, one that she says included "feelings." McDougal said she and Trump saw each other a minimum of five times per month, starting in the summer of 2006, just weeks after Barron was born. "Did Donald Trump ever say to you that he loved you?" Cooper asked. "All the time. He always told me he loved me," McDougal replied. "When I look back, where I was then, I know it's wrong. Like, I'm really sorry for that," said McDougal, who said she never really talked about Melania with Trump, but that he once gave her a tour of their penthouse, pointing out a room that was Melania's, where she went when she wanted to be "alone." Via CNN, she apologized to Melania. "I'm sorry. I wouldn't want it done to me. I'm sorry."

The very next day, Melania was due to give a speech at the State Department honoring, of all things, the annual Women of Courage Award. I was curious if she would back out, considering that the salacious interview with her husband's alleged mistress had aired just hours before. But Melania did not cancel and, instead, focused her brief remarks on the meaning of courage. "Courage sets apart those who believe in higher calling and those who act on it. It takes courage not only to see wrong, but strive to right it. Courage is what sets apart the heroes from the rest; it is equal part bravery and nobility." The speech was written in large part by Grisham, by now a trusted aide; Melania had made only a few changes.

Outwardly it may appear as though Trump has the power to play God with her emotional well-being, but I suspect that it's a very different power dynamic on the inside. Trump, by several accounts, is desperate for her approval, and he relies on her—her punishing coldness in the wake of the affair headlines and rumors took a toll on him. His moods in the West Wing at the time rolled from aloof and distracted to straight-up sour and fuming.

According to Bob Woodward's book *Fear,* Trump was concerned about how Melania would react to the stories of dalliances with Russian prostitutes, telling his lawyers, "I've got enough problems with Melania and girlfriends and all that. I don't need any more. I can't have Melania hearing about that." However, a former West Wing staffer who was frequently present in the Oval Office with the president told me that when the story about Trump and the alleged Russian hookers broke, the lewd details of the "dossier" leaking (no pun intended) to include accusations of golden showers, Trump actually called Melania to tell her, incredulous to the point of laughter. "You won't believe this," the source tells me he told her. She thought it was funny, too, and the two of them, together, remarked how ridiculous it was.

There are those who see Melania as the complicit wife, sticking around in a damaged marriage for money, perhaps, or power, or whatever the trade-off might be. And there might be some truth in that.

There are many women who marry for money and who, because of it, turn a blind eye to infidelity—or worse. Part of the country was slim on empathy for Melania, as they often were, pegging her emotional maturity at the same level as her husband's, which was basically that of a petulant child. Marist even conducted a poll asking respondents whether Melania should leave Trump—43 percent said she should stay, but more than one in three thought that she should go.

But Melania, say friends, wasn't ever going to leave. "What about after the White House?" people would ask me at every D.C. cocktail party or soccer game with our kids, desperate to know what I knew. "Would Melania Trump leave Donald Trump?" was everyone's favorite parlor game for the many months during the Daniels and Mc-Dougal scandals—add to those scandals the white State of the Union suit, the canceled trips, the curtailed public appearances, the solo motorcades, and it was enough to make a very unsexy Washington somewhat hot and bothered. "Is she going to divorce him?"

But I would say then what I still say now: "Maybe. But I don't think so." I refer back to the fact that Melania was raised in a tight-knit family, that her parents are still together, that she has faith in her Catholicism, that she is a product of where she came from, and that she typifies an old Slovenian proverb: the woman of the house controls three of its corners; the man, just one. Melania is definitely a woman very much in control of her three corners.

17

A Room of Her Own

Reporter: "Do you love your husband?"
Melania Trump: "Yes. We are fine. Yes."

Melania and Donald Trump are the only first couple since the Kennedys and the Johnsons to have separate bedrooms in the White House (excluding the handful of months in 1998 when Bill Clinton was forced to sleep on the sofa in the private study attached to the master bedroom, having been kicked out by Hillary after his affair with Monica Lewinsky came to light).

Their relationship might not take the form that most marriages or relationships do (by all accounts, Trump didn't have separate bedrooms with his two previous wives; it's worth noting that those relationships lasted nowhere near as long as his current one), but that doesn't negate that, for them, it is what works, and—with her tendency to need alone time and his to be bolstered by sycophants—it is strong.

The Trumps live their lives with a good deal of physical detachment. That includes their separate bedrooms, a setup they have had in place for many years. Especially after Stormy and McDougal, there was heightened hyperbole that Melania had somehow kicked him out of their marital bed, assigned him to the doghouse. However, I think it's important to note here that the reality of that scenario simply isn't possible. Trump still occupies the master bedroom in the executive residence, and it is Melania who doesn't sleep there, according to those familiar with the layout.

"There are classified structural assets [in the master bedroom], essential to protective needs," a Secret Service agent who worked the presidential detail said. "Since he was at the White House first, and there are some major security protocols in place in the presidential bedroom, he is more than likely in there." The other big bedroom on the second level of the residence is the Queen's Bedroom, but a source tells me it has a "horrible bathroom" connected to it and the decor—pink, with a canopy bed—is neither the style of Trump nor Melania. The other bedroom on the second floor of the residence is the Lincoln Bedroom—again, not an option for long-term stay. (Though the Lincoln Bedroom was a favorite place for the Clintons to host guests.)

There are, however, two smaller bedrooms on the floor, each with a connecting bathroom, and those could be an option for Melania, but that's not where she is. Melania likes her privacy, she likes her space, so she selected living space on the third floor of the executive residence, not the second. I'm told she prefers to stay in the room Marian Robinson, Michelle Obama's mother, lived in during the Obama years.

It's more like a small two-bedroom apartment than a simple bedroom. It has its own master suite and another, smaller bedroom, plus a living room area and two bathrooms.

Mrs. Robinson may have avoided the spotlight during the years she lived in the White House, but she was a beloved and constant presence to the staff and the Secret Service. They all adored her. She was friendly but sassy, and she had her own life in Washington separate from that of her family, and she had her own rules that she refused to change, even though she had agreed to be a live-in grandma. (For example, she would occasionally step out onto the patio area of the third floor for a cigarette.)

Michelle Obama said that the fact her mother had her own space on a different floor than the rest of the family made her feel slightly better about marginalizing her independence for eight years. "There are many times when she drops off the kids, we hang out and talk and catch up, and then she's like, 'I'm going home.' And she walks upstairs," Michelle once told Oprah Winfrey about her mother's White House habits.

From what I have gathered, Melania also appreciates the privacy afforded by the third floor, which is also where she has her "glam room," the space where she does her hair and makeup, located on the east side. Someone familiar with her habits says she often likes to wear a silk robe while she gets herself together, a garment she is prone to wear when she is home and begins or ends her day. Again, the third floor feels more like a private space in which she can do just that. She can also use what was once the Carter Doll Room (a fan of dolls, this is where Rosalynn Carter kept some of her collection) for her dressing room and storage for clothing. A private gym is up there too, and it houses Melania's pilates machine, which she uses with some regularity.

The Obamas used some of the third floor's many spare bedrooms for staff "employee quarters"; their chef, Sam Kass, was a frequent overnight guest who happily, and with his boss's invitation, would stay for several nights when workdays went long into the evening. The Trumps, however, have chosen not to use the spare bedrooms in that way. Instead, the empty rooms mostly remain empty. Sometimes Melania's parents will stay there or a friend of hers from New York will come for a visit, but it's rare they are occupied for long periods.

The real secret of the third floor, and probably its peak allure, is the solarium, a massive sun-filled space where, since the beginning of the twentieth century, first families have enjoyed relatively more comfort than in other spaces in the residence. First lady Grace Coolidge was the first to build out the space, calling it her "sky parlor."

Jackie Kennedy turned it into a kindergarten for Caroline and some of her friends, portioning off some of the space with cubbies and a chalkboard; Ronald Reagan liked the natural light and spent most of his recuperation from his gunshot wound in the solarium; the

Clintons loved to use it for family nights and board games. Melania likes it, too. She had it redecorated when she moved in, as she wasn't a fan of the beige and burnt orange palette the Obamas' decorator, Michael S. Smith, had done the room in. Smith, in general, is prone to using earth tones and taupe, an occasional faded sage green; when *Architectural Digest*, the interior-decorating magazine of note, did a feature on Smith's work for the Obamas in the White House, it was photo after photo of brown, beige, orange, and tan. Only the Family Dining Room had bold color, in the form of blue striped wallpaper.

Melania kept very little of the Obama decor, which the Obamas reportedly paid for out of pocket, to the tune of $1.5 million by the end of their eight years in the White House, according to NBC News. (Congress provides $100,000 for each new first family to redecorate the residence to their liking, but Trump, like Obama, didn't use it and personally paid for redecorations.) Melania hired a woman named Tham Kannalikham to overhaul the residence to her liking. Kannalikham was hardly a celebrity designer in the vein of Smith. She had done some work as an in-house designer for Ralph Lauren, mostly decorating his lavish boutiques and showrooms. She is quiet and personable and has maintained an excellent reputation with the White House Historical Association, with which Kannalikham must work to ensure she is respecting the rules and guidelines of decorating the White House. Kannalikham's main point of contact was the White House curator, William Allman, who, though looking forward to retiring after forty years in the job, agreed to stay on to help with the Trumps' transition to moving in. He officially retired in June 2017. As curator, Allman's role was essentially to oversee the museum component of the White House and to ensure that a family could live and work as seamlessly as possible among the American art, treasures, and historical items without disrupting them and while abiding by the family's taste. It should be noted that the White House Historical Association, the nonprofit that Jackie Kennedy started in 1961 to help oversee all aspects of the executive residence, has by several accounts a solid working relationship with Melania. "We love her," one board member told me. It's the historical association that approves and allocates private funds to update certain items in the White House.

Kannalikham's work on the White House residence was mostly done while Melania wasn't even living there yet. She sent detailed instructions, however, with inspirational photos and examples of what she wanted.

For the solarium, as is typical of Melania's aesthetic, most of the furniture is white and warm, the artwork traditional, and the vibe luxe comfort. She has showcased the most stunning part of the room, the view, by not distracting from it with gaudy furnishings and too many knickknacks. The room's massive windows look out to the south all the way past the Washington Monument and beyond; you can even see Reagan National Airport in the distance.

Another bonus of the third floor, and one that appeals to Melania, again for its privacy, is the wide promenade that goes all the way along the uppermost level, running outside on the south side of the White House roof. Unlike the Truman balcony, or really any of the outdoor space below the third floor, the first lady, even the president, can step out on the promenade, which is basically like a big terrace, and be perfectly fine from a safety perspective (although for the president, a Secret Service detail is never too far away). When they're on the promenade, there is no need to shut down pedestrian walkways or close traffic on the busy streets around the perimeter of the White House, as must often occur nowadays when the first lady or the president wants to go outside, even for a few minutes.

Several years ago, when Barbara Bush returned to the White House for the unveiling of George W. Bush's official portrait, she lamented to a staffer how security had changed there since 9/11. Bush used to walk their family dog, Millie, all around the White House grounds, even right up to the gates, where she used to talk to people. "It was such a different world then," she said. Today that's an impossibility, which is why the outdoor space on the third floor is so appreciated by the first family.

The Trumps spend time together when they can, and when they

want to. In the morning, they see each other typically until Trump makes his way to the West Wing, which can sometimes be as late as 10 A.M. During the day, the president calls Melania on the phone when he wants her advice, something he does often.

"Once while I was visiting Melania and Donald, they were both working on separate issues but in the same room at the residence," Melania's close friend tells me of a trip she made down from New York to visit Melania. "I observed him over the course of an hour, look up about every six to seven minutes, and say to her, "'Baby, what do you think, is this guy full of crap? Is he jerking me around?' It was funny and real and very much how he looks to her for her opinion, an opinion which he knows will always be an honest one."

The friendly rapport between the Trumps that some of their friends told me existed might very well be a symptom of their sleeping arrangements and separate quarters. In their Trump Tower penthouse, there are reports that Melania sleeps in a separate bedroom; she definitely has her own office, her own bathroom, her own dressing room, and her own sitting room. Same for Mar-a-Lago, where the Trump family living quarters are only about three thousand square feet, large by American standards, beyond cozy by Trumpian ones. Melania's bedroom there opens up to a balcony that overlooks the grounds of the estate cum private club, all the way to the ocean. Her parents, by the way, have their own suite of rooms at Mar-a-Lago and, like their daughter, choose to spend their time there engaging in leisure activities like going to the spa or sitting in the sun.

Back at the White House, Melania runs her home as traditionally as she is able to, considering Trump's work hours and his obsession with watching television news. For Barron's sake, she wants things— meals, playtime, and so on—to be as comparable to pre-Washington times as possible. Melania redecorated the White House bowling alley, which has been around since the Richard Nixon administration, updating the paint colors and fabrics, redoing the couches in a tufted royal-blue velvet. She even redesigned the actual bowling balls in red, white, and blue, each emblazoned with a drawing of the north entrance of the White House and the words THE PRESIDENT'S HOUSE above. (It's actually known as "the People's House.") Trump even got his own "toy," a $50,000 golf simulator, fitted inside one of the third-floor residence rooms, where he can hit a golf ball toward a large video screen. Trump's version is more sophisticated—and expensive—than the golf simulator Barack Obama had in the White House. (Trump paid for the simulator and its installation from his own funds.) It might seem like an extravagance, but many presidents put in hobby systems at the White House, like Nixon and his bowling alley. It was Obama who turned the White House tennis courts into a full basketball court; Dwight Eisenhower carved out space on the South Lawn for a putting green. Trump's simulator, however, has not cut down on his days spent actually golfing, which three-quarters of the way through 2019 is pushing 180 days.

Much was made of the fact that Trump had a lock put on his bedroom door (even though the Secret Service can break it down at a moment's notice). Clearly these are a man and a woman who like their privacy, and living in the most famous white fishbowl is not going to change that.

18

A Health Crisis

"A sincere thank-you . . . to all who have sent good wishes and prayers!"

—MELANIA TRUMP

It was April 2018 or thereabouts when Melania began experiencing some nagging pain. She visited her doctor and was told that she had a fairly severe issue with one of her kidneys; several more appointments with specialists followed. Her condition, they told her, would require surgery. For an intensely private person like Melania, the idea of undergoing a medical procedure was intimidating and scary; as first lady it was downright daunting. She didn't want anyone to know she was sick, her Slovenian upbringing compelling her to accept the bad news without showing it on her face, rejecting any impulse to slow down or ask for help or show the slightest hint of weakness. She carried the burden of her medical issue mostly on her own shoulders, conferring with her mother and father, her sister, and Trump, while knowing he wasn't comfortable with medical issues. He is famously squeamish about hospitals and doctors and germs—Melania didn't want to alarm him, but she also didn't want to deal with his anxieties. He is prone to stress when it comes to health and well-being. And his concern for her could teeter on obsessive, so she was careful to avoid throwing him into a spiral of worry.

The public didn't know a thing, of course, and she wanted to keep it that way, insisting on maintaining the date she had selected for finally unveiling her first lady initiative, Be Best. She was adamant that the announcement of her program be made in the Rose Garden, a spot more aligned with West Wing importance and sweeping ceremonies for announcing things like Supreme Court justice nominees and the passing of laws—it wasn't really first lady turf. Which is exactly why Melania wanted to do it there.

On a sunny May 7, most of Trump's cabinet, as well as Ivanka Trump and Melania's parents, joined the president in the front rows of the audience and watched as Melania, at this point grinning through near constant discomfort, emerged from the West Wing and walked the length of the colonnade, alone, dressed in her favorite white pencil skirt—likely the same one she wore on "hat" day the month before (along with a $6,000 tan leather trench-style jacket by Ralph Lauren)— to unveil her platform. Be Best was sixteen months in the making, and it was a lot. There were three parts: children's overall well-being, fighting opioid abuse, and focusing on kids' being positive on social media. "I feel strongly that as adults we can and should be best at educating our children about the importance of a healthy and balanced life," she said in her remarks. The title Be Best was immediately ridiculed by the public for its odd grammatical phrasing. "Shouldn't it be, 'Be THE Best?'" people said. Or, possibly, "Be YOUR Best?" Yes, it probably should. But it wasn't. Again, Melania cared little about what people were saying about the title; she was riding a surge of popularity, spurred on by how she handled the events of the past few months, including the Daniels and McDougal headlines. Being quiet and fighting back by going solo to events and insisting on her own motorcades were apparently viewed favorably by the public, who, in an April CNN poll, boosted her positive impression from 47 percent in January to 57 percent, her highest number yet, higher than any favorability rating earned by her husband in the network's Trump polling history, going back to 1999.

She spoke for ten minutes that day, sharing her thoughts about Be Best, whose logo Melania had designed herself, writing the two words in marker in her own handwriting. Admittedly, vast parts of her remarks were awkward because they addressed the importance of being nice and kind online and setting a good example for children—while Trump, who let fly Twitter name-calling on the regular, sat feet from her in the front row. Smiling afterward, he, the giant elephant in the Rose Garden, sat at a small desk and signed a proclamation marking the day Be Best Day, handing Melania the pen when he was done. "I think you all know who's going to get the pen."

Asked later how the president felt about his online behavior in the light of his wife's new platform, press secretary Sarah Sanders said, "I think the idea that you're trying to blame cyberbullying on the president . . . ," she said, trailing off. She didn't really have an answer, in other words.

The strange part of Be Best is that to this day it has no publicly stated framework, timeline, or markers for progress. Melania has done events to promote her platform, but she has mainly done so in conjunction with other government entities that already have programs that dovetail with Melania's Be Best initiative, like the Department of Education and the Department of Health and Human Services. She is still "gathering information," says Grisham, about whether we can expect policy changes in the future or if Melania is going to seek funding or legislative support from Capitol Hill. She has, however, visited more than fifteen states and nine countries, participating in Be Best–related experiences. But the likelihood that it will ever have the impact of Michelle Obama's Let's Move campaign or Nancy Reagan's Just Say No is slim to none.

Melania's chief concern about Be Best that day was simply that she would be able to make the announcement—her family had tried to convince her to put it off until after she had taken care of her kidney issue. Melania didn't listen. She felt like the unveiling of Be Best had to get done before she had her surgery; otherwise, it would be lost in the swirl of stories about her health. Also, doctors had warned her that the recovery time could be long, an undetermined period that might be as little as a week or as long as a month, possibly longer still if there were complications.

On Sunday night, May 13, Melania Trump slipped out of the White House and motorcaded the twenty minutes to Walter Reed National Military Medical Center in Bethesda, Maryland, settling into pre-op mode to await her early-morning surgery. She was not accompanied by Trump, who was beside himself with worry and very much wanted to go along. Trump is not good with illness; it stresses him out. While he's gotten better with visiting wounded or sick military personnel, first responders, and others, because he has to, he was practically crippled by the thought of Melania in pain, in a hospital, undergoing a surgery. He wanted to be with her, but she didn't want to raise suspicions or incur undue press attention by having him there. He is also not good at a ruse. And sneaking the first lady out of the White House and into a hospital required extreme secrecy.

Melania knew well that if Trump went anywhere, with him would have to come a far more intense security profile, and the protective press pool. There was also always the chance that if he went, he would spill the beans, either directly to the press or to one of his staff, who would turn around and leak it. Melania knew her husband: he wasn't good at keeping his feelings to himself, and he liked to be the one to announce things. If he were to wait at the hospital during the procedure, she was concerned that in his fit of worry, he would let it slip out. Fiercely determined to undergo her hospital stay exactly the way she wished, Melania wasn't going to divert from her strategy. That included not alerting the media, or the public, until she was out of surgery.

"This morning, first lady Melania Trump underwent an embolization procedure to treat a benign kidney condition. The procedure was successful, and there were no complications," said a written statement issued by Grisham that I received under embargo minutes before it was to be released widely. "Mrs. Trump is at Walter Reed National Military Medical Center and will likely remain there for the duration of the week. The first lady looks forward to a full recovery so she can continue her work on behalf of children everywhere," the statement read.

At 5 P.M. that afternoon, Trump tweeted that he was departing the White House to pay his wife a visit. "Heading to Walter Reed Medical Center to see our great First Lady, Melania. Successful procedure, she is in good spirits. Thank you to all the well-wishers!" he wrote. There was a sense of disbelief among the public that Trump hadn't been present for his wife while she was having surgery. People and pundits were appalled. Certainly, Melania could have, and perhaps should have, corrected the misperception by issuing another statement via Grisham that stated something like, "While the president wanted very much to be by his wife's side, for the sake of privacy and out of concern for the sensitive nature of the medical procedure, Mrs. Trump requested the president visit when she was out of her procedure." But Melania wasn't big on statements about her feelings, and bailing out Trump from a touch of bad press wasn't high on her list of things to do that day.

That the first lady of the United States had undergone a medical procedure serious enough to warrant a weeklong hospital stay for recovery, without anyone finding out ahead of time, to me was remarkable, and it spoke to the intense loyalty her staff felt toward her. Trump, on the other side of the White House, couldn't keep a lid on anything—his staff was like a sieve, so frequent were the leaks. But Melania not only suffered a debilitating medical issue for weeks without anyone finding out but also checked into a hospital and had an operation. And not a peep from anyone.

Melania was the first U.S. first lady to undergo such a serious medical procedure while in the White House since Nancy Reagan had a mastectomy in October 1987. Rosalynn Carter underwent surgery to remove a benign lump from her breast in April 1977. Weeks after

Betty Ford became first lady, she was diagnosed with breast cancer and underwent a mastectomy in September 1974. Melania's procedure, which is what the White House was calling it, and therefore what the press was instructed to call it, was rare.

"An embolization procedure to treat a benign kidney condition" said a couple of key things, without revealing any details. One, it confirmed embolization, which means there had to be a closing off of blood vessels, commonly done to cut off or stem growth. Two, a benign kidney condition indicated the thing that was embolized was likely a growth of some kind, but it was not malignant. Yet after a couple of days in the hospital, the public was beginning to wonder why she was still there. Medical experts were all over cable news channels speculating that the length of her stay indicated a more complex situation than is normal for what was described, since some patients who undergo embolization are free to leave a medical facility the same day. Not so Melania.

She waited two days after her surgery to tweet about how she was feeling—really, an unheard-of length of time for the first lady of the United States to update the American people about a hospital stay and well-being. "A sincere thank you to Walter Reed Medical Unit @WRBethesda & to all who have sent good wishes & prayers! I am feeling great & look forward to getting back home @WhiteHouse soon," she tweeted. It did little to shed light on her condition, the procedure, or how long she would really be in the hospital. Grisham was on high alert and would ping me whenever CNN strayed into speculation territory—pointing me back to her initial statement. I understood what she was trying to do, but I also argued it was difficult to have it both ways. Her statement was lean, and it was also days ago, and the job of every journalist was to get the real story of what was happening, and in our lightning-fast news cycle, that meant bringing out any sort of medical expert or historian or reporter or doctor or anyone who could attempt to dig at the story to help it make sense to a curious and anxious public.

By Friday, with Melania still at Walter Reed, the speculation had ballooned into straight-up conspiracy-theory status. I was getting e-mails from colleagues and friends, people I respected and trusted, telling me that they had heard Melania had possibly undergone cosmetic surgery, augmenting her breasts, getting a facelift, or having liposuction—or that she actually did have something more serious, like cancer, and the statement had been a lie.

"I am not going to expand beyond the statement I put out," Grisham told me on Tuesday, a full day after the procedure, when there was no other information offered to the public or the press. I kept asking why the routine procedure would require a multiday hospital stay. "The first lady is in good spirits and she is resting. There are HIPAA laws to consider, but she also deserves personal privacy," Grisham shot back.

I am not naïve. And I am a reporter in the Trumpian era of dramatic falsehoods and exaggerations and lies, many from the mouth of the president himself. The thought that something was fishy obviously occurred to me, and those suspicions were influenced and amplified, I will admit, by the Greek chorus of people telling me something wasn't on the up-and-up.

Again, I went back to my closest Melania sources, over and over again; I hunted every weird and obscure lead. But I kept coming back to the fact that, while Melania might withhold information, while she might be the most opaque first lady in history in terms of being forthcoming, she wasn't a liar. I also had a source whom I trusted implicitly, who shared with me that Melania's medical issue was indeed not minor—and that an embolization of a growth of some sort, small or large, when attached to the kidney, as hers might have been, made for a dangerous and complicated operation. In no way was it ever intended to be an outpatient situation. Couple that with the amount of pain she had apparently been in, according to close friends, and how long she had had that pain prior to the surgery, and there was concern that if her recuperation was not careful and extended, her type of condition could possibly result in the loss of her kidney.

I pressed Grisham, and she pressed back. "Every patient is different," she told me. "The medical professionals who have been giving opinions to the media based on one statement are uninformed. Mrs. Trump has a medical team that is comfortable with her care, which is all that matters. Her recovery and privacy are paramount and I will have no further comment beyond this. Anyone else who chooses to speak with the media will only be speculating."

On Saturday morning, May 19, six days after she had checked in, Trump welcomed her back by tweeting. "Great to have our incredible First Lady back home in the White House. Melania is feeling and doing really well. Thank you for all of your prayers and best wishes!" he wrote, after initially tweeting and deleting the same message with a typo of his own wife's name, spelling it "Melanie."

However, the return home to the White House didn't put a stop to the speculation about her health or what she may have had "done" (there were still soooo many people who thought she went under the knife for cosmetic purposes), because no one would see Melania in public for weeks. In fact, the last time anyone had laid eyes on her publicly was more than three weeks before, when she accompanied Trump on a middle-of-the-night trip to Andrews Air Force Base to welcome home three American hostages returned from North Korea.

Grisham told me that Melania was fine and that she was working on upcoming events like the Congressional Picnic, scheduled for June, and the annual July Fourth festivities, but still, no public sighting? Not even a glimpse? A tweet with a photo? Couldn't she just pop out to a school for an hour? Drop off some Be Best supplies or maybe even just host a few kids at the White House garden? How about even a wave of a hello from the Truman Balcony, to make sure the first lady wasn't, well, pulling a *Weekend at Bernie's*? The conspiracy theorists had a field day with each passing hour that Melania didn't appear in public.

But, like anything else in Melania's world, she wasn't going to be forced into faking something—and she wasn't going to step in front of the cameras just because the media was demanding she do so. In fact, like Trump, she would double down and stay inside even longer, just to shove it in the face of everyone who wanted to make sure the first lady was still the first lady and that she didn't have a new nose or something. I understood this, but only because I was used to covering her. Everyone else was perplexed. But as fourteen days stretched into twenty, and twenty stretched to twenty-five, I too was wondering where the hell she was.

Finally, Melania did go to an event on June 4 at the White House, honoring more than forty Gold Star families. It was her first public appearance since having a medical procedure for a benign kidney condition on May 14, but, though she tweeted about it, the event was closed to the press.

On June 6, she emerged, more than three weeks since anyone had seen her in public: Melania joined Trump for a trip to FEMA (of all places) to sit in on a meeting about hurricane preparedness. I covered her that day, just as I had broken the news the day before that Melania was finally scheduled to emerge from her recovery. I watched as she silently entered FEMA headquarters in downtown D.C. and sat beside the president at the head of the table, filled with other cabinet members, the vice president, and other officials. It was an odd place for her to reappear. She was wearing a tan trench-coat dress and her signature heels. How did she look? To me? The same. "Of course, we have to start with our great first lady, Melania," said Trump to the assembled people of the . . . Federal Emergency Management Agency. "Thank you, Melania. She's doing great. We're very proud of her. She's done a fantastic job as first lady," he went on, oddly referring to her in the third person, even though she was sitting right next to him. "People love you. The people of our country love you." Now he was going on too long, rambling a bit. "She went through a little rough patch, but she's doing great"—back to the third person. The whole minute or so was bizarre.

That morning he had tweeted in defense of Melania: "The Fake News Media has been so unfair, and vicious, to my wife and our great First Lady, Melania. During her recovery from surgery they reported everything from near death, to facelift, to left the W.H. (and me) for N.Y. or Virginia, to abuse. All Fake, she is doing really well!"

Two days later, with speculation about her medical procedure still hanging in the air, Trump did what Melania was worried he would do a month before—he spilled the beans. After all that quiet, all of the cloak-and-dagger ops to keep her condition and her medical procedure secret, her own husband played her out. "First lady's great, right there," said Trump, who was answering questions from the South Lawn of the White House, en route, alone, to the G7 summit in Charlevoix, Canada. He pointed to the upper windows of the White House, to the residence level. "She wanted to go," said Trump of his wife, who had been so fiercely private about her health. "Can't fly for one month, the doctors say," Trump continued. "She had a big operation, that was close to a four-hour operation. And she's doing great." With one quick sentence, Trump had elephant-plodded right into Melania's orchestrated, tidy, and very private persona—and trampled all over it.

Trump's statement made her reemergence into the public eye tougher and more complicated. But as with most things, Melania knew she could catch attention again, under her own terms, whenever she wanted to—without ever saying a word.

19

The Fashion

"I wish people would focus on what I do, not what I wear."

—MELANIA TRUMP

The spring of 2018 had been difficult for Melania Trump, to put it mildly. Part of a difficult year, actually, if you chuck in the stories of Stormy Daniels and Karen McDougal and the rumors about Russian hookers and lewd sexual exploits, all of which heated up or broke after January 1, 2018.

But Melania had weathered it. Unlike almost every other political spouse before her, she had not gritted her teeth and held her husband's hand. If anything, she'd hung him out to dry. But mostly she had disappeared, retreating even more deeply than the public had come to expect of her.

It was April 2018, two days before Melania's forty-eighth birthday, and she wanted to show off a bit, make it clear she was still there, alive—turn the focus toward herself for once. She thought about what her predecessors had done before her, like Jackie, who, when she wanted to steal the spotlight from Jack, wore something she knew would make headlines—for example, the couple's first trip abroad to

France would never have been as big a sensation had Jackie not been keen enough to wear Givenchy, designed by the master of French couture Hubert de Givenchy. For that trip, Jackie had asked Givenchy to make more than a dozen pieces, but it was the floral embroidered satin gown she wore to a formal dinner at Versailles that sealed her popularity abroad. Afterward, Jackie sent Givenchy a personal note of thanks, adding that the French president Charles de Gaulle, at the dinner, had told her, "Madame, this evening you look like a Parisienne." "I am the man who accompanied Jacqueline Kennedy to Paris, and I have enjoyed it," JFK famously joked, slightly passive-aggressively, in his speech to that nation at the end of the trip.

Jackie and Melania were both loath to continually be written about for what they wore, but they also knew it came in handy when the need presented itself.

So on that April day, Melania wore a hat. A big white hat.

The occasion was her first major hostessing duty as first lady; she and Trump were welcoming Emmanuel and Brigitte Macron, the president and first lady of France, to the White House for the first official state visit of the administration. She had been prepping for months. Not just the menu—goat cheese gateau with tomato jam and buttermilk biscuit crumbles, rack of spring lamb with Carolina Gold rice jambalaya, and nectarine tart with crème fraîche ice cream for dessert—but what, precisely, she would wear.

She turned to her stylist, Hervé Pierre, who had proved himself up to the challenge several times before, always nailing what Melania was thinking, as able to interpret her thoughts as well as anyone could. Pierre, who spent fifteen years at the house of iconic designer Carolina Herrera, doesn't call himself a stylist for Melania, at her insistence, but rather an "adviser," though his primary role for Melania includes selecting and shopping for wardrobe items, tailoring fit, and offering up accessories. These are all things a personal stylist does, of course, but it's very Melania to not want to admit she has a stylist, even though she sort of does.

Melania wants everyone to know that she, Melania, picked out her outfit, that it was her decision to wear a certain dress or a suit or a coat. If Pierre gets involved in the shopping, it's mostly because he has been tasked by her to find something specific or sees something that might work in tandem with one of Melania's ideas.

Michelle Obama also liked to make her own choices, but they were choices she was making from a plethora of options that her personal stylist, a young woman named Meredith Koop, had selected already, knowing Michelle's taste and the occasion. Koop started as a sales associate at Ikram, the iconic Chicago boutique run by Ikram Goldman. Michelle Obama was a regular. When then–senator Barack Obama decided to run for president, Michelle turned to Goldman for help with her wardrobe. By the time Obama entered the White House, the job of helping dress Michelle—by now an icon of style herself—was too big for Goldman to handle alone, so Koop, ever the able assistant, stepped in. Koop has been a thoughtful shopper for Michelle for almost a decade now. It's Koop's job to keep her in clothes that not only reflect her taste but also highlight the many facets of fashion design, combining emerging designers with well-known names, high-end price points with affordable ones, and forward-focused sartorial choices.

Melania didn't want that. She didn't want someone else pulling items. One of her favorite pastimes is perusing shopping sites like Moda Operandi, which carries thousands of high-fashion looks and caters to women already thinking of the season ahead of the current one. Or Melania's most frequent online shopping destination, Net-a-Porter, where she often buys her clothes, just like you or me, or anyone, really, and has them delivered to her home, which, unlike you or me, happens to be the White House. Most of the time, Pierre does the buying for some of the bigger, more important stuff that requires longer-term planning, and when he does Melania receives the packages directly from him. She tries things on, decides what she likes and what she doesn't, and Pierre or one of his helpers will send back the discards.

"My role is to dress the First Lady and advise her—I'm not a stylist; I am an adviser, and she is adamant about that," Pierre has said. "Who, as a free woman, is going to be told what to wear? It's a conversation, a collaboration. Without intellectualizing, my advice is respectful and it makes sense." Melania and Pierre have found a vibe that works for them, with Pierre making sure tailoring is impeccable for a dress or a coat, but avoiding being too involved in the acquisition of that dress or coat. He does, however, plan for Melania's bigger moments: with her, he makes sure her trunks and suitcases are packed with essentials for each of her lengthier trips.

For the Macrons' elaborate official arrival ceremony—a fancy deal on the South Lawn of the White House with military bands, flags, marching, anthems, and such—Melania had already selected her outfit. It was a bright white Michael Kors Collection skirt suit with an asymmetrically hemmed jacket and a wide white belt to match, very much in the vein of Melania's usual sartorial silhouette. She would buy a new pair of Christian Louboutin So Kate stilettos, too, in blue denim with a white patent leather 4.75-inch heel, for $775.

The ensemble, while good, needed something else, thought Melania. Something extra. Something fabulous. Pierre suggested a hat. Melania agreed.

Pierre reached out to Michael Kors's team and asked for several yards of the white suit fabric, as he was commissioning the hat to be specially made—so for those of you who thought at the last minute Melania had decided to add a generous accessory to her outfit, you're wrong. The hat was planned, well in advance, and it was custom made, by hand, by a hatmaker commissioned by Pierre. Kors is persnickety about Melania wearing his clothes, which she does with frequency. During the presidential campaign, the Manhattan-based designer was a vocal champion of and a donor to Hillary Clinton. When Melania wore her first real headline-grabbing Kors outfit, for Trump's first special address to Congress a month after his inauguration, the designer had to accept that the new first lady was going to wear his clothes, whether he liked it or not. It's a free country: the first lady can walk into any store that sells Michael Kors and buy whatever she likes—or order it off the Neiman Marcus Web site.

Melania entered the Capitol gallery that evening wearing a black belted Michael Kors suit, adorned with delicate sequin flowers. The price tag was just shy of ten thousand dollars. "Mrs. Trump has been a longtime client at our New York boutique. She has a keen understanding of what works best for her and her lifestyle," said Kors when asked to comment. Translation: she went into the store and bought it like anyone else, I had nothing to do with it. Kors, who tweets constantly when celebrities—who are not Melania Trump—wear his clothes, didn't do anything to herald the new first lady's taking a shine to his designs. And he hasn't since, more than two years into her tenure and more than a dozen significant Kors designs worn by Melania later.

So it was a bit of a surprise, back to the hat, that he agreed to give Pierre that extra fabric.

The hat became a defining moment for Melania, who kept it on all day long, even for a tour of the Cézanne exhibition at the National Gallery of Art, which she took with Mrs. Macron. She kept the hat on, even inside. *The Washington Post*'s Pulitzer Prize–winning fashion critic, Robin Givhan, dedicated an entire column to the hat: "The hat, broad-brimmed with a high, blocked crown, announced the first lady's presence as boldly and theatrically as a brigade of trumpeters. It was the bright white hat of a gladiator worn on an overcast day, a kind of glamorous public shield when sunglasses would not do at all. That hat was a force field," Givhan wrote, "that kept folks, the wrong folks, from getting too close." A "diva crown," she called it. It was true, the circumference of the thing meant she couldn't hug tight or kiss beyond a smooch into the air that would hopefully land somewhere near a face. Trump certainly couldn't get close. But, honestly, as soon as Melania stepped out in that hat, was he even there? I think he gave remarks at the opening ceremony, but no one knew what he said. Cable news panels for once dropped the Trump coverage and started talking about hats and Beyoncé and Olivia Pope.

Had it been any first lady other than Brigitte Macron that Melania chose to literally and figuratively overshadow with her hat, she might have had some trouble, but Brigitte was #TeamMelania all the way. Nine months earlier, in Paris, Brigitte got a taste of what being married to Trump must be like, in terms of having to conform to his ideal of physical beauty. When they met during their visit on Bastille Day, cameras rolled as Trump looked at the sixtysomething French first lady and objectified her, eyeing her up and down before saying, "beautiful. You're in such good shape." He then turned to her husband, several years his wife's junior, and said, "She's in such good physical shape." Like, can you believe it? This older broad is actually a pretty hot piece! The video clip was incredibly awkward to watch—cringeworthy is being kind. I can't imagine what it must have been like to be there in person, but in that instant Brigitte bonded with Melania, so sympathetic was she to the fact Melania had to be married to this person, or that was how she saw it. Melania, of course, didn't feel that way and had long ago tried her best not to let her husband's numerous social gaffes get to her. But she did take it into account when she decided on that hat. While most other first ladies would be annoyed Melania stole their spotlight, Brigitte was basically like, "Go girl."

But such is the power of Melania's clothing choices. They are complex, they are impeccable (mostly), and they often leave Americans with more questions about their first lady than answers.

Did she wear the white Christian Dior pantsuit to the State of the Union address in 2018 to mess with her husband's head after news broke of his alleged affair with porn star Stormy Daniels? What does one wear to recover from that sort of public humiliation? A white, "I'm fine—just look at me" suit in a sea of congressional black and navy? Was that the trick? That it harkened to suffragettes and Hillary Clinton and the resistance certainly didn't hurt either. Melania may not have been sending up a Bat signal of solidarity, but she certainly didn't mind if women, or Democrats, or Democratic women, thought she did. I have a theory that when the Trumps are unhappy with each other, Melania wears menswear—because Trump notoriously likes to see women in tight, short, übersexy and feminine dresses. In 2018, Melania wore a lot of pantsuits.

Pierre had first become acquainted with Melania quite out of the blue, when she cold-called him mere weeks before her husband's inauguration, asking if he would make her gown. She phoned him early one morning and asked him to send over some sketches of ideas—by 4 P.M. that same afternoon.

"I was surprised, yes," Pierre told me. "But I was so excited." He didn't know Melania in a personal way. But she had chosen well, because Pierre wasn't afraid to dress the woman who, for so many in his industry, represented the man that beat their beloved Hillary Clinton. Anna Wintour, the doyenne of fashion, had unabashedly fund-raised and sanctioned the use of *Vogue* editorial pages in support of Clinton. Other designers had already stated on the record they would not work with Mrs. Donald Trump. Pierre put it to me this way: "The amazing thing about America and about freedom is that if you don't want to do something, you don't have to do it!" Born in France, Pierre, who is small in stature and almost always has a flower in the lapel of his jacket and Converse sneakers on his feet, became a United States citizen in August 2016. Dressing the first lady, for him, was an honor beyond compare.

Pierre's job might be more complex than that of Michelle Obama's stylist, because he can't simply call up any designer in the Rolodex (and neither can Melania) and ask that a dress be made for her for such and such occasion. And that's because, essentially, the fashion world does not like her, mostly because of her association with her husband. So polarizing is this president that wearing a certain designer, no matter how often Melania is photographed or written about for what she has done, is not an option. No one wants to claim her.

There have been designers who have said they won't dress Melania—quite vocal ones at that. Having decided her husband's politics are not for them and, by extension, therefore neither is she, certain designers would rather forgo the business of dressing a first lady, which used to be considered an honor. Before Trump took office, Tom Ford said on a talk show, "I was asked to dress her quite a few years ago and I declined. She's not necessarily my image." It was stinging enough that Trump took notice and remembered: two months later, speaking at a luncheon in Washington in January, he remarked, "Tom Ford came out and said he was not dressing Melania. He was never asked. I never liked him or his designs." He then gestured to Melania, seated in the audience: "He's never had something to dress like that." Marc Jacobs, Zac Posen, Phillip Lim, Sophie Theallet, and Naeem Khan (all avid Michelle Obama designers) have said they would also avoid dressing Melania. It's not something that Melania particularly cares about, say those who know her. Unlike Michelle Obama, Melania rarely asks designers for customized looks.

Designer Alice Roi, who dressed Melania in the high-profile custom navy coat she wore for the inaugural weekend prayer breakfast at the National Cathedral, and made her a similarly tailored red coat that March, won't do so again, because of the backlash she faced after her name was attached to Melania Trump originals. For Roi—who delighted in a round of interviews about dressing the first lady after the inauguration, explaining how Melania favored a "1950s silhouette, in which the waist is emphasized"—the degree to which her business suffered was eye-opening, someone close to Roi tells me. Making it worse, the two women were longtime friends, and Roi was one of the few designers Melania felt truly comfortable working with. Two handmade outfits within three months of each other, both made in collaboration between designer and client, signaled Roi could very well become one of Melania's go-to couturiers, at least that's what both envisioned, until Roi faced the wrath of anti-Trump fashionistas. The hit Roi took, both in her revenue and reputation, in the wake of dressing her friend, the first lady, was too much to bear. Melania, gracious as ever, completely understood that Roi would no longer be able to make clothes for her.

If that stings, and people who know her say it does not, Melania doesn't show it. She still has a stable of favorites, if a small one (in addition to those Web sites, which don't discriminate), including Christian Dior, Dolce and Gabbana, Chanel, Raf Simons (when he was with Calvin Klein), Roland Mouret, and of course Ralph Lauren, who custom made her baby blue Inauguration Day suit and several other pieces.

For her inaugural gown, Melania gave Pierre some words to help him come up with what she wanted—"powder," "pale blue," "vanilla"—and she said that, for fit, she wanted it to be tight but also have movement. Basically, she handed him the fashion equivalent of finding the needle in a haystack. They went back and forth for days until they landed on the final sketch of the gown: an ivory, silk crepe, off-the-shoulder column sheath with a high slit in the skirt and a ruffle trim that went to the floor. For a special touch, Pierre and Melania added a thin red ribbon, tied at the waist in a tiny bow. It was modern and simple but laboriously constructed. And it was unlike any other inaugural gown a first lady had worn before, which is how Melania liked it. If she has a sartorial pet peeve, it's dressing anything like anyone before her has already dressed. The gown now lives in the Smithsonian Museum of American History's First Ladies exhibition, like several of her predecessors' gowns. The exhibition is one of the most popular of all the Smithsonian museums in Washington. It not only serves as a historical document of sorts illustrating what the times were like and what was in fashion during each first lady's tenure but also defines each first lady's personality. Was she rich and extravagant like Abigail Van Buren's blue velvet gown suggests? Or modest and practical, like Eleanor Roosevelt's long-sleeve pink crepe inaugural gown? Was she a follower, which Mamie Eisenhower's taffeta evening dresses with full skirts and cap sleeves, all the rage in the 1950s, suggest? Or was she a leader, like Nancy Reagan, whose sleek, one-shouldered James Galanos gown broke the mold of flouncy, überfemme dresses?

The museum collection itself was started back in 1930 by first lady Lou Henry Hoover, President Herbert Hoover's wife, who was, like Melania, a private person. She preferred to work behind the scenes, once making a painstaking list of every item of furnishings from the James Monroe presidency to preserve for posterity, since Monroe was the first president to move into the rebuilt White House after it had been set on fire by the

British during the War of 1812. It was under Monroe that much of the furniture was restored; Lou Hoover thought it important to document his efforts. It was she who first donated her dresses and personal artifacts to what was then the "national museum," which eventually developed, with her initial assistance, into the Smithsonian it is today.

Whether clothing is a fair assessment of who a first lady is—and it's not fair—the world is going to look at what she wears. It just will. We have no royalty, our celebrities are fads, presidents are boring, sartorially, at least, so a nation turns its lonely eyes to the first lady. There's an innate tendency to judge her by what she is wearing, and it happens whether there's style there or not. (We still pulled something from Barbara Bush with those pearls, didn't we?)

What a first lady chooses to wear speaks to many other components of life that aren't just about her. It can reflect a mood, hers or the country's; it can be subject to interpretation, intended or not; it can signal wealth or wealth adjacency. It captures the period of her tenure to such an exacting degree the Smithsonian has an entire section dedicated to first lady fashion in the Museum of American History. A rite of passage—one that Melania performed in 2017—is the induction of the first lady's inaugural gown into the exhibition. Yet discussing a woman, any woman, via her clothes feels sort of icky in modern times, as does expecting her not only to be smart and cultivate a policy platform but also to reveal her favorite cookie recipe in an issue of *Good Housekeeping*. When was the last time Melania Trump whipped up a batch of homemade sweets in the kitchen? Try never.

In lieu of understanding our current first lady by looking at how she communicates verbally with regularity, makes speeches, does interviews, talks about her feelings, maybe even does push-ups on a late-night talk show or sings carpool karaoke, we are forced to look elsewhere to understand who she is. Reading her clothes and nonverbal clues is a simple method of trying to understand who the person is who's married to the president of the United States, made even more curious by the fact that president is Donald Trump. In the case of Melania Trump, what she wears, in part because she is unwaveringly stylish and well dressed, is sometimes all we have to analyze what she might be thinking behind those $500 sunglasses. The non-verbal cues Melania gives with clothes have served at times to help us read her feelings, and at others to make them murkier.

But if Melania gets annoyed at how much people talk about her style, it's yet another thing she should come to anticipate and get used to. After all, as far back as the 1880s the public and the media were riffing off what a first lady wore. Frances Folsom, the youngest first lady in American history, was twenty-one when she married Grover Cleveland, who was forty-nine, in a White House ceremony (there were almost the same number of years between them as between Melania and Trump). Frances quickly became the talk of the town, wearing dresses many believed were too "revealing," if revealing meant exposing elbows. Long before Michelle Obama was dragged through fashion think pieces for her affinity for sleeveless dresses, poor Frances was fending off the press for her choices. Frances used a Parisian designer to custom make most of her gowns; some were copied by American dressmakers. The press paid attention to how she adorned her clothes with flowers and her hats with feathers.

Frances, like Melania and Michelle, was young, beautiful, and stylish—catnip for an anxious public in need of someone to tear at. Her necklines often exposed what prudish observers thought was too much décolleté, but younger women in America took to copying her, ditching the bustles on the backs of their skirts and tailoring skinnier straps on their shoulders, happy that the first lady was shaking off stuffier "rules" about the amount of skin that was acceptable to show.

Frances also did what Melania apparently cannot do, which is help her husband dress for his . . . girth. Cleveland was a big man, but with Frances's help, he changed the cut of his suits to help hide his midsection. Melania clearly has had little effect on Trump's style, which consists of three basic looks: work Trump (oversize dark suit, white shirt, ridic-ulously long red tie), sporty Trump (white polo shirt, red MAGA hat, long Bermuda shorts), and casual Trump (open-neck button-down shirt, windbreaker, red or white MAGA hat, pleated khakis).

Clearly, this is why it's more interesting to stay in first lady style territory.

Melania and Michelle Obama will likely both bear the legacy that Frances Cleveland did, at least in part. Frances was America's first real first lady remembered for being stylish. Like it or hate it, Frances's clothes gave people something to talk about, and the press was grateful.

Grace Coolidge was another first lady who paved the way for the rest of American women, wearing the drop-waist flapper dresses of the mid-1920s while first lady, showing everyone else it was okay to do so. She embraced sportswear and, with it, the notion that women could and should be athletic. Grace wore pants, too. And cut her hair into a bob. She was modern and cool, and her style reflected as much. Where Grace was edgy and sporty, other first ladies, like Mamie Eisenhower, were girly and feminine. Mamie was a different kind of trendsetter for America, with her "Mamie Pink" everything (flowers, dresses, the White House private residence, which reporters dubbed the "Pink Palace"); because of Mamie, pink really became the "girl" color, such was the power of her influence. Mamie was also a bit kooky and kitsch with her clothes. When Dwight Eisenhower had a kickoff picnic for his reelection campaign in 1956, Mamie wore a dress with a giant print reproduction of the White House on the bodice, which was repeated on the pleated skirt. Her purse was embroidered with a symbolic elephant.

Jackie Kennedy was no doubt paying attention to all that style influence, good and bad, as it was she who got the world obsessed with the fashion of first ladies—where once it was a hobby or a light aside to a political piece about a president, with Jackie clothes became a calling card. Jackie was smart about it, too, creating a movement with her look that lent fortitude to her husband's vision of youthful exuberance. If Mamie was dainty in grandma's pink sparkles and tight curls, Jackie was chic in her mohair jackets and knee-length skirts and stylish brunette bouffant. Jackie cultivated a relationship with her favorite designer, Oleg Cassini, who would be instrumental in preparing her looks, be they for a state dinner or a White House social function. Cassini was her personal couturier, meaning he created her clothes, and as such was informally dubbed the Secretary of Style, an ancillary member of Kennedy's cabinet.

Jackie in 1960 wrote Cassini a letter asking if he was sure he wanted to commit to being her fashion designer. "ARE YOU SURE YOU ARE UP TO IT, OLEG?" Jackie wrote to him in capital letters, adding her joy that he would even entertain what could be undue criticism from a zealous public. "One reason I am so happy to be working with you is that I have some control over my fashion press, which has gotten so vulgarly out of hand," she wrote. "You realize that I know that I am so much more of fashion interest than other first ladies." Jackie also wanted the clothes Cassini designed exclusively for her to be hers alone, no mass knock-offs. "I want all of mine to be original and no fat little women hopping around in the same dress," she wrote in the same letter. Melania must not care about such a thing, because anyone with the money can buy at least 70 percent of the items she has worn as first lady.

But Jackie's letter to Cassini also includes sentiments that Melania might relate to, all these decades later. Though Melania may or may not deal with the scrutiny better than Jackie did, she too thinks of her fashion as protection, armor from a world examining her every move. "Protect me," Jackie wrote to Cassini, "as I seem so mercilessly exposed and don't know how to cope with it."

Cassini's background was dressing Hollywood starlets (he once had a love affair with Grace Kelly), which made it even savvier of Jackie to think to make him her dresser, adopting a built-in celebrity element to her entourage. Like Melania, Jackie understood the power of aspirational fashion and was keenly aware that a designer or an outfit could elicit flattery or garner prestige at a public appearance, a visit to a foreign nation, or a "casual" moment at home. Clothes, Jackie understood, were the armor or the costume, the billboard or the subliminal message.

Melania's personal adviser Pierre has had many more hits than misses with Melania. For her first international viewing as American first lady, joining her husband on a lengthy trip abroad, Melania plotted her approach several weeks in advance, calling on Pierre to prep outfits for at least twelve public events on the nine-day trip. With each stop, the world got to know a bit more about this mysterious first lady who wasn't afraid to wear expensive labels—and no American ones, at that—and who was clearly aware that how she dressed and was photographed were paramount since otherwise she was going to be nothing other than an accoutrement to her husband on the trip. Traditionally, first ladies will showcase American designers as much as they can, especially on trips abroad. Michelle Obama was particularly good at selecting designers who were American but had origin in or connection to the country she was visiting. Melania has little care for those sorts of rules—again, she's not prone to doing anything that feels inauthentic to her, even if that means wearing an international designer in Trump's "America First" world.

Pierre also designs custom pieces for Melania: in addition to the inaugural gown, Melania wore a Pierre original as she departed Washington with Trump for that first trip abroad. He had made her a high-waisted orange leather skirt with white piping. Another leather pencil skirt by Pierre would be worn by Melania months later, this one in chestnut brown to match the colors of autumn at the White House Thanksgiving turkey pardon. It was his original green dress design with a shawl collar and belted waist that Melania wore the first time she and Trump hosted the king and queen of Jordan at the White House. Entire articles were written about what Melania was doing or not doing to promote the cause of "fashion diplomacy," a phrase that Michelle Obama had raised to an art form during her eight years in office. Did she wear green because it's in the Jordanian flag? Or did she just like green? As usual, everyone would have to settle with the gray area because Melania would not do interviews about her clothes or anything else, thank you very much. Previous first ladies have done more press, more glossy magazine interviews, more open discussion about sartorial pressure or choices. Melania? No thank you.

The truth, however, falls somewhere in between. Did she contemplate the green because of its association with the country's flag? Certainly. Did she pick it just because of that? Not likely. Does she want the king and queen of Jordan to think she did? Yep.

When Melania's official first lady portrait was unveiled, think pieces were written about how she wasn't wearing an American designer. Instead, she wore a black suit by the Italian design house Dolce and Gabbana. But, honestly, what most people were staring at in the portrait wasn't the suit but the huge diamond ring—her upgraded 25-carat emerald-cut engagement ring that Trump had given her two years before to mark their ten-year wedding anniversary. It is fifteen carats more than the original—one carat for every year she had been married to him, plus five for extra measure.

For Melania's first official state dinner, with the Macrons, she did what was anticipated, selecting a haute couture Chanel gown, one of two she asked to be sent to her to choose from. At the last minute, she opted for the one she wore, a long, sleeveless dress, simple in silhouette but covered in silver sequins and hemmed in lace at the bottom. On the Chanel haute couture runway, the look was originally shown as a jumpsuit, which Melania had toyed with wearing, but she went with the gown version, which likely cost over $100,000, as one-of-a-kind pieces from Chanel often do.

Price doesn't necessarily seem to matter much to Melania when it comes to her clothes—I was the one who first noticed she had selected a $680 Balmain plaid shirt for her debut public foray (the only one so far) into Michelle Obama's beloved White House kitchen garden. But unlike Michelle, whose very adept longtime stylist, Meredith Koop, would pluck selections for the first lady, hyperaware of the situational atmosphere of each event, Melania for the most part wears off-the-rack items, which is fashion speak for "you can buy them in a store or online, just like anyone else." Koop would no sooner put Michelle

Obama in a $680 plaid shirt in the garden with kids from an inner-city D.C. school than she would in jeans for a state dinner.

Michelle's everyday looks and dresses typically didn't retail in their original form for more than a few hundred dollars. But Koop, knowing her boss's preferences and what looked best on her figure, would often have the dresses modified and customized. Sometimes that meant turning a dress with sleeves into one without or a sheath into an A-line, a mini into a midi. The designers were only too happy to oblige. Unlike Melania, Michelle was worshiped by the fashion crowd; she had the sartorial power to literally make a career—as she essentially did for designers like Jason Wu, Prabal Gurung, and Tanya Taylor, among others. The Koop-requested customization meant the price would be higher, but many designers would trip over themselves to design for Obama, so they would often be generous and not charge exorbitant amounts.

Which brings us to the rules about first ladies and clothes. It's a sort of a fuzzy area of ethics, but the basic gist is that first ladies are prohibited from accepting clothes for free, per government finance rules. However, they can accept free garments for one-off, very special occasions, as long as the item in question is then donated to the National Archives after it has been worn. As such, most of the first lady state dinner gowns were "donated" by designers. Anything else a first lady wears must be purchased on her own, with her own personal money. Again, it's another weird rule of the job that reeks of unfairness. Here the first lady is supposed to be impeccably dressed for each public occasion, ostensibly to look good representing the country and her husband, but really so a catty public can dissect every stitch. And yet everything she wears she has to pay for out of her own pocket. For women like Melania, whose clothing budget has always been on the high side of generous, this isn't necessarily a problem—and good for her, because unlike Michelle, who oftentimes received generous markdowns from designers, Melania never gets a price break from Seventh Avenue.

Fashion was something Melania had always been thoughtful

about, and over her almost two decades with Trump, she had gone from sexpot slips with too much décolletage to tailored suits, smart jackets, and coat dresses. And coats that aren't dresses—just coats. In the fall and winter of 2018 and early 2019, Melania would be photographed in more than twenty different coats at various public events. She had several of the same color, blue being a favorite, and for one spell of about five weeks, wore seven different coats, all in varying shades of plaid.

Melania has pretty much single-handedly brought back the coat as principal player, not just an accessory to be added later. She has coined her own twist by regularly wearing one of her $2,000 cashmere coats and not even fully putting it on, leaving it resting on her shoulders, her arms at her sides and not through the sleeves. It's the ultimate "rich person" move. If you're balancing your coat on your body, you can't really use your arms or the coat would fall off. So all the things you need arms for—opening the car door, carrying groceries or your children, driving a vehicle, toting shopping bags, and more—you either don't need to do or don't have to do.

One of the outfits Melania worked on the most was the one she wore to be introduced to the world as first lady of the United States. The baby blue Ralph Lauren dress with the matching cropped jacket—the one that when most people saw her step out in it they whispered one word: Jackie.

True, it was reminiscent of Jackie Kennedy's style, but Melania had a clear idea of what she wanted, and no comparison was going to stop her from seeing her vision through. "She knew the fabric, the fit, the color. She even knew the shoe she wanted and the exact heel height," one of Melania's close friends tells me. "She knew that a hat would not work, but that gloves in the same shade of blue would." The friend tells me that Melania designed the look in collaboration with Ralph Lauren himself, along with members of his team. Of course, for most of the campaign, Hillary Clinton had worn Ralph Lauren suits, which would have made Melania's choice of him for her inaugural look a little bit odd, if it weren't for the fact that Lauren was the iconic American designer, so it felt like less of a personal jab. Lauren, philosophically, doesn't have a partisan feel for designing; his team designed for Clinton, and they just as easily designed for Melania.

Melania has morphed her style into what I like to call "Lady Melania," the farthest cry from what she looked like in those naked modeling pictures, splayed out on a carpet. There are three components to "Lady Melania" looks. One: hair up. She wears her hair up for very lady-important occasions and meetings. Examples: Inauguration Day; meeting Pope Francis, the queen of England, the emperor of Japan; when wearing Dior in Paris (because that's almost as iconic as meeting a pope or a queen); and, again, wearing Dior in Paris (she's done it twice). Two: wearing gloves. Examples: Dior in Paris, funerals of important people (the Reverend Billy Graham), at Buckingham Palace for a state banquet, and when the coat is just too good not to add a matching glove. Three: Christian Dior outfits. Examples: to meet royalty (Prince Harry and the aforementioned queen, the emperor of Japan), galas (the Red Cross gala at Mar-a-Lago), on important trips (her first international trip with the president), any trip to Paris, unveiling her first Christmas decorations at the White House.

Another interesting thing Melania does that is unlike her predecessors when it comes to her clothes (and fashion diplomacy, those words again) is purposefully *not* wear designers associated with the places she is visiting but rather wear clothes that in some small way resemble the culture of where she is going. Michelle Obama would often plan to wear designers from the countries she visited or from the countries of visiting leaders. For the India State Dinner, Michelle picked Naeem Khan, who is American of Indian descent. When the Obamas hosted President Xi Jinping of China, Michelle Obama commissioned a gown from Vera Wang. Visiting England, she wore Roksanda Ilinčić, a London-based designer, as well as Peter Pilotto, again, a British designer. Hosting the leader of South Korea, she wore an outfit by Korean-American Doo-Ri Chung. And so on.

Melania doesn't showcase particular designers as did Obama, who

championed them to the point of shifting the bottom line of the fashion industry by the billions, according to some studies. Rather, she
picks according to the place, whether her Felliniesque Dolce and Gabbana floral jacket in Sicily; the floor-length Gucci gown, trimmed in
pink fur with a floral pattern, that looked very similar to a cheong-
sam, a traditional Chinese dress, worn to a state dinner hosted by
President Xi in China, a simple black coat tied with a thick silk belt,
reminiscent of an obi, in Japan at a dinner with the Abes, or, the next
evening, a long gown by Valentino, in bold red, the emblematic color
of the Japanese flag; or a custom-made suit jacket and skirt, designed
by Christian Dior in echo of the original Dior silhouette of the 1960s,
an homage to the design house's seventieth anniversary, when in Paris
for the first time as first lady.

Mordechai Alvow was born in Israel, but when he was in his twenties,
he moved to Los Angeles with the hopes of doing hair for celebrities.
Within a few months, he was. (It was the late eighties, and he landed
no bigger name, with no bigger hair, than the lead singer of the band
Whitesnake, David Coverdale.) Alvow built a loyal clientele after
moving to New York, where through the years he has often been
sought after for editorial photo shoots for magazines. He met Melania Trump thirteen years ago on an assignment for Japan *Vogue*. The
magazine wanted a bridal photo shoot with Melania, photographed at
Mar-a-Lago. The two hit it off right away, and she loved what he did
with her brunette locks. Before he left that day, an assistant got his
contact information, and soon he was Melania's go-to stylist.

They would collaborate for years before Melania's big move to
the White House, which, of course, Alvow made with her, at least
in terms of her hair. When Alvow can't be in Washington, Melania
will fill in with someone local to do the regular, simple blow-dry, but
Alvow is typically with her for every major event. When Melania
returned from Asia, I flew with some members of the press on her
plane home. Unloading at the White House, late at night by the south

doors, one of the vans was filled with relatively small and different sized Louis Vuitton luggage. I assumed they belonged to the first lady, which they did, but they were labeled for Mordechai, who had come along on the Asia trip and needed his styling tools. He did the same when Melania went on her first big solo trip abroad, to Africa in October 2018. To anyone else, he appeared a regular member of her entourage, but I had long ago started to follow his Instagram page and can always spot Mordechai—he is tall, skinny, and handsome, with salt-and-pepper hair and a warm, friendly grin. At an orphanage in Kenya where Melania stopped to visit, her staff all held babies in the nursery—and Mordechai did, too, cradling a tiny infant in his arms, smiling and cooing. We made eye contact and he looked at me and looked at the baby, *Can you believe this?*

Melania also has a trusted makeup artist whom she uses not so much for trips but for events and major photo shoots, including for her official portrait. Like Alvow, Nicole Bryl met Melania more than a decade ago on a photo shoot for a magazine—specifically, the story Melania did for *People* just after Barron was born. And, also like Alvow, the two had great chemistry and trust, which was all Melania needed from those she let into her very small private world. Bryl also had to make Melania look great, which she did by keeping Melania in a year-round state of perpetual bronze glow. Bryl likes to fangirl a bit over her most famous client, but she is protective of her, once in an interview going off on people who judge Melania the person because of her husband's political views. "The only one who gets flustered about this sort of talk is me, and those who know her and care for her the most," said Bryl, who posts photos of Melania with some frequency on her Instagram page, tagging the captions with heart emojis and x's and o's, and the occasional "my Queen."

As with Alvow, Melania doesn't *need* Bryl to do her makeup. Surprisingly, she often does it herself, which is a feat she mastered years ago when she made the transition from working model to Donald Trump's girlfriend. Today, it is oftentimes she who applies her thick, long false eyelashes, perfectly, at the ends of her shaded lids, which are usually dark slate gray, just a hint of silvery shine across the brow bone.

It was Bryl who spilled the beans about Melania's significant renovation of the White House residence's beauty salon area, called the Cosmetology Room since Pat Nixon was first lady. Bryl dished to *Us Weekly* before Inauguration Day, "Melania wants a room with the most perfect lighting scenario, which will make our jobs as a creative team that much more efficient, since great lighting can make or break any look."

The resulting room is all pristine white—Melania's favorite, clean palette. A large crystal chandelier hangs from the ceiling, because it is a glam room, after all, and she is a Trump. A giant flat-screen television is mounted on the wall as well, so Melania can watch "whatever she chooses" while she does her hair and makeup, which typically takes well over an hour, start to finish.

It is here that Melania sometimes does tune in to CNN, and, like her husband, she is avid about taking notes when she feels news reports unfairly paint her in a negative light. Other reporters and I who cover her are no strangers to real-time e-mails or texts from Grisham, asking about a certain story angle, headline, or chyron. While Melania doesn't particularly care about many things, she does read her press— and she knows the bylines of and backgrounds and beats of everyone who writes about her. This year, in Brussels for NATO, I had the chance to shout a question to Trump, simply because I was stationed where I could watch the leaders and spouses enter a dinner. I asked the president how he felt his day of meetings had gone (it was the day he had whipped up a frenzy about relations between Germany and Russia). Trump stopped, looked at me, looked at my CNN-branded microphone, and looked back at me. He was puzzled because he didn't know who I was, hadn't seen me often enough before to place my face; he knew every other West Wing CNN reporter, trust me, but I was new to him. Melania held a smile. "Very good. Beautiful. Really well," said Trump to me, adding he was having a "very good time at NATO." The first couple then proceeded inside for the private dinner, but I learned from a dinner attendee that later Trump had turned to Melania and asked who I was, and she gave him my name and said that I primarily focus my reporting not on him but on her.

Yet unlike her husband, Melania isn't a complete and total news junkie when she does turn on the television. She's prone to the occasional binge-watch (she was hooked for a while on *The Crown*), and she has said in the past that her favorite show is *How to Get Away with Murder*.

What she watches and what she does when she's in the presence of her hair and makeup people aren't all that different from what other women in this country do with the people who see them, quite literally, at their most bare. She is honest and funny and forthcoming. There is gossip, there is chatter about celebrities and pop culture and headlines. This is a safe zone.

Melania treats Pierre and Alvow and Bryl much the same way Michelle Obama treated her glam squad of Meredith Koop, Johnny Wright (her hairstylist), and Carl Ray (her makeup artist). Obama brought the three into her inner circle, where they remain to this day, with the exception of Wright, who was replaced on hair-care duties by one of his protégés, Yene Damtew. Damtew worked with Michelle when she was first lady, but typically assisting Wright or focusing on Malia and Sasha Obama. Damtew stepped into the top spot after Obama left the White House (and Wright moved to Los Angeles) and has remained Obama's chief hair guru. In September 2017, Obama made a rare social appearance, attending the opening party for Damtew's small new salon in Arlington, Virginia. Obama's support for Damtew, Ray, Koop, and Wright is, like Melania's for her own team, genuine, thoughtful, and trusted.

When you're a first lady, new friendships are hard, if not impossible, and finding some way to connect to anyone who doesn't understand the life in the fishbowl is also incredibly rare. That both Melania and Michelle bonded so tightly with their beauty team is not a coincidence. Although the relationship is employer/employee (both women pay for their glam teams with their own money; they are not taxpayer funded), there is a deep bond of loyalty that goes beyond a paycheck. They are paid minimally, but they accept the skimpy salary because they serve at the pleasure of the first lady of the United States, and they're seeing the world and quietly becoming famous on their own, with the knowledge that after her tenure, they can, and should, smartly parlay their lean years of White House tutelage into a more profitable job.

But while it's ongoing, the FLOTUS glam squad is on the same hectic schedule as their boss, being shuttled from place to place, surrounded by armed Secret Service agents, reading the same headlines about what's being worn and why and what it means.

For Melania, the fashion stories are constant. A few things contribute to the fascination beyond your average first lady, of course. Melania was a fashion model. She has been defined for most of her adult life by what she wears. And there is the obvious wealth and luxury level in which she operates, and which influences her choices. She's been a celebrity for close to two decades—C-list, perhaps, for the bulk of that time, but a celebrity nonetheless.

For Michelle Obama, the transition from corporate lawyer to fashionable-yet-approachable FLOTUS was quite simply more groundbreaking than Melania's path, if only because people were already looking at her (and judging Melania) solely by what she looked like. Obama had to create and cultivate a sense of style that worked for her, without breaking budgets or putting it too far out of reach for the average American woman—and she very much succeeded. For Hillary Clinton, fashion was the annoying reality of being a woman in the political spotlight. Years ago I once interviewed Nina McLemore, who designs the primary-color power suits worn frequently by Clinton (and Elizabeth Warren and Valerie Jarrett and others). You've seen the ones I'm talking about: bright shades, long jackets, stand-up collars, turned-up sleeves at the cuff. McLemore is a fashion realist when it comes to women of authority, and her goal is to literally design an outfit that no one notices, a jacket so utilitarian that it's a non–talking point. Pretty much the exact opposite of Melania Trump, or even Michelle Obama. For Hillary Clinton, what she wore had to, by desire and necessity, be irrelevant. McLemore is good at making decent-looking, incredibly irrelevant clothes.

Because of her background and her years being scrutinized by old-money Manhattan doyennes as she circled the wealthy landscape of New York on the arm of Donald Trump, Melania is hyperaware of what she wears, what it means, and how it fits. Now, she is also clued in to the fact that she must shed the public perception of her, an almost insurmountable task: going from naked model to first lady of the United States is a fairly remarkable, and historically unprecedented, undertaking. She approaches it with daily consideration to the event, her role, what's expected of her, and how much she likes something. In some ways, her current mode of belted coat dresses and tailored suiting separates is antithetical to the Melania of even ten or fifteen years ago, when she would accompany Trump to an event in a barely-there slip dress or cloaked in a fur cape, fashion choices that could be an entire course of study at the Fashion Institute of Technology.

As first lady, her dresses are typically A-line, with a tight bodice, sleeves or sleeveless, and a billowing skirt. To keep track of what she has on, both for clarity of repetition and historical record, there is a notebook kept as a diary of each look, updated by one of her communications staff members. Often a look is chosen weeks in advance for big events or trips, though Melania has been known to change her mind at the last minute and do her own thing. If that happens, the notebook gets updated.

I remember how quickly my in-box filled at work when Melania appeared at her first White House Easter Egg Roll (remember, at that point she wasn't yet living in Washington, so a Melania sighting at the White House was like seeing a chupacabra). I think people thought she might appear in a tight Hervé Léger cocktail dress, a strapless mini of some sort? Instead, she wore a tea-length, light pink dress with flowing organza layers in the skirt and a simple tank-shaped bod-ice, designed by Pierre specially for the occasion. It was casual and sweet, feminine and pristine—like a mom should be, if she was in the 1950s and about to serve lemonade to a bunch of kids. "What a weird choice," friends and coworkers said to me. "Her dress is so not like her!" was another note. But reclassifying herself sartorially as a "proper" middle-aged woman will be a long and uphill road for Me-lania, and the frothy dresses, demure hemlines, and pastel palettes go a long way in making that possible. She has been successful in letting people assume what she *might* wear and then appearing in something radically different from what's expected. The dismantling of an image as indelible as her wearing a see-through Lucite bodysuit in a fashion spread almost twenty years ago, let's face it, requires some thought.

Out of the gate, she defined what her style would be, mostly tai-lored looks and belted suits and coats, with the occasional dress or evening gown thrown into rotation. I recall the Alice Roi coatdress Melania wore to the prayer breakfast and services at the National Cathedral during inauguration weekend and, knowing she would be photographed from behind, her insistence on the perfect triangle bell shape the back would make. Roi said dressing Melania was easy be-cause she has inherently good taste and is "meticulous, impeccable, simple and not glitzy."

Melania's style helped immensely on her first overseas trip with Trump in 2017. Ahead of the travel, which included stops in Saudi Arabia, Israel, Belgium, and Italy, Melania studied intensely. She knew where she would be going and whom she would be visiting, and she also had noted how previous first ladies had dressed for sim-ilar trips. By that time in Trump's presidency, with no major public speaking roles under her belt, no formally announced first lady "plat-form," and no particular reason to go besides accompanying her hus-band, Melania understood it was important to lead with her looks—a no-brainer approach she'd picked up as a young girl in Slovenia, where it was her beauty that caught attention.

In the days before her departure for the Middle East and Europe,

Melania's small staff of helpers packed for her, assigning a separate bag for each outfit for every single one of her events. Pierre had been instrumental in the final run-through of looks, making sure each detail was finalized and each piece was impeccably tailored. Melania's luggage is always packed into her Louis Vuitton suitcases, trunks, and hanging bags, and for trips like this one, they often take up an entire separate vehicle. On the LV bags are her custom luggage tags. She has tan leather ones embossed with gold initials, MTK, for Melania Trump Knauss, and others made in red, the letters FLOTUS in gold across the middle. That government van with all its precious fashion cargo is then driven to Andrews Air Force Base ahead of the president and first lady, with the rest of the trip's necessities, and pulled up to the doors of Air Force One, where each piece, carefully and discreetly labeled and organized to prevent confusion, is loaded onto the plane.

Melania had spent time getting information from State Department officials regarding wardrobe protocol for each country on the journey, and her outfits reflected immense care and detail as a result. While Trump stuck to his ubiquitous oversize Brioni suits and way-too-long ties, Melania stepped off the plane at the couple's first stop in Riyadh, Saudi Arabia, wearing a black, long-sleeve, wide-legged Stella McCartney jumpsuit, reminiscent of an abaya, the loose, robe-like garment worn by Islamic women in the region. However modest the gesture of solidarity, it was present. And not to leave anyone out, Melania accessorized her jumpsuit with an oversize, $485 python-embossed Yves Saint Laurent belt. Naturally, it was gold. As if to say, "Hey, Saudi Arabia, friend. We like gold, you like gold—we get you. Everything is cool." That evening at a private formal dinner with Saudi royals, Melania again reflected the traditional covered-up dress of the women in her host nation, with a cape-sleeve raspberry floor-length gown by Reem Acra and a diamond collar necklace.

That first trip overseas showcased other important fashion diplomacy and heralded Melania Trump on the global stage in an appropriate and style-savvy way. For her audience with Pope Francis at the

Vatican, Melania wore a black lace dress with matching black lace overcoat by Dolce and Gabbana, her hair up and discreetly covered by a black lace mantilla. For other events it was coatdresses by Michael Kors, a tan leather suit by a Belgian designer while in Brussels, and a shimmery silver evening dress for a closing dinner with Trump in Italy. It was all very high-fashion, but the takeaway headline would be the $51,500 Dolce and Gabbana jacket at the G7 summit, a price tag she would neither explain nor live down.

Grisham, Melania's spokeswoman, and Melania herself, often grow frustrated with all the focus on her fashion. It's a double-edged sword, though, and thanks in large part to her predecessor, whose looks made her a powerful force in the fashion industry by association, Melania must contend with observers of her style. She might get frustrated with everyone talking about how she looks, but the simple fact is, her appearance is something Melania excels at, and as a former model, it's what she knows. Part of the job is very much about what a first lady wears, and in this age of bloggers and style watchers and red carpet vultures, the scrutiny is unavoidable.

In Africa in October, her looks were particularly bold, almost costume-like. On safari in Kenya, she looked like she'd borrowed from Meryl Streep's Karen Blixen in the movie *Out of Africa*. Jodhpurs, crisp white shirt, knee-high brown leather boots, and, yes, that white pith helmet—it was all, well, a little much. The helmet would see her crucified in the press, as it recalled for many Africans a painful time in the continent's history. Colonialists were avid wearers of the pith helmet, and sporting one, even without intentionally sending a message, was unforgivable. For someone as meticulous as Melania is about observing history and custom, it was a definite misstep.

Along for the Africa trip, I hadn't noticed the helmet when we first saw the first lady that particular day. We were ushered to the Shelldrick Animal Preservation Reserve to hold for her arrival—she was to feed a small herd of orphaned and rescued baby elephants—and when she finally appeared, clutching a giant baby bottle of milk to stick into the mouths of eager elephants, she wasn't wearing the hat. But as we moved to phase 2 of the day, piling into open-air Land Rovers for a safari (or, safari lite, really, with Nairobi's skyline in the distance and Secret Service agents dotted throughout the bush, it was hardly the stuff of the wild), our two press vehicles pulled close enough to Melania's rover to note she had added the pith helmet to her ensemble.

What struck me wasn't the hat, however, but more how alone she seemed. It was just her and her safari guide and a couple of Secret Service agents. She was shooting photos with her iPhone, just like any of us would, and each time we would spot a herd of zebras or pull up as close as we could to a giraffe, her vehicle would come to a stop and she would sit and stare, quietly, keenly aware of how she must have looked in profile to our cameras. Her chin jutted out just slightly, her eyes a tad squinty, her arm resting gently on the side of the vehicle, she looked as though she was posing for an imaginary glossy magazine.

It should be noted that so far, there has indeed been no splashy spread of the first lady in the pages of *Vogue*—although sister Condé Nast publication *Vanity Fair* did ask if they could send along a writer and a photographer on the Africa trip. The request was denied.

Compared with Michelle Obama, Hillary Clinton, and Laura Bush, all of whom had several features in *Vogue* through the years, Melania hasn't been treated well in the pages of the fashion bible thus far. Nor have writers on *Vogue*'s digital pages been kind; they've hammered her with unflattering headlines after her events, mocking her outfits, her relationship with Trump, and her sporadic adherence to traditional first lady rites of passage.

Of course, should she have wanted a *Vogue* feature or *Vanity Fair*, Melania would have had to consent to an interview for the magazine, and she could obviously be asked about everything from her husband's infidelities to her unconventional attitude toward her role, and his. I would imagine with the promise of a *Vogue* cover (something Wintour *never promises to anyone*), Melania *might* have been coaxed to

participate, but it's now a moot point, even though I am told Wintour
has asked more than once that Melania be in the magazine, no matter what her public protestations have been. Indeed, *Vogue*'s fabled
editrix has extended the invitation for Melania to be in the fashion bible's pages, and it has been Melania who has said no, says my source.
Mainly because, like Trump, she believes the magazine is not loyal.

Vogue's iconic September issue featured Stormy Daniels in 2018.
She was dressed in a navy fitted Zac Posen gown, given full hair
and makeup treatment, and photographed by the one and only
Annie Leibovitz. That Wintour put the porn star in the pages of
her magazine before the first lady pretty much sealed the deal. Not
only would she not be guaranteed a cover, she would have to follow
Stormy.

Months after the Africa trip, Wintour seemed unable to let her
deep distaste of Melania go. She publicly said in an interview that she,
as the overlord of *Vogue*, preferred to use its pages for women whom
she felt met her own definition of strong. In other words, Democrats.
Kamala Harris had a spread, and so did Alexandria Ocasio-Cortez
and Amy Klobuchar; Elizabeth Warren and Kirsten Gillibrand had
already been in *Vogue*'s pages. "You have to stand up for what you
believe in and you have to take a point of view," Wintour said about
her choices, which translates to, "If you don't agree with me, you don't
get in." Not exactly a democratic way to run a magazine, but Wintour has never been known for running her empire like a democracy.
Wintour never mentioned Melania by name in the interview about her
"rules" for getting ink, but the message was clear, as Melania remains
the only sitting first lady not to have a *Vogue* cover in over a decade.
"We profile women in the magazine that we believe in the stand that
they're taking on issues. We support them in the fact that we feel
they are leaders. Particularly after the defeat of Secretary Clinton in
2016, we believe that women should have a leadership position and
we intend to support them," said Wintour. It was so clearly pointed
at Melania that Grisham, her spokeswoman, shot back a response:
"To be on the cover of *Vogue* doesn't define Mrs. Trump, she's been

there, done that long before she was first lady," a reference to the 2005 wedding cover. "Her role as first lady of the United States and all that she does is much more important than some superficial photo shoot and cover." Grisham kept going—calling the queen of fashion a couple of names, for good measure. "This just further demonstrates how biased the fashion magazine industry is, and shows how insecure and small-minded Anna Wintour really is. Unfortunately, Mrs. Trump is used to this kind of divisive behavior."

So with that hat, the white outfit in Africa, that backdrop, that pensive face in the Land Rover, Melania was also showing Wintour what she had missed. She was art directing, styling and posing for the spread that would never be, and doing so in a way that would make Wintour lust for what could have been.

I shared my theory with my fellow journalists on the trip, a small and talented crew that included Katie Rogers of *The New York Times*, another frequent chronicler of Melania Trump. I'm not sure if anyone bought what I was saying then, but by the time we landed in Egypt the following day and Melania got off the plane in wide-leg trousers, cream blazer, and black necktie, it became more feasible. I also thought it notable that she was wearing a menswear-inspired look in a country with a not-stellar track record on women's rights. Again, there are no coincidences when it comes to Melania Trump and her clothes.

And, oh, the memes. There were dozens and dozens—the most popular mocked her look, spawning all sorts of "Who Wore It Best?" tweets comparing her to Kentucky Fried Chicken's Colonel Sanders or Michael Jackson in the "Smooth Criminal" video or the villain from *Raiders of the Lost Ark*—even Agatha Christie's Hercule Poirot. (I for one thought immediately of Diane Keaton in *Annie Hall*.)

As she closed out her Africa trip that day in a face-to-face meeting with the Great Sphinx of Giza, one of the most mysterious symbols in the world, she may very well have been mapping the backstory of the *Vogue* cover feature that wasn't to be—the "Slovenian Sphinx," as *The New York Times*'s Maureen Dowd has dubbed her. It was a fitting end to the weeklong journey to Ghana, Malawi, Kenya, and Egypt for Melania.

The visit to Africa did little to quell the ongoing who-is-she, who-is-she-not debate, but it did provide an opportunity for Melania's debut impromptu press conference in Egypt with the group of seven reporters who crisscrossed the continent with her throughout the trip. She talked to us about the Brett Kavanaugh debate raging back home—a story line that had all but usurped any chance of her Africa trip's making a substantial dent in the airwaves. (I should know: most of my scheduled TV hits for CNN were pushed to make room for Kavanaugh bits; I was relegated to a handful of phoners from the road.) She agreed with Trump that Kavanaugh was "highly qualified" for the Supreme Court justice job, but she was also "glad" that his accuser, Dr. Christine Blasey Ford, was heard. The answer was classic Melania—she didn't take a stand either way, and in giving a middle-of-the-road response, she did enough to prevent headlines stating that she broke from her husband's thinking, while still managing to show a more liberal angle. And she discussed her thoughts on her husband's Twitter habits ("I don't always agree with what he tweets, and I tell him that. Sometimes he listens, sometimes he doesn't"); the #MeToo movement ("We need to help all the victims, no matter what kind of abuse they had"); whether she had purposefully visited a continent her husband had reportedly referred to as home to "shithole" countries ("I never heard him saying those comments and that was anonymous source and I would leave it at that"); and if she felt that Trump's administration had too drastically chopped the budget of USAID, the government entity with which she had partnered for her Africa trip ("I saw successful programs that USAID is providing to the countries, and we are helping them on the journey to self-reliance"). It was Melania's first-ever off-the-record press "gaggle," as we call these quick, unplanned scrums with a principal, and she was prepared, even seemed to me more relaxed than she had with press in the past.

When it was my turn to toss a question, I asked her about the previous day's scandal of cultural insensitivity, what she thought of the drama caused by her wearing that pith helmet in Kenya—and she snapped at me. In her Ralph Lauren cream slacks and jacket, draped on her shoulders, her white Chanel blouse and tie, her Chanel ballet flats, and, yes, her ivory Chanel fedora, with its black band and signature fabric camellia, Melania trained her steely blue eyes on me and hissed, "You know what? We just completed an amazing trip. We went to Ghana. We went to Malawi. We went to Kenya. Now here we are in Egypt. I want to talk about my trip and not what I wear."

It was the peak of irony.

I understood what she was saying, of course; there is an inherent and deeply unfair bias about clothes that men never have to face, but at the same time she is Melania Trump. It is unavoidable, part of the turf. And, quite frankly, what she wears and how she wears it to draw attention is in her wheelhouse.

Just minutes after she answered me, Melania walked like a runway model back and forth across the panoramic vistas of the Great Pyramids, photographers clicking away. Though maybe not for *Vogue*, she was posing for us, for someone, somewhere, perhaps all the editors who had ignored her, who hadn't put her on the cover of their periodicals, who didn't climb over themselves to plaster a newsstand with her face. Dramatic instrumental music played loudly from speakers on a nearby stage on which a dance troupe performed whom no one was watching—because all eyes were on Melania Trump, alone.

20

The Melania Effect

"It's called 'Melania.'"

—DONALD TRUMP, ON THE NEW-ERA FIRST LADY

It would be months into her tenure as first lady before the world witnessed a break in Melania's unsmiling facade. She was thought to be a robot, a Stepford wife, devoid of feeling. So when she flared, it made headlines.

Donald Trump had done it again. Pushed her out of the shot. Forgotten she was there. It was supposed to have been a four-person photo op—simple, something a monkey could do. But as was often the case, Trump forgot about his wife, and by the time he remembered she was there, it was too late.

The walk on the red carpet at Ben Gurion Airport in Tel Aviv, Israel, in May 2017 wasn't more than one hundred yards. One carpeted section led from the steps of Air Force One to a podium on the tarmac, where Trump was to give brief remarks at a formal welcoming ceremony, having just touched down in the second country of his first major international trip as president. Another identical carpeted path led from the podium to the edge of the tarmac and a cordoned-off audience area lined three deep with photographers and news cameras, plus two rows of seated dignitaries they would walk over to meet.

The movements were fairly simple: they'd gone over them with the White House protocol team and been reminded of the choreography before departing the plane. After remarks, the two couples, the Israeli prime minister Benjamin Netanyahu and his wife, Sara, and the Trumps, would walk side by side in a show of solidarity, both literal and figurative, on the second carpeted portion, away from the podium. Then the Trumps would shake hands with the VIPs and subtly peel off, hopping into the Beast, the president's armored limo, and then move on to the other random diplomatic stops they had to do. But dammit if he couldn't get right just one rehearsed fifteen-step walk.

As the foursome made its way toward the cameras, already not in sync, the Netanyahus holding hands, the Trumps not, Melania fell behind, sort of spilling off to the side of the carpet. Wearing a bright white Michael Kors Collection skirt suit, picked especially to honor the white in the Israeli flag, as well as the symbol of peace, Melania dropped behind, the five-foot-wide swath of red carpet not quite big enough for Trump's girth and his penchant for easy distraction. Thus Melania lagged, unable to fit next to the other three, awkwardly relegated to unintended submissive "walk behind the man" positioning. And she didn't like it.

There's a split second, maybe two, before Trump, as he often does after that approximate amount of time, remembers his wife is actually there and that he's supposed to walk next to her, be aware of her, hold her hand. Trump's synapses fire in a pretty obvious real-time way when you watch the moment on video playback. Suddenly, he realizes he has forgotten something, like his keys going out the door. With hardly a turn of his head, he absently reaches back with his left arm, bending his hand at the wrist, a glance over his shoulder that doesn't even do the courtesy of meeting her eyes. Melania isn't having it and—with a swat, as fast as lightning—she bats his hand away and turns her head.

Trump had made the "leaving her behind" mistake several times before, and would continue to do so, in a variety of iterations, throughout the course of the first half of his presidency. While one could have a field day speculating what it means about the state of his marriage to Melania, a virtually futile exercise regarding any married couple since every marriage is different, it was for the public a rare peek behind Melania's veil.

Perhaps Trump's most notable "forgot her" episode happened almost immediately in his tenure as president, right off the bat, on Inauguration Day. Trump and Melania had pulled up to the north side of the White House in their black Secret Service Suburban to greet Barack and Michelle Obama on the front steps. It was a traditional moment, time-honored, between the outgoing president and the incoming; a "welcome to the house, here are the keys" gesture of goodwill between old and new, this one bound to be especially dissected after such a brutal campaign.

Trump was just hours from being sworn in as president when he got out of the back seat on the side of the vehicle closest to the front door of the White House. Melania got out of the back seat on the driver's side, facing Pennsylvania Avenue. Yet by the time Trump had made it up four of the steps on the stairs to clasp hands with Obama, Melania had barely rounded the rear bumper. When Trump was awkwardly cheek-kissing Michelle Obama, Melania was finally standing on the porch with the rest of them, having hustled to catch up, and likely unaware that behavior she was so used to would be humiliatingly called out over and over again in the days and weeks to come as a curious public analyzed the first couple's marriage.

"He just . . . left her," an incredulous Greek chorus of Americans would say to one another around the proverbial water coolers the next day. "*Can you believe it?*" "*I would kill my husband if he did that!*" "*Barack would never have done that to Michelle!*"

Standing on the front steps of their new and profoundly unfamiliar home, holding a blue Tiffany gift box, wearing her matching Tiffany-blue suit and gloves, abandoned by the man she was expected to stand beside with honor and respect for him as he leads the country, Melania seethed. Trump had put his third wife in second-thought status too many times to count before, yet it was in that moment that it must have become clear to Melania the title of president of the United States probably wasn't going to change anything about his boorish behavior. It certainly wasn't going to change whether he got the door for her or waited for her to catch up to him so the two could walk alongside each other.

Exceedingly independent and very clear about how and why she moves through life, Melania was not experiencing that car-to-greeting series as the bone-chilling disappointment that the rest of the world was. She was angry he had done it so publicly. In her previous life as "model wife of Donald Trump," she didn't freak out when her husband neglected to participate in the chivalry expected of most men of his age and status. "Why change him?" had been Melania's mantra for the nineteen years she had known Trump. This wasn't a man who had wooed her with roses and poetry.

Because, for the most part, Melania didn't mind the slights; they had become a regular part of the marriage. It was more that now everyone else would see the behavior she grew to recognize, accept, live with, and ignore.

As perhaps the most technically unqualified modern first lady in recent history, Melania had none of the experience to strategize a defense about how to handle the public scrutiny of her marriage. So insular was her life in New York that, while she knew she would be a global fascination, she didn't really have a buffer to protect her when she entered Washington. She barely had a team, and she had basically zero in the way of public sympathy at that point to help her combat the force of nature that was her husband. She just had herself. Her introduction to being first lady was lonely and bizarre.

So, she swatted.

The hand swat was the first time Melania Trump really got noticed. She had been first lady for just four months; she hadn't even moved into the White House full-time yet. Up until then, the biggest headlines about her were all will-she, won't-she speculation about whether she would fulfill her promise to move to Washington after Barron's school year in New York ended. But with that one emotional swatting-away gesture, the perception of Melania shifted from stone-faced trophy wife cum first lady to human with feelings—or, more likely, "Human? With feelings?!"

As such, the Israel incident put her on the map in a new way, spawning endless stories on cable news and digital front pages with exclamatory headlines like "Melania Trump Hates Holding Donald's Hand" (a story by Huffington Post with an accompanying video of the moment that a year later had nine hundred thousand views). A *Newsweek* headline asked, "Did Melania Trump Smack Donald's Hand at Israeli Airport?" And while every intern at every news organization across the globe was tasked with finding other moments when the couple did or didn't clasp fingers, Melania, virtually nonplussed considering it all, sat back and watched her stock rise.

Google searches for "Melania Trump" and "Melania" had two notable spikes in 2017. The first was Inauguration Day; the second accrued over the course of a couple of days in May, picking up steam on May 22 (or, swatting day) and peaking on May 24, as the story reached fever pitch.

Grisham never responded to press requests about the incident, nor did she comment on what exactly went down on that red carpet, which smartly left it up to observers to draw their own conclusion—a brilliant strategy and one Grisham would employ countless times in the months to come and which she may very well use now as the president's spokesperson, filling Sarah Sanders's shoes as press secretary. The bottom line for Melania's communications apparatus is "don't tell everyone everything." She has learned that keeping quiet usually ends up just fine in the end, as it did with the hand swat.

Red-meat conservatives simply chalked the tarmac dustup to the media's overzealous scrutiny of all things Trump. "Oh, now they're attacking their marriage!" was the battle cry. And liberals could point to it and say, "See? Even his wife hates him." Melania didn't care either way. Neither theory was necessarily true or untrue. The focus in general was ridiculous, she thought. She was never big on public displays of affection, which didn't essentially have all that much to do with Trump; it was just how she was. Years on the New York social circuit meant that Melania was an air-kiss expert, but gooey hand-holding with her husband? That she was happy to leave to the Obamas.

In all fairness, however, she would interlock pinkies with her husband literally seconds after the hand swat and fully grab his famously short fingers many other times throughout that same day and throughout the entire trip. Her temper flares were scary, but they were also infrequent and usually quite brief. Also, when the swat occurred, it's important to bear in mind they had just touched down in a country rife with Orthodox tradition, and Melania in her new role had studied the protocol. She had prepared extensively for this, her first big bow on the international stage, and getting off on the wrong foot in a country as important to her husband's administration as Israel was not in her playbook. Still, he wasn't supposed to forget that she was right next to him.

The following year, next to another first couple, Emmanuel and Brigitte Macron of France, Melania would again make headlines for pushing her husband's hand away, this time during a choreographed and rehearsed official state arrival ceremony on the South Lawn. In that instance, Trump reached for her hand almost too much, blindly trying to find her fingers while simultaneously paying attention to the audience in front of him. She kept trying to close her hand, signaling *no, not now, don't do this now*. But Trump would ultimately grab her fingers and hold tight, then nod his head toward hers as if to say, "Phew, thank you!"

What Melania learned in these moments was the power of the intense messaging she could render without saying a word. If she was merely quiet, she might be boring and shallow. But if she was quiet and did something outside expected protocol, she became interesting and savvy—*and* sympathetic. She didn't need the approval or the understanding of that knowledge to operate, but she was clearly clued into its impact. What the tarmac incident taught her was that next to her husband, whose bluster and bravado sucked oxygen out of everyone around him, she had an advantage.

The last time Melania had gotten that kind of ink and interest was a couple of weeks before the visit to Israel, back in Washington, with another silent and quick motion. She nudged Trump to put his hand over his heart during the national anthem at the White House Easter Egg Roll, a move that got past exactly no one. The entire national press corps seeks out examples of Trump not doing the right thing, for sport. Not showing proper reverence to the national anthem was kind of a big deal.

Melania and Barron, then eleven, were standing with Trump on the White House's Truman Balcony, next to a man dressed in a full Easter Bunny costume, a role Sean Spicer once played when he worked in the George W. Bush administration. Below them were visitors on the South Lawn who had been ticketed for the annual roll festivities. Mother and son, Easter Bunny, and the thousands facing them in the crowd had their hands over their hearts as the military singer, Gunnery Sergeant Sheffield, belted out the first bars of the anthem. But Trump just stood there with a goofy, somewhat self-satisfied smile, until Melania moved her left arm into his right, with some force. It was a subtle and stealthy reminder that got Trump's hand in the correct place by the time "dawn's early light" approached. "Watch the First Lady Nudge President Trump for National Anthem," wrote *USA Today*; "President Trump Appears to Get a Nudge by First Lady," said NBC News; "Did Melania Give Husband Anthem Nudge?" asked the BBC; "14 Hilarious Reactions to Melania Trump Nudging Donald for the National Anthem," wrote *Bazaar*.

In essence, Melania had launched the Melania Effect without really even knowing she had done so. How many millions of wives nudge their husband to remember to do something culturally and socially appropriate in a moment of forgetfulness? In an instant, Melania became all the more relatable, and more important, she became real.

And with each swat, poke, nudge, and pout, she becomes more and more a memorable and independent first lady.

It's in these moments that we see the real Melania Trump. A Melania who has scrupulously done her homework and knows what the protocol is that needs to be followed. A Melania who wants to make a good impression. A Melania who is not worried about making her husband happy or making him angry. She is a Melania who is not willing to be ignored.

Whatever you might think of Melania—insipid trophy wife, clotheshorse, tone-deaf Marie Antoinette, enabler of one of the most divisive presidents in recent history, or a woman who spent her childhood and formative years in a poor communist country, who speaks five languages, who privately spends her time visiting sick children, who is a fierce protector of her child and keeps a noble grace and silence—Melania Trump is impossible to ignore. Say what you will about her, what is clear is that Melania Trump is unlike any other first lady.

Acknowledgments

There are people who come into your life in the first place for a reason, and those who re-enter it by some sort of divine stroke of good luck. For me, that person is Colin Fox. Colin and I first met in our freshman year at St. John's College in Annapolis, Maryland, a small liberal arts school that focuses solely on a Great Books program, attended mostly by nerdy types and deep thinkers, college kids not interested in a traditional university Greek system, more the original one, with Plato and Aristotle and Homer. I won't embarrass Colin by going into our relationship, but it was important and formative and one of the greats. So I was thrilled when we kept in touch for years after college, here and there, and I watched from a distance as his storied career in publishing became the stuff of wild success. A couple of years ago, after I started my job at CNN, Colin would ping me from time to time, "I hope you're writing this stuff down." I said I was taking notes. Eventually, it became, "You might have a book there." And if Colin was telling me so, I probably did. I can't thank him enough for helping me formulate my thesis (just like we used to do back in school, arguing the opposite sides of theories, testing the limits of logic, questioning man's nobility and such), and for pushing me to New York to meet with the great Amy Einhorn of Flatiron Books. But I'm most grateful that I coaxed him out of his much-deserved early retirement to act as my agent—my publishing Sherpa, too—and guide me through this new territory I had landed in called writing a book. He has been my leader, my editor, my friend, my counsel, my sounding board, and my forever friend—all from afar in long phone calls, medium-sized emails, and short texts. He has virtually held my hand and many times agreed with me that I was crazy to take this on. (Thanks for that, by the way.) This book would not exist without Colin Fox.

I'd also like to thank my father, James K. Glassman. When Colin didn't have the answer, or wasn't sure he was giving me the right one, he would always say, "Ask your dad." Because that's just who my dad is, the guy with all the right answers. Mentor, idol, hero—my compass. He has also been editing my copy since the second grade. I don't know how I got so blessed to have him as my father, but it is my life's greatest gift.

I am also thankful for Cab Bennett, who for almost twenty years has been telling me I can do it—whatever "it" is—when I am certain I cannot. He's picked up where I have had to drop off, with parenting, with friends, with relationships, with taking care of a creaky house, or beloved and mildly neglected pets, or things that go bump in the night. He's the rock, the patient calm in my storm.

Deep thanks to my mother, Mary Glassman, and my sister, Zoë Miles. Both have taught me resilience and fortitude.

My talented colleagues and bosses at CNN have been generous with their time, support, and patience. They include Jeff Zucker and Virginia Moseley, and Wolf Blitzer, who for many months never failed to ask me how my book was going and who always had a minute for me, a piece of advice, and a funny story. I'd also like to thank Rebekah Metzler and Betsy Klein, for forever being a quick text away, and for long, celebratory dinners in faraway lands. To Glennon Gordon, my very best friend, thank you for keeping me on track, and loving me when I fell off it. And to Susanna Quinn and Elizabeth Thorp, and my Farmington friends, especially Sarah Tonetti, for their collective impeccable intellect and words of wisdom. To Ryan, who rode in on his white horse, thank you for making me feel lucky. And Lauren Pratapas, good egg, great PR woman. Mark "The Shark" London, who I am happy to say is both my lawyer and my dear friend. A special nod of gratitude to Maegan Vazquez, not only a fabulous and tenacious CNN White House reporter, but one hell of a book research assistant in her side hustle. To Stephanie Grisham, for a pretty stellar track record of getting back to me, even when doing so was probably the last thing she wanted to do. I am thoroughly impressed with and thankful for the countless journalists I interact with each day and in the many years that have made up my long and happy career. It is sometimes a challenging profession, but one of extreme importance—thank you for letting me read your work and form a better understanding of the world around me.

I reserve special thanks for my editor, Amy Einhorn, who I am really grateful didn't drop me when I missed, well, almost every deadline. She was there for me in the beginning of this process when I was super-confident, and also there for me when I lost all hope. Most important, she is the best in the business and I cannot believe how lucky I am that she agreed to take me on for my first book. Thank you to the Flatiron Books team: Bob Miller, Marlena Bittner, Keith Hayes, Cristina Gilbert, Nancy Trypuc, and most especially, Mr. Fix-It, Conor Mintzer.

Finally, I'd like to thank first lady Melania Trump, a fascinating woman who has been one of the most challenging, interesting, and inspiring subjects I have ever covered.

About the Author

KATE BENNETT, a CNN reporter, is the only journalist in the White House press corps to cover solely
first lady Melania Trump and the Trump family.
Bennett has been a lifestyle journalist for almost two
decades, chronicling the intersection of people, pop
culture, fashion, and politics. She is also the author
of a weekly CNN Politics newsletter about the social
and cultural climate in Washington. Bennett is a native
of Washington and a graduate of St. John's College,
where she majored in classics and philosophy, and
her work has appeared in Politico, *Washingtonian*,
and *Capitol File* magazine, where she was editor in
chief. She lives in Bethesda, Maryland.